1989

LONGMAN LINGUISTICS LIBRARY
Title no 29

DIALECTOLOGY
AN INTRODUCTION

LONGMAN LINGUISTICS LIBRARY

General editors
R. H. Robins, University of London
Martin Harris, University of Salford

Dialectology

An Introduction

W. N. Francis

LONGMAN

LONDON AND NEW YORK

Longman Group UK Limited
Longman House, Burnt Mill, Harlow
Essex CM20 2JE, England
and Associated Companies throughout the world

*Published in the United States of America
by Longman Inc., New York*

*First published 1983
Second impression 1987*

British Library Cataloguing in Publication Data

Francis, W. N.
Dialectology.
1. Dialectology
I. Title
417'.2   P367

ISBN 0-582-29117-8

Library of Congress Cataloging in Publication Data

Francis, W. Nelson (Winthrop Nelson), 1910–
Dialectology.

(Longman linguistics library; title no. 29)
Bibliography: p.
Includes index.
1. Dialectology. I. Title. II. Series.
P367.F7 1983   417'.2   82-20856
ISBN 0-582-29117-8 (pbk.)

Set in 10/11pt Linotron 202 Times Roman
Produced by Longman Singapore Publishers Pte Ltd
Printed in Singapore

Contents

List of maps

Preface

This book was undertaken at the suggestion of a former student who found himself required to teach a course in dialectology without a general text, at least in English, to give his students. Although this deficiency has recently been to some extent remedied, there is still a need for a text which surveys the discipline and introduces the student to the methods, goals, and results of dialect study. It is hoped that this book will fill that need.

Throughout, the emphasis has been placed on dialectology as a branch of linguistics, with much to contribute to the body of linguistic knowledge and theory. It has not always occupied that position, at least in the view of prevailing schools of linguistic theory. It has often been treated as a field for amateurs, collectors of linguistic curiosities which can be disregarded in the development of elegant theoretical models. To some degree, at least, this attitude is an excuse for neglecting stubborn facts of language variation and heterogeneity which are the central subject matter of the discipline and an embarrassment to theoretical generalization. Fortunately, as is pointed out in my final chapter, over the last two decades attempts have been made to incorporate the findings of dialectology into models of language which provide for 'systematic heterogeneity' as an inherent universal of language structure. From being a peripheral, if not irrelevant, aspect of linguistic study, dialectology is today being incorporated into its central core.

As is pointed out in the Introduction, the book divides itself into three parts: two introductory chapters on the nature and incidence of variation in language; four central chapters on methodology; and two final chapters on the relationship of dialect study to various schools of linguistic theory. I have attempted to main-

tain a balance between the traditional studies which have produced the great collections and atlases from Wenker and Gilliéron to the present day and the sociolinguistic studies which
have proliferated over the last fifteen or twenty years. Both are
essential to the good health of the discipline; it is just as unwise
for the modernist to write off as irrelevant the monumental work
of the last hundred years as it is for the conservative to reject the
sociolinguistic studies of Labov and others as violating the great
tradition of dialect study.

The book is directed primarily to university students who have
had some preliminary training in linguistics, especially phonetics
and phonology. But although this background is assumed, it
should still be possible for those with no formal linguistic training
to follow the material with little or no difficulty. Wherever technical vocabulary is used, the attempt has been made to introduce it
in an explanatory context; all special terms are printed in small
capitals on their first occurrence and either defined or used in a
way that makes their meaning obvious. Illustrative material, most
but not all from English, has been incorporated at every stage,
and the writings of master dialectologists of the twentieth century
have been extensively quoted in order to give the reader a sense
of the body of thought and speculation which has accompanied
the hard work of the field collector. Much of this writing – primarily in French, German, and Italian – has been neglected by
British and American dialectologists; one aim of this book is to
show the truly international nature of the discipline. All quoted
material of this sort I have translated myself, with occasional help
from colleagues who are native speakers of the languages
involved.

It remains to express my gratitude to those who have aided
and supported my efforts during the ten years this work has been
in process. A senior fellowship from the National Endowment for
the Humanities enabled me to spend a sabbatical year in preliminary reading and study. Several colleagues have read the entire manuscript, notably Robert Meskill, who helped particularly
with the generative phonology section of Chapter 7, and Wolfgang Viereck, who gave up time from a brief visit to Providence
to read the text and discuss it with me. Geoffrey Leech and R. H.
Robins, General Editors of the Longman Linguistics Library,
read the material chapter by chapter and contributed invaluable
comments. The staff of Longman have been cooperative and sup-
portive beyond the call of duty. I am especially grateful to
William Rice, Director of the Brown University Photolab, for ex-
pert and understanding work on reproducing maps and figures
and fitting them into restricted page space.

I cannot close without expressing my gratitude to two who introduced me to dialect study a quarter century ago: the late Harold Orton, who arranged a Fulbright fellowship for me at Leeds to work on the Survey of English Dialects, and Stanley Ellis, who took me into the field and shared his incomparable knowledge of field methods and problems with me. Without such an introduction to the discipline, this book would never have come about.

Providence, Rhode Island   W. NELSON FRANCIS
22 June 1982.

Key to symbols

Except where otherwise noted, transcriptions are in the International Phonetic Alphabet (IPA), with the following substitutions or additions:

š for ʃ
ž for ʒ
č for tʃ
ǰ for dʒ
r for ɹ in Chapter 8.
ü for y
y for j
/ / enclose phonemic transcriptions (systematic phonemic in the generative dialectology section of Chapter 7)
[ ] enclose phonetic transcriptions (systematic phonetic in the generative dialectology section of Chapter 7)
ˊ primary stress
ˋ secondary stress
+ morpheme boundary
# word boundary
→ 'rewrite as, is realized as' in synchronic rules
> 'changes to, is replaced by' in diachronic rules
≠ 'contrasts with'
~ 'varies with'
Ø 'zero'

La géographie linguistique n'est peut-être qu'une humble servante de la linguistique, mais une servante qui souvent fait marcher la maison en l'absence fréquente des autres membres et dont la voix doit toujours être écoutée même en leur présence.

Jules Gilliéron 1918

Chapter 1

Introduction

What is dialectology?

This book is about the study of dialects, which are varieties of a language used by groups smaller than the total community of speakers of the language. Any language spoken by more than a handful of people exhibits this tendency to split into dialects, which may differ from one another along all the many dimensions of language content, structure, and function: vocabulary, pronunciation, grammar, usage, social function, artistic and literary expression. The differences may be slight and confined to a few aspects of the language, or so great as to make communication difficult between speakers of different dialects. At some point on this graduated scale the differences may become so great that linguists speak of separate but related languages, rather than dialects of the same language. Actually there is no positive and clear-cut way to establish criteria by which separate dialects can be distinguished from separate languages. It thus appears at the outset that we cannot precisely define our subject matter.

This difficulty of definition is compounded by a difficulty of identification. The popular view is that the large area over which a single language is spoken – France or Italy, for example – is neatly divided into separate dialect areas, each set off by clear dialect boundaries. This view is supported by terminology: people speak of Norman, Parisian, Neapolitan, or Sicilian dialects, suggesting that the speech areas are as precisely defined as political cities or states. The truth is that dialect boundaries are usually elusive to the point of non-existence. Very seldom does a traveler cross an imaginary line and suddenly find the people using a new and quite different dialect from that used on the other side of the line. Usually the change is gradual and hardly noticeable. This was clearly expressed as early as 1888 by the famous French philologist, Gaston Paris:

> Actually there are no dialects. . . . Varieties of common speech blend into one another by imperceptible gradations. A villager who might know only the speech of his village would easily understand that of the neighboring village, with a bit more difficulty that of the village he would come to by walking on in the same direction, and so on, until finally he reached a point where he would understand the local speech only with great difficulty. (Quoted in Gauchat 1903, *p* 379)

There are some exceptions to this gradual transition across the countryside. When a pronounced non-linguistic barrier of some sort separates one group from its neighbors, that barrier may mark a sharp dialect boundary as well. The barrier may be geographical. The descendants of the *Bounty* mutineers and their Polynesian companions who settled on Pitcairn and Norfolk Islands in the South Pacific were cut off from contact with other speakers for many decades and to some degree still are, though they now have radio and contact with passing ships. They evolved a dialect of English which is used only by themselves, so that the shores of the islands where they live constitute a precise dialect boundary (Ross and Moverly 1964). This is, of course, a special, almost unique case. Similar, though less extreme, are the differences among the inhabitants of islands along the Maine coast of the United States. They have no difficulty in identifying a person as a speaker from another island, even one within a mile or two, and may treat him as a 'foreigner'.

On the other hand, the barrier which sets up a dialect boundary may be political or social. The educated speech of England, which is common to the upper classes throughout the country, is markedly different from that of Scotland and Ireland, not to mention the United States and Canada. There are, of course, geographical barriers here as well, but the major influence is that of political and social allegiance. In fact, political and social, and to some degree literary, affiliation may create supposed language boundaries where no real ones exist. Thus on one side of the political boundary between Belgium and the Netherlands people consider themselves to be speaking Flemish and on the other side Dutch, though the differences are slight and the transition gradual. Somewhat the same situation exists along the border between Norway and Sweden.

In spite of cases of distinct dialect boundary, however, the normal situation is that of gradual transition across a given area. Dialectologists use the concept of the ISOGLOSS, a line marking the limit of use of a word or other linguistic feature. A well-known isogloss in American dialectology is one that separates the users of *pail* from the users of *bucket* to describe 'a large, open vessel for water, milk' (Kurath et al. 1939, *p* 151). This runs across southern New Jersey, northwestward through eastern Pennsylvania, and westward across the rest of Pennsylvania and northern Ohio. To the north of this line the predominant word is *pail*, and to the south *bucket* (see Map 1.1). Because it runs close to a number of other isoglosses, Kurath uses it as a convenient bound-

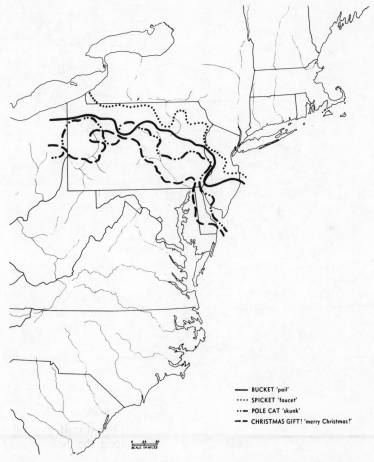

——— BUCKET 'pail'
···· SPICKET 'faucet'
··— POLE CAT 'skunk'
— — CHRISTMAS GIFT! 'merry Christmas!'

SCALE IN MILES

MAP 1.1. Four isoglosses in eastern United States (from Kurath, WGEUS).

ary line between Northern and Midland American English. But a closer look at the actual data on which the line is based reveals that it is by no means as sharp and clear as it is sometimes made to appear. Map 1.2 shows the detailed responses given for this item, usually by two or more people in each community visited. The following details can be observed:

1. There are localities in the neighborhood of the isogloss where one speaker (or INFORMANT) responded with *pail* and the other with *bucket*.
2. There are scattered occurrences of each word in the area

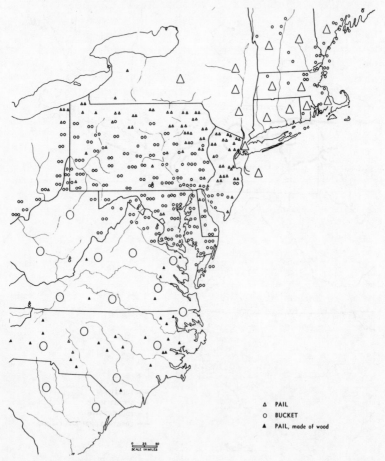

△ PAIL
○ BUCKET
▲ PAIL, made of wood

MAP 1.2. Distribution of words for 'pail,' eastern United States (from Kurath, WGEUS).

dominated by the other: of *bucket* along the Maine coast and inland in Vermont and New Hampshire, and of *pail* as far south as central North Carolina.

3. There are areas where both terms are used, but with different meanings: *bucket* for the common metal object and *pail* for one made of wood with one of the staves lengthened to serve as handle.

Closer investigation would probably reveal that most speakers over the whole area know both words, and in some areas the two words are interchangeable, perhaps with a preference for one over the other, while in other areas they have somewhat different meanings. The isogloss, therefore, does not mark a sharp switch from one word to the other, but the center of a transitional area where one comes to be somewhat favored over the other. The isogloss is a useful concept, as we shall see, but it must always be viewed as an abstraction and not a clear line on the land which one might step across from one dialect area into another.

The situation becomes more complicated when we try to find places where a number of isoglosses lie close enough together to constitute a BUNDLE (as in Map 1.1), and hence something approaching a true dialect boundary. Very seldom do even two isoglosses fall together along all of their length. The more common situation is as represented in the abstract and hypothetical Map 1.3. Here we have two linguistic features – it does not matter what kind – each of which has two variants, A and a representing one, and B and b the other. It will be observed that the two isoglosses run close together but only coincide for about one-third of their length. In the center, the B : b isogloss is to the north (above) the A : a one, and to the west it is south of it. The area is thus divided into four subareas: two large ones, 1 and 2, which have AB and ab respectively, and two small ones, 3 with aB and 4 with Ab. How are we to describe the dialect situation here? We have three choices:

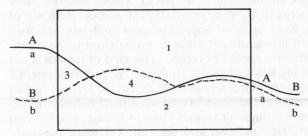

MAP 1.3.   Hypothetical isoglosses and dialect areas.

1. Each numbered area can be called a separate dialect.
2. One or the other of the isoglosses can be said to predominate over the other. If the A : a isogloss is used as the dialect boundary, the northern dialect includes all of area 1 (the AB area), plus area 4 (the Ab area), and the southern dialect includes areas 2 (ab) and 3 (aB). Conversely, if we choose the B : b isogloss, then area 3 goes with the northern dialect and area 4 with the southern.
3. Areas 1 (AB) and 2 (ab) can be called the 'true' northern and southern dialects, and 3 and 4 'mixed' or 'transitional' areas, belonging to neither main area, but constituting a broader segment of the dialect boundary.

Any one of these conclusions may be adopted by the dialectologist, depending on many other factors that he may wish to take into account, such as the linguistic or political history of the area. As more isoglosses are added, each following its own route, it is clear that solution 1 would splinter the area into many subareas, each with a unique set of features. On Map 1.1, for example, where there are four isoglosses, there would be nine separate areas. Solution 3 would change the dialect boundary into a broad band across the map, containing all the isoglosses within it, but never narrowing to a single line. Again referring to Map 1.1, this band would range between 50 and 150 miles wide. This has led some dialectologists to conclude, with Gaston Paris, that dialect boundaries are a myth. And if there are no dialect boundaries, how can we say that there are dialects?

But to come to this conclusion would be to abandon the study of dialectology altogether. It is obvious that there *are* dialects; that people in, for example, Charleston, South Carolina, use different words, different pronunciation, and different grammar from people in Boston or New York. There are, therefore, dialect centers and dialect areas, even though their boundaries may be fuzzy and the transition from one to another gradual. Dialectologists speak of the centers as FOCAL AREAS and the fuzzy boundaries between them as TRANSITIONAL AREAS. Both are of interest: the focal areas as supplying clear contrasts one with another, and the transitional areas as giving clues to how individual features may spread or recede. This kind of pattern is not unusual in many fields of study. Biologists make a fundamental distinction between plants and animals, but at the level of certain one-celled creatures the boundary between them is fuzzy. Physical geographers distinguish various kinds of terrain: tropical rain forest, desert, high plateau, and the rest. On maps these are often shown in contrasting colors with sharply defined boundaries, but there may actually be a gradual transition from one to the other. So dialectologists also make maps with dialect areas sharply bounded, though they know that in actuality the boundaries are broad areas of gradual transition.

Why study dialectology?

So there are such things as dialects. The question then arises, why do we study them? What are the motives behind the considerable expenditure of time, money, and energy which is needed for the serious collection, presentation, and analysis of dialect data? Some answer to this question is essential as a justification for a book such as this.

There are at least four kinds of motivation for dialect study, which can be called the curious, the anthropological, the linguistic, and the practical.

The curious

Whenever people from different parts of the country get together, conversation frequently turns on language differences. People are curious about different words for familiar things or different meanings for familiar words. Differing pronunciations also arouse curiosity. People from the Middle Atlantic area of the United States are curious as to why New Englanders pronounce *barn* something like *ban*, while Texans may pronounce it like *born*. The New Englander is amused by the Southerner's pronunciation of *fan, fine,* and *find*, which all sound alike to him. Dialect is a frequent source of humor; it can also lead to or reinforce prejudice. But most people find it interesting and are curious about its origins and distribution.

Allied to the curious interest is affection, even sentimentality, about dialect. People who themselves may be educated speakers of standard dialect may read or even write stories, poems, and newspaper columns in what they conceive to be a local dialect. There is a respectable body of dialect literature, including such classics as Mark Twain's *Huckleberry Finn*, Harris's *Uncle Remus*, Burns's poems in Lowland Scots, and Tennyson's Northern Farmer poems in broad Lincolnshire. But there is also a large body of dialect writing which, though definitely second-rate, is much read and loved. Both in England and in the United States provincial newspapers often have weekly columns of jokes and anecdotes in local dialect. With our increasing sensitivity about ethnic minorities and their language and customs, this sort of essentially innocent humor has much declined in recent years. The blackface minstrel show is no more, 'Pat and Mike' jokes about the Irish are scarce, and even Yiddish comedy is on the decline. But there are still many who openly or secretly retain affection for a non-standard dialect and among themselves make and repeat dialect stories, rimes, and anecdotes.

The anthropological

This is a convenient cover term for all those studies which deal with human societies and cultures, their histories, and the many ways they are organized. Language is an essential part of culture, and language differences are often indicators of deep-seated social and cultural phenomena. In some societies, for example, the language or dialect of women is quite different from that of men; this says much about the relationship between the sexes. There may be other types of social differentiation marked by dialect differences. Patterns of dialect are often indicators of the movements and interrelationships of various groups, and are thus of interest to historians. Much of the earlier settlement history of the United States is mirrored in dialect differences and their distribution.

Recently there has been a great deal of interest in SOCIOLINGUISTICS, the study of linguistic reflections of social customs, structures, and differences. It has long been realized that many linguistic differences are closely related to such sociological variables as education, economic status, occupation, race or class identification, political and religious affiliation. But until recently this aspect of dialect has not been much studied by dialectologists, whose interest has lain more in the geographical distribution or history of language variety and language change. Hence they have usually restricted themselves to one type of dialect, commonly that of uneducated country people, who were thought to preserve older forms of the language longer and in a 'purer' form. Nowadays there is much more interest in the language of the towns and cities and that of younger speakers, who often are the innovators.

It is not always easy to distinguish between the sociolinguist and the dialectologist. A rough distinction, which not all of either group would accept, is that the sociolinguist is primarily interested in the people themselves, and hence in the language for what it can reveal about them, while the dialectologist is interested in the language itself and studies the social aspects for what they can reveal about it. Since our concern is with dialectology as a branch of linguistics, we shall concentrate on the linguistic aspects of sociolinguistic dialectology, which will be dealt with in Chapter 8.

The linguistic
The linguist in the narrower sense of the term is interested in the systematic structure of language. He deals with points of pronunciation, grammar, meaning, and vocabulary not as isolated phenomena, but as parts of an elaborately integrated system, which is learned more or less well by all members of a speech community. The theoretical linguist is often rather disturbed by dialect variation, which may disrupt or complicate an overly abstract view of language structure. But he cannot overlook the facts, and many modern linguists are trying to find ways to deal with dialect differences as an integral part of language, not just as something rather messy and embarrassing which they wish would go away. We shall look at these attempts in Chapter 8.

The linguist is also interested in language history, which implies linguistic change. Dialects are often a source of valuable evidence to the historical linguist. Dialect differences are commonly the result of changes taking place in different ways or at different rates in different places. It is not true, as it is often said to be, that people in the Appalachian region of the United States 'speak pure Elizabethan English'. Since they did not get there until 200 years or so after the death of the first Queen Elizabeth, it would be remarkable indeed if they preserved unchanged the language of their sixteenth-century ancestors. But their dialect does have many features of pronunciation and especially grammar which are relics of older English no longer current in other varieties of English (See Wolfram and Christian 1976). By collecting and studying these, the dialectologist can help the historical linguist in his studies of how and perhaps even why language changes – or does not change.

The practical
In an older and more élitist society, the speaker of dialect was considered provincial, uncultivated, uneducated, and even stupid. Much dialect humor preserved this stereotype, which was to a certain extent true; after all, dialect was considered to be characteristic of the rural and uneducated. The upper classes commonly used language considered more refined than that of the local peasants or craftsmen who worked for them. Hence those dialect speakers who had the opportunity to rise in the world made it one of their first goals to acquire a reasonably accurate form of the language of the gentry, which was considered to be *the* language, of which local and lower-class dialects were corrupt and degenerate relatives. It was not necessary for schools to teach the 'correct' language, since most of those who went to school were already speakers of it, and the rest were soon forced by

their own social uneasiness or the pressure of their schoolmates to acquire it.

Much of this feeling about the relationship between the STAN-DARD language and the local, ethnic, or class dialect is still with us. But in those countries where education is no longer the privilege of an élite group but is available to the masses, teachers are often faced with pupils or even whole classes whose speech is a dialect different in many ways from that of the teacher himself or that of the educational, political, economic, and social establishment. This poses a problem for the teacher, for the school system, and for society as a whole. Two extreme positions can be – and often are – adopted. On the one hand, the older view, that non-standard dialect is a corrupt and degenerate version of the standard, may be maintained and enforced. This imposes the difficult task of teaching the standard and attempting to eradicate the non-standard. The paradox about this view is that if the pupils themselves see no advantage in changing their language, the task is virtually impossible, while if they do see the advantage, it is largely unnecessary. Those who wish to alter their way of speaking usually succeed in doing so with little or no instruction. In extreme cases, this attitude may break down the cooperative relation between teacher and pupil which is essential for a successful school program. The teacher accuses the pupils of being stupid and wilful, and the pupils condemn or disregard the teacher as being unreasonable and autocratic.

On the other hand, the school may adopt the position that since a person's speech is an intimate part of his personality, any attempt to change it without the voluntary and enthusiastic participation of the person himself is bound to be resisted as a personal attack. Hence whatever version of the language the pupils use is to be accepted and encouraged. It is, after all, adequate to the daily needs of the speaker, which he carries on with fluency once he is out of the classroom. The idea is that this fluency is the desirable aim, within the classroom as well as outside. Thus if the teacher is not already familiar with the dialect of his pupils, it is his responsibility to become so, so that he can understand them and perhaps modify his own speech at least enough so that they can understand him more easily. The problem here is, of course, that no matter how understanding and tolerant of dialect differences the teacher and the school may be, this attitude does not extend throughout society, which is likely to close doors of educational and economic advancement on non-standard speakers.

Dialectology cannot point out the solution to this dilemma, which has social complications extending far beyond language alone. What it can do is to ascertain the facts about dialects and make them available, in order to supersede the ignorance and prejudice which cloud the subject. Accurate and detailed knowledge about language and its varieties – including the standard dialect – must be the foundation of any serious approach to the dilemma sketched above. There is thus a very practical and useful side to the study of dialects.

Plan of this book

It remains to outline briefly the approach and sequence of ideas that will be adopted in this book. As has been suggested above, the approach will be primarily linguistic, rather than anthropological or practical. Dialectology will be considered a branch of linguistics, which is the formal study of the organization and content of language as it is known and used by native speakers. Our contention is that this approach must precede the others. Before we can consider the uses and functions of language diversity in society, and before we can decide on what educational maneuvers can and should be taken to alter those uses and functions, we must understand the dimensions, origins, and range of that diversity. The sociolinguist and the educationist can then carry out their special tasks on a basis of fact and understanding. Likewise the linguist will be able to undertake the study of language as it actually exists, not as it might be in an ideal world of perfect communication.

The emphasis throughout most of the book will be on how dialectologists have conducted their studies in the past, as well as on new concepts and techniques now coming into use. Illustrations of method and theory will be drawn from work on various languages, primarily the Germanic and Romance languages of western Europe and the New World. These are the areas where most of the pioneering and innovative study has been carried on, and where the most extensive published materials are found. But it should be stressed that dialectological study of other languages and language families has been and is being pursued. No attempt is made in this book to survey the results of this study worldwide. Our aim is rather to familiarize the reader with the discipline itself – the problems it encounters and the methodology that has been developed to deal with them.

Chapter 2 deals with the central concern of dialectology: variation in language. Variation is assumed to be a universal characteristic of language, rather than an occasional accidental feature. Various types of variation will be illustrated and their distribution across the speech community discussed.

Chapters 3–6 deal with the methodology of dialectology, as it has developed over the last century. Since the dialectologist, by the very nature of his subject matter, must deal with large bodies of language data, the discipline has been much involved with problems of collecting and handling this material. The first problem that faces the collector of dialect is how to sample the language and the community of its speakers. Since even unsophisticated users of a language are familiar with a large vocabulary, running to many thousands of words, it is evident that a collection attempting to encompass the complete lexicon of any dialect is an impossibility. The number of grammatical features, syntactic and morphological, while presumably smaller than the lexicon, is still very large. Only in phonology is anything like completeness reasonable to expect. Therefore the dialectologist must decide upon the sample of language he wishes to collect. This question is dealt with in Chapter 3.

The number of speakers in a dialect community is also likely to be quite large. Only in the case of an in-depth study of the language of a single village or other small community is it possible to interview all the speakers. Usually the dialect collector must be content with a sample of the population, and the larger the population is, the smaller the relative size of the sample must be. There are, after all, limitations of both time and cost, so that compromises must be made with an ideal of completeness. Thus attention must be given to the number and type or types of speakers to be interviewed, and to the procedures by which they are to be selected in order to guarantee that they accurately represent the population or segment of population to be dealt with. Chapter 4 deals with these problems.

Once the samples of language and of speakers have been decided upon, the dialectologist must decide how the actual collecting is to be managed. Chapter 5 discusses various methods that have been used in the past, and new methods made possible by technological aids like the tape recorder. Much forethought must go into planning the actual format of the records, so that they will be optimally accessible to editors and researchers. After all, a large collection of data, no matter how carefully planned, is of little use if it is disorganized and chaotic to such a degree that it is difficult and time-consuming to find what one is looking for. The larger the collection, the more careful and systematic must be its organization. Attention must also be given to the actual methods of collection – whether it is to be done by individual interviews in the field, by group interview at some central point, by checklists or tape-recordings solicited by mail, or whatever. And who is to do the collecting? In the past collectors have ranged from amateurs – local schoolteachers or clergymen, undergraduate or graduate students – to highly-trained professionals, capable of making rapid and accurate phonetic transcriptions of what they hear. The problem often resolves itself into a question of quantity versus quality. Since resources are always limited, those planning a collection of dialect material must decide whether they want a large body of material which may have considerable inaccuracy and incompleteness, or a smaller but more carefully collected sample, which makes up in accuracy and completeness what it lacks in number of speakers represented or number of linguistic items obtained.

Finally, decisions must be made as to how the collected material is to be made available. Here again the range of possibilities is great. At one extreme, the field records just as they are brought in by the interviewers may be published, possibly by some relatively inexpensive facsimile method. At the other extreme, the material may be subjected to a great deal of selection and editing, ultimately to be published in collections of elaborate and expensive maps, as in the great dialect atlases of the earlier part of this century. Tape-recordings are easy to collect but almost impossible to use until they are transcribed. Maps may be simply a presentation of raw data, or they may be carefully edited to display particular dialect features thought to be important or revealing. All these questions of editing and publication are discussed in Chapter 6.

These four chapters present the methodology of dialectology in considerable detail. There are several reasons for devoting so much space to what some might consider mere mechanics. In the first place, any interpretive study of dialect, whether linguistic or sociological in emphasis, can be no better than the corpus of language upon which it is based. Careful and intelligent planning of the collection phase of the discipline is essential, and has been the mark of the most successful ventures into the field. Secondly, a proper appreciation of the amount of labor that has gone into this phase of the study should lead the beginner in the discipline to a wholesome respect for the accomplishments of his predecessors, as well as a realistic appreciation of the problems and obstacles facing the dialect investigator. Finally, in spite of the importance of this aspect of the discipline, it has been given relatively little attention in recent general treatments of the subject (*eg* Kurath 1972; Petyt 1980; Chambers and Trudgill 1980).

Nevertheless, it is true that the ultimate aim of dialectology is to broaden and deepen our knowledge about language by taking into account all the facts about linguistic variation that can be assembled. Our last two chapters, on the relationship of dialectology to linguistic theory, survey the field and present illustrative examples of the application of various types of linguistic theory to dialect study. Four different approaches are discussed and illustrated: the traditional, which focuses on individual items; the structural, which views a language or dialect as a self-contained system; the generative, which uses the data of linguistic performance as a key to the speaker's internalized knowledge of his language; the sociolinguistic, which investigates the relationship between linguistic facts, including dialect variation, and the social organization of the speech community. Although these four approaches have appeared chronologically in the order given, the last three at least are still active. They are not mutually exclusive; the student of dialect should be familiar with the advantages and shortcomings of them all.

The Bibliography lists not only all the books and articles that have been specifically referred to, but also an ample selection of other materials that have influenced the writing of this book and may suggest further lines of study to the reader.

Chapter 2

Variation in language

Differential change

Variation in language results from differential change. If we could assume, quite hypothetically, that at a certain point in its history a language is homogeneous – the same for all speakers at all times – and further assume that either no changes take place or that such changes as do take place are adopted by all speakers, the language would remain free from variation. But these assumptions, while they might be useful for establishing linguistic theories, are obviously false. No language spoken by more than a very small number of people is homogeneous, and when changes occur, they characteristically affect the speech of only a part of the population of the total language community. Some speakers will adopt an innovation, others will either not be aware of it or will reject it, and in both cases the response may be conscious or unconscious. Some innovations, like slang, may be confined to a single social group and may remain completely unknown to others outside the group. It is seldom easy, and often impossible, to find a simple cause for a linguistic innovation, because the factors involved are many and complex. But whatever the motivation, it is normal for an innovation in language to be differentially accepted across the speech community. Thus each change that occurs is likely to increase the amount of variation in the language.

There is a paradox here, which may be put in the form of a question. If the purpose of language is communication, it would seem that the more homogeneous the language, the more efficient the communication. Why, then, does the increasing variation resulting from differential change not make communication difficult, unreliable, and eventually impossible? If so, the propensity for language to change would ultimately lead to a breakdown in the principal function for which language exists.

One answer to the question is that in some cases this is exactly what does happen. When two varieties of a language have changed to the point where their speakers cannot communicate, we recognize that they have actually become separate languages. The process is usually so slow that it cannot be observed taking place, but the results remain and the historical linguist can reconstruct what has happened. We know, for example, that some 2,000 years ago there was a single Germanic language, probably exhibiting dialect variation (as all languages do), but not so differentiated as to make communication impossible. But the process of differential change has proceeded so far that today there are many mutually unintelligible Germanic languages: English, German, Dutch, Swedish, and the rest. The same is true of the Romance languages – French, Spanish, Italian, Romanian, and others. In this latter case we know a good deal about the common language from which they all descend, Latin, though the Latin we encounter in school is the standard literary language, not the spoken dialects which eventually became so different as to be no longer viable for communication outside their own subdivisions of the Latin speech community.

So it is true that differential change does cause variation to the point of communication failure. But this only occurs when the need for communication is no longer urgent. Those who must communicate frequently with one another are constantly engaged in adapting their language to counteract the effects of differential change. The result is that they preserve a relatively homogeneous variety of the language, which makes communication with speakers of other varieties feasible. Changes occur, but those which have a serious effect on communication either spread through the whole language community or die out. So we can visualize a kind of tug-of-war between the natural tendency for innovation and change and the practical necessity for sufficient homogeneity to make communication possible and not too difficult.

Redundancy

One major reason that speech communities can tolerate considerable variation in their language lies in a quality that differentiates natural language from other communication codes. This quality is REDUNDANCY. In simple terms it means that a normal utterance in natural language, unlike a code such as telephone numbers or artificial languages like symbolic logic, contains more information

than is necessary to convey the message. Compare, for instance,
the following sentences:

[1] that man is my friend
[2] those men are my friends

The only difference in meaning between these is that [1] deals
with a single man, while [2] deals with more than one; they exhibit the contrast between singular and plural. If there were no
redundancy, this contrast could be indicated by a single change,
from *that* to *those*, for example, or from *man* to *men*. These
changes would produce the following variants of sentence [2]:

[2a] *those man is my friend
[2b] *that men is my friend

The star here indicates an ungrammatical sentence – of the kind
that might be used by a learner of the language, but not by a
native speaker. Actually, the notion of plural is signaled four
times in sentence [2]: by the changes of *that* to *those*, *man* to *men*,
is to *are*, and *friend* to *friends*. This is a rather large amount of
redundancy, but by no means unusual.

Redundancy allows a message to get across in spite of what information theorists call 'noise in the channel'. Here NOISE means
anything that interferes with accurate reception. In the case of
speech, the noise could be real noise, preventing the listener from
hearing all of the phonetic material, or linguistic noise, such as a
different intonation pattern or subphonemic variation in pronunciation. In writing, noise may be difficult handwriting or
erroneous spelling. In either case, the receiver often can fill in the
parts obscured by noise. In written English, for example, one can
usually make out the meaning of a sentence even though all
vowel characters are deleted:

[1a] th–t m–n –s m– fr—nd

Dialect variation can be looked at as a kind of noise in the
channel, which alters the surface form of an utterance without
destroying the message. Returning to the redundant signals in
sentence [2], we may observe that there are speakers of English
who do not signal number in the verb *be*, but either extend *is* into
the plural or use the base form *be* for both singular and plural.
The following versions of sentence [2] would result, whose meanings would be perfectly clear to those who themselves would produce the standard form, as in [2]:

[2c] those men is my friends
[2d] those men be my friends

These forms have not been starred, because while they are incor-
rect in the standard dialect of English, they are perfectly grammatical in the dialects of their speakers.

Other types of dialect variation might alter or obscure some of the other signals of plural in sentence [2]. The following are grammatical sentences in their own dialects, and both are clear enough to speakers of standard or of other dialects:

[2e] them guys is my friends
[2f] them dudes, they my frien'

It is clear, then, that redundancy is a principal reason for the fact that dialect variation does not destroy communication – though the noise it sets up may provoke annoyance with or even condemnation of the dialect speaker by the hearer.

Receptive adaptation

Another reason why communication does not necessarily fail in the presence of variation is to be found in the ability of the hearer to adapt his interpretive faculties to the language he is receiving. Since the speech community is not homogeneous, all members of it are familiar with different ways of speaking and capable of adjusting to them, consciously or unconsciously. In pronunciation, for example, we are not usually aware that a change in fundamental pitch, as from an adult male speaker to a child, makes quite drastic alterations in the acoustic signal. Yet the hearer is able to shift his interpretation to accommodate these differences, usually without knowing that he is doing it. Similar adjustments, somewhat more conscious, are made to speakers with foreign accents, speech impediments, and other more or less pathological forms of interference with normal phonological patterns. Adjustments are also quickly made to different phonological systems. The speaker who himself makes a phonemic distinction between *hoarse* and *horse* or between *cot* and *caught* has no trouble understanding the speaker who does not, since the context is usually redundant enough to prevent confusion.

What all this comes to is that the receiver of a linguistic message is not a passive machine reacting only to overt and explicit items in a code. He is instead a partner in the enterprise, constantly making use of his own experience with variation to reconstruct the message as it comes in, by means of all kinds of associations, contextual information, and awareness of the situation and of the idiosyncrasies of the speaker. This adaptability helps make communication possible in spite of the fact that the surface codes of speaker and listener may differ in many ways.

When we come to examine dialectal variation in some detail, it becomes apparent that there are two aspects to be considered: on the one hand the forms and systems of the language which are affected, and on the other the distribution of variation among the individuals and subgroups of the speech community. In the former, we consider the ways in which variation appears in the language, and in the latter the ways in which it is distributed in the overall community of speakers of the language. Both must be taken into account in a realistic total picture of the language and its users.

The incidence of variation in the language

Variation is to be found in all parts of the language: in the lexicon, the phonology, the grammar, and, superficially at least, the semantics. All of these are subject to change, and in all of them change can be differentially received, with resulting variation. At the outset, we should distinguish between casual or INCIDENTAL variation, which can affect individual linguistic items without upsetting the system, and SYSTEMATIC variation, which affects the language in more fundamental ways. As an illustration, consider the DEICTIC system of English – the system of modifiers and pronouns used to indicate the location of some referent in space, not absolutely, but in relation to the speaker, and to some extent the hearer as well. The system of modern standard English and of most dialects is BINARY, that, is, two elements are contrasted, one locating the referent as nearby and the other as further away. The basic system is this:

relation to speaker	demonstrative	locative adverb
near	*this – these*	*here*
far	*that – those*	*there*

Especially in the demonstrative set, some dialects use other forms, such as *this here, that there*, and *them* (for *those*). These are incidental variants, since they merely replace items without changing the system. But some dialects of English (especially in Scotland) have a three-way system of place:

relation to speaker and hearer	demonstrative	locative adverb
nearer to speaker	*this – these*	*here*
nearer to hearer	*that – those*	*there*
away from both	*yon (yonder)*	*yonder*

This is a systematic variation, since the semantic area covered by *that, those*, and *there* has been divided into two parts. Historically, in fact, it goes the other way. Early Modern English had a three-way system, but it has been abandoned in standard usage, except for archaic and poetic use. It was still quite normal for Shakespeare; witness Horatio's poetic description of dawn:

> But look, the morn, in russet mantle clad,
> Walks o'er the dew of *yon* high eastern hill. (*Hamlet* I.i.166f)

An example of incidental variation in phonology is the pronunciation of *tomato*. Three variants exist in American speech: /təméto/, /təmúto/, and /təmǽto/ (in all three the final vowel may be reduced to /ə/). This variation affects this word only, and since the particular vowel used is already present in the relevant dialects, it does not influence the phonemic system. In contrast, the fact that many American speakers, particularly in the South, make no contrast between /ɛ/ and /ɪ/ before nasals, is clearly a phonemic fact which affects one part of the total system. It means that many pairs of words are identical for these speakers, though they contrast for others: for example *pen : pin, tent : tint, hem : hymn/him, wench : winch*, and many more. In this respect their phonology shows a systematic variant.

Lexical variation

Since the lexicon, with its thousands of items, is the least structured part of language, it is more susceptible to incidental variation than to systematic. It is relatively easy to add a new word to the vocabulary without causing a systematic upset, especially when a need is created by some new object, event, or circumstance in the world around us. All of us have seen the rapid growth of the vocabulary of space in the last two decades. The new vocabulary consists partly of new creations, like *astronaut*, and partly of new meanings for old words, like *satellite*. Owing to great public interest, resulting in widespread dissemination via the mass media, there is little variation in this kind of vocabulary. But other new developments of more local interest do tend to give rise to varying local terms, which may be confirmed by official sanction. Thus that modern phenomenon, the high-speed limited-access divided highway, for example, is variously called an *expressway*, a *freeway*, a *throughway*, or a *turnpike* in the United States, and a *motorway* in Britain. There is no evidence at present that any one of these is becoming the single standard that will render the others obsolete. Possibly the reason that there are multiple terms in the United States and a single one in Britain is the fact that in America each of the fifty states has its own high-way bureau, while in Britain there is only one.

Lexical variation, whether involving different words or different meanings for the same word, is not confined to new things which must be named. Often it deals with common matters of everyday life and goes back a long time in the history of the language. A common cause is contact with another language, from which familiar words are borrowed. In the north of England, for example, a broad band of territory lying diagonally across the country from the northwest to the east was occupied by the Danish invaders of the ninth and tenth centuries, many of whom set-

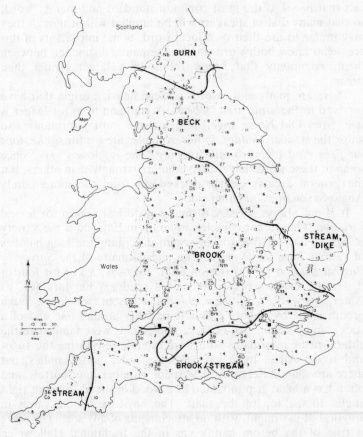

MAP 2.1.   Words for 'any running water smaller than a river' in England
(data from SED, IV.1.1).

tled down, intermarried with the local English, and soon lost their ethnic and linguistic identity. But the English of the region took many words from their language, which was closely related to English, and many of these words still remain. Map 2.1 shows the distribution of one of these words, *beck*, from Old Norse *bekkr*, the name of a body of running water smaller than a river. As can be seen, this word of Scandinavian origin appears in a wide band separating two Anglo-Saxon words, *burn* to the north and *brook* to the south. Even further south, along the southernmost row of counties, the favorite word is yet another Anglo-Saxon word, *stream*, though through most of this area most of the informants also use *brook*. The reason for that is undoubtedly the fact that *brook* is the most common standard and literary word, so that many dialect speakers will be familiar with it though they may prefer to use their own local word. Some informants in this area who knew both words made a semantic distinction between them, commonly that *brook* refers to a larger rivulet than *stream*.

There are many more words of Scandinavian origin that have survived in the same area as *beck*. A common term for *ladder* is *stee*, from Old Norse *stige*, though again most informants also know the standard *ladder*. Other examples are *lea* for *scythe, lops* for *fleas*, and the verb *laik* for *play*. The isoglosses vary, since some of these words have survived more strongly than others, but the general area is clearly marked off from the more purely Anglo-Saxon ones on either side.

It is not always so easy to find a historical reason for lexical variation. One rather complex situation in England is the variety of words, all Anglo-Saxon in origin, describing the long handles of various farm implements. The questionnaire of the *Survey of English Dialects* (SED) (Orton et al. 1962–71) asked for four of these: the handles respectively of a spade, a hay-fork (or, as Americans would call it, a *pitchfork*), a besom (which is a rough broom made by lashing a bundle of twigs around one end of a stick), and a scythe. All of these implements were familiar to the elderly rustic informants who were interviewed during the 1950s and 1960s. All of them have rather slender, long handles, but there are some differences. The spade handle is the shortest, and often has a hand grip mounted in a wood or metal frame at right angles to the top of the shaft. The hay-fork handle varies in length, but is straight, with no attachments of any sort. The same is true of the besom handle, as in the traditional Hallowe'en witch's broomstick. The scythe handle, unlike the others, is curved and has two short pieces fastened to it at right angles, by which it

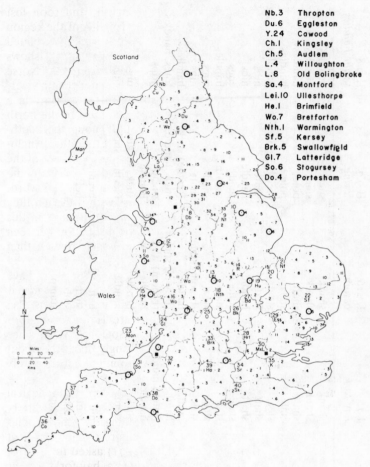

Nb.3	Thropton
Du.6	Eggleston
Y.24	Cawood
Ch.I	Kingsley
Ch.5	Audlem
L.4	Willoughton
L.8	Old Bolingbroke
Sa.4	Montford
Lei.IO	Ullesthorpe
He.I	Brimfield
Wo.7	Bretforton
Nth.I	Warmington
Sf.5	Kersey
Brk.5	Swallowfield
Gl.7	Latteridge
So.6	Stogursey
Do.4	Portesham

MAP 2.2.   Localities listed in Table 2.1.

is held and swung. These details are important, since they seem to be influential in determining the choice of words to name these handles.

The upper part of Table 2.1 lists the responses given to the relevant items in the SED questionnaire at seventeen localities in various parts of England. The localities themselves are shown on Map 2.2. It will be seen that they extend from Northumberland, next to the Scottish border, to Dorset in the extreme south.

Each item on the table is of interest in itself, as showing both the variety of terms and their regional distribution. Taken

TABLE 2.1 Handles of farm tools (data from *Survey of English Dialects*)

Locality	I.7.7 *spade*	I.7.12 *hay-fork*	I.3.16 *besom*	II.9.7 *scythe*	II.9.8 *scythe handles*
Nb.3	shank	shank	shank	sned	handles
Du.6	shaft	shank	shank	snid	handles
Y.24	shank	shaft	shaft	pole	handles
Ch.1	shaft	stale	stale	pole	handles
Ch.5	tree	steal	steal	(scythe) pole	handles
L.4	shaft	shaft	shaft	shaft	nibs
L.8	handle	shaft	handle	handle	nibs
Sa.4	stale	stale	stale	sned	cogs
Lei.10	handle	stale	stale	sneath	handles
He.1	(spade) tree	steal	steal	sned	cogs
Wo.7	handle	stale	(besom) stale	shaft	nibs
Nth.1	graft	graft	handle	(scythe) stick	handles
Sf.5	handle	handle	(broom) stick	stick, handle	fotes, handles
Brk.5	handle	(pitch) handle	(broom) stick	snead	grips
Gl.7	handle	handle	handle	handle	
So.6	stick	stick	handle	stick, snead	tugs
Do.4	stem	stem	handle	(scythe) stick	tugs
	helve (2)	hilt (2)	heft	beam	
	helm	foot	stem	heft	
	hilt	stake	stub		
	hean	strap	stump		
	jump				
	span				
	stock				
	strap				
	tiller				

together, they are even more interesting in what they show of varying degrees of semantic differential in various localities. Some observations that can be made are the following:

1. In only two of the localities is the same word used for all four: *shaft* at L.4 and *handle* at Gl.7. Since only one informant was interrogated for each question in each locality, this might simply indicate that the informant chosen had a limited vocabulary. Actually at both of these places the *scythe* question was answered by a different informant from the one who answered the other three. All were farm laborers, however.

2. At no locality were four different words given for the four types of handle. Most commonly, the same word was used for the fork and besom handles and different ones for the spade and scythe. This is true at seven of the seventeen localities: Du.6, Y.24, Ch.1, Ch.5, Lei.10, He.1, and Wo.7. At two others, one word serves for the first three items, with a separate word for the scythe: Nb.3 and Sa.4. Six localities use the same word for the spade and fork handles, and different ones for the other two; these are Nth.1, Sf.5, Do.4, and So.6.

3. Certain words are used only for one of the types of handle. This is most noticeable in the *scythe* column, where *sned, snid, snead*, and *sneath* account for seven of the seventeen localities. These are all phonological variants of the same word, descending from the Old English (OE) word *snæd*, which has always meant 'scythe handle'. It does not appear in any of the other columns. Likewise *tree* appears twice in the *spade* column, but is not used for any of the others.

4. Certain words seem to have regional distribution, while others occur in all parts of the country. *Shank*, for example, is a northern word: the three localities where it appears are in Northumberland, Durham, and Yorkshire, all in the north of England. But this distribution is limited to this meaning; in the original sense of 'leg' or 'leg-bone' the word is universal. *Stick* in this meaning is confined to the southern half of the country. The various descendants of OE *snæd*, on the other hand, range from Northumberland in the far North to Somerset in the Southwest.

5. In the last column, the local words for the two short hand grips attached to the scythe handle are given. It is noteworthy that these are called *handles* at eight of the seventeen places, but not at those where the same word is used for the large handle. It obviously would lead to confusion if both were called by the same name.

The great diversity of terminology here is typified by the fact that two villages only 35 miles apart (Lei.10 and Nth.1) use completely different sets of words for the four types of handles.

In the lower part of Table 2.1 are listed all the other words recorded at any of the 314 localities surveyed. (Each form occurs in only one locality except the two marked as occurring twice.) It is hard to explain why there are more different words for the spade handle than for any of the others: 17 as compared with 11 for the fork, 9 for the besom, and only 7 for the scythe (counting the phonological variants of *snead* as one).

One common source of lexical variation is differing response to the need for new words resulting from cultural or technological change. We have already noted the different terms given a new type of road in different parts of the English-speaking community. Another, more complicated example is the terminology created in Britain and America in response to two new modes of transportation: the railroad and the automobile. Both of these came into existence after the major breach in the English-speaking community caused by first the geographical and then the political separation of Americans from Britons. Although there was fairly constant intercommunication between the two major communities of English speakers, they to a considerable extent went their own ways in creating the vocabulary of the railroad

TABLE 2.2   Railway and motoring terms

British	US
Railway	
railway	railroad
line	track
level crossing	grade crossing
points	switch
shunt (vb.)	switch
carriage	car
goods van	freight car
guard	conductor
left luggage office	checkroom
Motoring	
motor car	automobile
tonneau	back seat
bonnet	hood
boot	trunk
saloon	sedan
change (gears)	shift
petrol	gas (oline)

and the motor car (*cf* Lane 1980). Table 2.2 gives illustrations of the differing terminology.

There are, of course, many terms common to both countries: in motoring: *car, clutch, brakes, carburetor, radiator, steering wheel*, etc. and in railroading: *train, locomotive, station, ticket*. Some of the original terms in each country have given way to the rival transatlantic ones as well. But the two vocabularies still retain considerable variation.

A more subtle, and sometimes more confusing, form of lexical variation is the use of the same word to mean different things in different dialects. This can be seen in Table 2.1. At Du.6 and Y.24, two localities only 65 miles apart, the words *shank* and *shaft* reverse themselves: at Du.6 *shank* refers to the handles of the hay-fork and besom and *shaft* to that of the spade, while at Y.24 the opposite is the case. Even within a single county (Norfolk), the term *daddy-long-legs* refers in some localities to a spider-like creature (as in the United States) and in others to a crane fly. In the southern United States a *gopher* is a hard-shelled land tortoise, while in the West it is a kind of burrowing rodent, similar to a prairie dog. Since neither animal occurs in the other's territory, confusion seldom arises from this ambiguity of reference.

In fact, lexical variation seldom leads to confusion or ambiguity when speakers of different dialects attempt to communicate. The usual response, at least among native speakers, is amusement. The tendency of speakers of other dialects to use 'funny words' for things is taken as one more example of the perversity of strangers and foreigners. This is undoubtedly part of the reason for the popularity of word collections in dialectology, particularly of an amateur sort. The technicalities of phonology and grammar may interest linguists, but everybody is interested in words.

Phonological variation

Earlier in this chapter the distinction was made between incidental and systematic variation. Both kinds may appear in phonology. Thus two speakers whose pronunciation is alike in most respects may have differing pronunciations of certain words. The example of *tomato* has been cited above. Other examples are *economics* (/ik-/ or /ɛk-/), *athlete* (/ǽθəlit/ or /ǽθlit/), *hostile* and other adjectives in *-ile* (/-ɪl/, /-əl/, or /-aɪl/). The adoption of one or the other pronunciation by individual speakers hardly constitutes dialect variation; it is primarily idiosyncratic. It may be motivated by a conscious desire to be 'correct', by the fact that the word was first encountered in print and the speaker devised his own pronunciation on the basis of the spelling, or merely by whim. This kind of incidental variation in pronunciation may become so widespread that differing versions are both accepted as 'correct' even within the standard dialect. This is true of the examples given above, all of which are cited in Webster's *Third New International Dictionary* (though /ǽθəlit/ is marked 'chiefly substandard'). Some variations of this sort may have a regional distribution as well; pronunciation of the suffix *-ile* as /-ɑɪl/ is much more common in England than in the United States; in fact, the pronunciation with /-ɪl/ or /-əl/ marks the speaker as American, though the reverse is not true.

This kind of incidental variation, though sometimes marking regional or class dialect, is relatively unimportant linguistically. More significant are those differences which, taken cumulatively, make up an ACCENT. This is a common term for a variant pronunciation system, as in 'Oxford accent', 'southern accent'. It is also used technically by linguists, especially in Great Britain, to describe a variety of speech differing from others only or primarily in pronunciation. As David Abercrombie puts it: '*Accent* and *dialect* are words which are often used vaguely, but which can be given more precision by taking the first to refer to characteristics of the medium [*ie* speech] only, while the second refers to characteristics of language as well.' (Abercrombie 1967, *p* 19; see also Abercrombie 1965) These differences can be of four principal kinds:

1. differences in the number of phonemes constituting the system or a subsystem within it;
2. differences in the feature constituency of the phonemes;
3. differences in the allophonic realization of the phonemes;
4. differences in the incidence of the phonemes, *ie* in their distribution through the lexicon.

It is obvious that these types of difference are not wholly independent: (1) and (4) are related by the fact that if one variety has, for example, three front vowels and another has four, the sets of words having specific front vowels will differ; (2) and (3) are related by the fact that allophonic representation of a phoneme is controlled by its distinctive features. It is convenient, however, to deal with these four types of variation separately.

1. Number of phonemes

English is somewhat unusual among languages in that almost all varieties use the same set of consonants, but the number and nature of vowel systems vary greatly. An attempt was made thirty years ago by G. L. Trager and H. L. Smith, Jr, to establish an 'overall pattern' of nine basic vowels, which they claimed encompassed all dialects of English, though some dialects might lack one or more of the nine (Trager and Smith 1951). Other linguists objected to the proposal on various grounds, principally that it set up a straitjacket into which some systems could be fitted only by distorting or disregarding phonological facts. The assertion that Dialect A 'lacked' a certain vowel seemed to suggest that

MAP 2.3.   Scottish vowel systems (data from Catford 1957).

that dialect was somehow deficient, or even that it also lacked the words which had the missing vowel in other dialects. This, of course, is not the case; two varieties of English may have identical lexicons while using different vowel systems to express them. On the other hand, it was shown that certain dialects, in the American South, for example, have ten or more simple vowels. Given these facts, there is no way of establishing a specified number of vowels as normal or standard for English.

An interesting presentation of varying numbers of phonemes within subvarieties of a regional variety of English is that of J. C. Catford on Scottish vowels (Catford 1957). In a single environmental pattern, words of one syllable ending in /t/, Catford finds that Scottish vowel systems range in number from eight to twelve. Simply on the basis of the number of vowel phonemes, the distribution of various systems is as shown in Map 2.3. A count shows that of the 69 localities mapped, 3 have eight-vowel systems, 27 have nine, 11 have ten, 15 have eleven, and 13 have twelve. The favored number is nine, but it still accounts for fewer than half the localities. Isoglosses have been drawn to include the nine-vowel area (also the three eight-vowel localities and one ten), which covers the industrial center of the country, including the large cities of Edinburgh and Glasgow. Around the fringes of this area to the north, west, and south the vowel systems range from ten to twelve, with the twelve-vowel areas in the northeast and southwest furthest from the center. This is a characteristic pattern which dialectologists recognize as a FOCAL AREA with RELIC AREAS surrounding it. Catford concludes: 'This suggests that the 12-vowel system is a survival, and that 16th century "standard" Scots may have had such a system.' (p 115)

2. *Feature constituency*[1]

To say that two varieties of a language have the same number of phonemes but that the feature constituency of some members of one set is different from that of another is, in effect, to say that the two sets do not match, that some of the phonemes in one set are different from those in another. To take a simple example, consider the two vowel systems which Kurath and McDavid call American Type II (Metropolitan New York, the Upper South, and the Lower South) and Type V (Standard British English) (Kurath and McDavid 1961, *pp* 6–7). These systems are given in Table 2.3.

It will be seen that both systems have thirteen vowels and three diphthongs. But they differ in three respects:

1. The vowel of *crop* (and the other 'short o' words) is [−round] in Type II and [+round] in Type V.

2. The vowel of *sun* (and most other 'short u' words except *put, pull*, etc.) is [−high, −low, +back] in Type II and [−high, +low, −back, −front] in Type V.

3. The vowel of *car* (also *father, calm*) is [+back] in Type II and [−back, −front] in Type V.

These differences in feature constituency account for three of the characteristics of what Americans call an 'English accent'.

TABLE 2.3   American English vowel systems (after Kurath and McDavid)

Type II

crib : three	ɪ	i			ɷ	u	wood : tooth
ten : ate	ɛ	e		ɜ	ʌ	o	sun : road
hat : (man)	æ	(æː)				ɔ	law
					ɑ	ɒ	crop : car
five		aɪ	au			ɔi	boil
			thirty				
			down				

The vowel in parentheses is a long, tense, somewhat raised low front vowel, which appears in some dialects, particularly Philadelphia, New York, and the Middle Atlantic region. Its development as a distinctive phoneme is subsequent to the data on which the Kurath–McDavid analysis is based (see Ferguson 1972).

Type V

crib : three	ɪ	i			ɷ	u	wood : tooth
ten : eight	ɛ	e		ɜ		o	road
bag	æ		ʌ ɒ		ɒ	ɔ	crop : law
five		ai	au			ɔi	boil
			thirty				
		sun : car					
			down				

An even greater difference appears in the Scottish nine-vowel systems, which Map 2.3 shows to predominate in central Scotland. They are divided into two sets, one having an extra high central round vowel and the other having an extra low back vowel, which may or may not be round. These contrasting systems are marked 9_1 and 9_2 on the map, and their vowel systems are:

System 9_1			*System 9_2*		
i		u	i	ⓤ	u
e	ɜ	o	e	ɜ	o
ɛ		ʌ	ɛ		ʌ
a	ⓞ		a		

In each case the extra vowel is circled. What this means is that in a 9_1 system a word like *taut* contrasts with *tot*, while in a 9_2 system they are homophonous; and that in a 9_2 system *bit* contrasts with *boot*, while in a 9_1 system they are alike (as /bɛt/). Reference to Map 2.3 shows that these two systems are distinctively located, the 9_1 systems in the center and west, and the 9_2 systems in two areas, one in the extreme east (Berwick) and the other in the south central area (primarily Dumfries). It is clear that though they have the same number of phonemes, these two types contrast both in phoneme membership and in distribution.

3. Phonetic realization

Differences in the phonetic realization of phonemes are very common; it is probable that they constitute the major part of what ordinary speakers of a language recognize as different accents. Some of them may individually be too slight to be explicitly recognized, except by those trained in phonetics. Others may be quite conspicuous, to the point where they are identified by all as markers of specific accents. Among these might be mentioned the 'Northumbrian burr' and the Canadian rendition of the diphthong /aw/ before voiceless consonants as [əɷ] (this also occurs in regions of the United States, such as the coastal South).

One particularly interesting example of allophonic variation is the wide variety of phonetic realizations given to the English phoneme /r/ in postvocalic position. In Great Britain, six main types are recognizable, each having its own regional distribution. They are:

[r] a dental or alveolar tongue-tip trill
[ɹ] an alveopalatal frictionless continuant, formed by bunching and retracting the tongue
[ʈ] a retroflex continuant, formed by turning the tip of the tongue up toward and nearly touching the hard palate.
[ʁ] a uvular fricative, rather similar to the /r/ of Parisian French, northern German, or Danish
[ə] A mid-central non-syllabic vowel
[:] lengthening of preceding /ɑ/ or /ɔ/.

Some linguists do not consider the last two of these as allophones of /r/. Instead, they assume either that /r/ has been replaced by another phoneme, /ə/, or that it has been deleted, with resulting 'compensatory lengthening' of the preceding vowel. Dialects or accents showing these realizations of postvocalic /r/ are called 'r-less' dialects. This is a misnomer, since these dialects have a genuine /r/ in other positions, such as word-initial or intervocalic. But since these two phonetic elements occur in the same

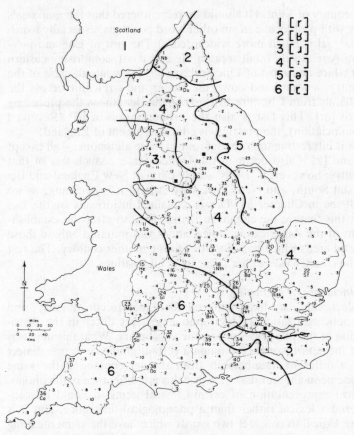

MAP 2.4.   Varieties of /r/ in *arm* (data from SED, VI.6.8).

position as the other four and in complementary distribution with them, it seems most logical to consider them allophones of /r/.

These six renditions of postvocalic /r/ have clear-cut regional distribution in Great Britain. Map 2.4 shows the variant pronunciations of the /r/ in *arm*, as recorded by the SED. The trilled [r] is characteristic of Scottish English; it was recorded by the SED in only one location in England, Longtown in Cumberland. The uvular trill or fricative [ʁ] is restricted to the extreme north of England; it is the 'Northumbrian burr'. The retroflex variety is standard in the West Country and the South. The frictionless continuant [ɹ], which is the most common type in America, is limited to two widely separated and rather small regions, one in Lancashire in the northwest and the other in the extreme southeast-

ern county of Kent. (It should be remembered that the map deals
only with postvocalic /r/; in other word positions, especially word-
initial, [ɹ] is much more widespread.) The rest of England is 'r-
less.' A relatively small area on the east coast, comprising eastern
Yorkshire and most of Lincolnshire, has [ə], while the rest of the
country, a wide band down the center and stretching across the
Midlands from Cheshire to East Anglia, lengthens the preceding
/ɑ/ to [ɑː]. This last is also the pronunciation in RP (Received
Pronunciation), the prestigious educated accent of England.

It is interesting to note that four of these allophones – all except
[r] and [ʁ] – also occur in the United States. Much less of that
country, however, is 'r-less' – only parts of New England and the
coastal South, and New York City (where it is declining, as we
shall see in Chapter 8). This is explained historically by the fact
that this feature developed in British English after the establishment of the American colonies, and it was imitated only in those
coastal areas which had close ties to the mother country. The rest
of the country uses either [ɹ] or [ɽ] in all positions.

4. Incidence of phonemes

Dialects may be alike in the number, feature constituency, and
phonetic realization of their phonemes, yet differ in the distribution of the phonemes across the vocabulary. What this means is
that the set of words containing a certain phoneme in one dialect
has a different membership from the set containing the same
phoneme in another dialect. Since this is a difference in the phonological representation of certain lexical items, it could be considered a lexical rather than a phonological difference. But it is
more logical to consider two words which have the same meaning
and grammatical function in two dialects and differ in only one or
two phonemic segments as the same word. An example from
American English is the contrast between /u/ and /ɷ/ as the stem
vowel of words spelled with *oo*. All American dialects have two
contrasting high back round vowels, tense /u/ and lax /ɷ/. The former is virtually universal in *pool, fool, mood, loop, boon, doom,
loose*, and many more. The latter is standard in *good, foot, cook*,
etc. But quite a few words vary between the two; among them are
hoof, roof, root, soot, room, coop, hoop. The distribution of these
words between the /u/ set and the /ɷ/ set varies greatly, both re-
gionally and individually. Even speakers native to the same community may have different patterns.

Another example showing clear regional variation in the United
States is the so-called 'broad *a*'. Most varieties of English have
both a low-front /æ/ or /a/ and a low central or back long /ɑː/ (represented as /ɒ/, following Kurath, in the charts of Table 2.3). For

the majority of speakers of American English, the latter vowel is relatively rare, occurring principally before /r/, as in *barn, car, heart, card*, and in a few individual words like *father* and -*al*- words such as *calm, palm* (but not *half*). But in the eastern New England area, /ɑː/ appears instead of /æ/ in quite a large number of words before /f, v, s, θ, ð/ and the combinations /nt, ns, nd/, such as *half, pass, path, can't, dance*. This pronunciation also characterizes British RP and other British dialects. At one time it was considered prestigious in the United States and was assumed by speakers who wished to indicate their superior education or social status. Unfortunately for them, no simple rule applies; the 'broad *a*' does not always replace /æ/ before the indicated consonants. So the pretentious speakers often revealed that they were not native speakers of a 'broad *a*' dialect by using /ɑː/ not only in *glass, bath, laugh, can't*, and *dance*, which was correct, but also in *lass, math, graph, pant*, and *romance*, which did not belong to the the /ɑː/ set in any native variety. Linguists call this *hypercorrection*.

A recent change in RP is the shift of quite a few words from the /ɔ/ set to the /ɒ/ set, among them *coffee, lost, often, boss*, and many others having a voiceless fricative after the vowel. Most American speakers retain the /ɔ/ in these words. This, then, represents a case where the difference between British and American pronunciation has increased rather than diminished during the last generation.

The examples of phonological variation so far cited mostly have to do with single phonemes, their distribution and realization. But variation is found in other parts of the phonological system. Stress, and its frequent concomitant, vowel reduction or deletion, may vary from one dialect to another, as in British *secret'ry, diction'ry, labórat'ry*, compared with American *secretary, dictionary*, and *láb'ratòry*. Intonation patterns may differ to the point where serious misunderstanding may result: some British intonations are interpreted as offensive or hostile by Americans, and the wider pitch range sometimes used quite normally by British men may be interpreted as effeminate by Americans, who associate wider pitch range with women's speech. On the other hand, the narrower pitch range of American speech can sound dull and monotonous to a Briton. It is differences of this sort that led Bernard Shaw to remark that England and America are two countries kept apart by a common language.

Grammatical variation

Morphology
The field of grammar is commonly divided into two parts. MOR-PHOLOGY and SYNTAX. Roughly speaking the former has to do

with the phonological shapes of words that adapt them to specific grammatical functions, principally by the application of various affixes or by compounding. INFLECTIONAL morphology is related to the morphophonemic rules at the end of the syntax, while DE-RIVATIONAL morphology is related to the adaptation of lexical forms to accommodate the word-class subdivisions of the lexicon. The past-tense modifications in which, for example, *walk, drag, bat,* and *sit* plus PAST become /wɔkt/, /drægd/, /bǽtɪd/, and /sæt/ exemplify inflectional morphology, while the creation of nouns from the adjectives *hard, difficult,* and *native* by adding the suffixes *-ness, -y,* and *-ity* to give *hardness, difficulty,* and *nativity* is an example of derivational morphology. Variation may appear in both of these.

A field of inflectional morphology of English where much vari-ation appears is the plural forms of nouns. English forms noun plurals in four basic ways:

1. By suffixing the regular plural ending. This has three allo-morphs: /-ɪz/ or /-əz/ after stems ending in a [+ strident] con-sonant (*ie* /s, z, š, ž, č, ǰ/), as in *horses, roses, wishes, mirages, matches, judges;* /-s/ after stems ending in other voiceless con-sonants (/p, t, k, f, θ/), as in *caps, hats, ducks, laughs, myths;* /-z/ after stems ending in other phonemes (voiced stops and fricatives, sonorants, glides, vowels), as in *jobs, waves, buns, walls, doors, sofas,* etc.
2. By using the singular form unchanged, as in *sheep, fish, species.*
3. By changing the stem vowel, as in *feet, mice, men, women.*
4. By adding or substituting an irregular suffix, either native or derived from a foreign language, as in *oxen, children, alumni, strata, criteria, seraphim.*

Variation of one sort or another occurs within or between all of these. One of the most common forms is to use (1), the regular suffix, for words which in standard or conservative English use (4). Thus *geniuses* alternates with *genii* and *corpuses* with *cor-pora.* This is in line with the general pressure of analogy to regu-larize the language. Alternatively, some words for which the standard language uses the regular form have in some dialects plural forms in *-en* or *-n,* representing survival of older forms of the language. Thus some dialects have *toen, eyen,* and *housen* in-stead of *toes, eyes,* and *houses.*

Another common variation is to extend group (2), especially to nouns of measure or quantity: *four mile down the road, it weighs six pound, I've lived here five year.*

One interesting variant occurs within the regular rule. In some

areas of southern England the allomorph /-ɪz/ (or /-ɪs/) is used instead of the expected /-s/ after stems ending in -*st*. Thus the dialect of Dorset has the plurals *fistes, postes, nestes, chestes*, and
ghostes (Widén 1949). This may be a survival from the fifteenth
century, or it may be an innovation resulting from the insertion of
a vowel to break up the difficult consonant cluster /sts/. It will be
further discussed in Chapter 7.

Another part of English inflectional morphology where much
variation occurs is the past tense forms of irregular verbs, those
that change the stem vowel instead of or in addition to adding the
regular suffix in /-t/, /-d/, or /-ɪd/. There were more of these verbs
in older English; the process of analogy has resulted in many of

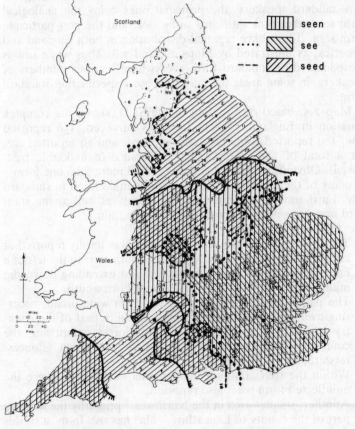

MAP 2.5. Irregular past tense forms of *see* in England (data from SED,
VIII.2.5).

them shifting into the regular class. But dialects, both regional and social, often preserve older irregular forms, either in place of or in alternation with the newer regular forms. Examples are *clum* (*climbed*), *holp* (*helped*), *swole* (*swelled*). Conversely, analogical regular forms may be used in place of irregular forms still considered standard; for example, *throwed*, *catched*.

A notable fact about morphological variation in English is that it is more likely to be a matter of social or class-based variation, unlike lexical and phonological variation, which are mostly regional. In some cases, both kinds of variation may occur within the same form. A case in point is the past tense forms of the verb *see*. Throughout the English-speaking world, the standard past tense form is *saw*. But variant forms are common in the usage of non-standard speakers, the principal ones being the analogical form *seed*, the form with zero suffix, *see*, and the past participle form *seen*. These have regional distribution in both England and America, as illustrated by Maps 2.5 and 2.6. Thus while *saw* is the educated or standard form everywhere, various numbers of speakers, in some areas the majority, use a specific non-standard form.

Map 2.5, based on the data of the SED, shows the complex situation in England. Of 314 localities surveyed, 136 reported *saw*, 180 reported *seen*, 129 reported *seed*, and 86 reported *see*, for a total of 531 (there was one instance of a double past, *sawed*). Obviously many localities reported more than one form – in many of them two non-standard forms in addition to standard *saw*. Furthermore, the non-standard forms, as well as the standard *saw*, have definite geographical distribution.

The following facts appear from the records:

1. There is a rather large area where *saw* was hardly reported at all. It includes most of the West and Southwest, to the left of a line starting in northern Lancashire and extending down the middle of the country to the coast near Portsmouth.
2. The past participle form *seen* is the most widespread, occurring everywhere in the central and southern part of the country except for an area in the Southwest comprising the counties of Somerset and Dorset and parts of Devon, Gloucestershire, and Wiltshire.
3. Within the *seen* area is a smaller area in the East where the uninflected form *see* is also reported.
4. Another, smaller area in the Northwest–primarily the western part of the county of Lancashire – also has *see*. In most of this area it is the only form; even *saw* is not reported (it is to be kept in mind that most of the informants for SED were relatively uneducated farm workers).

5. The analogical form *seed* occurs in two areas, one covering the whole Southwest, and the other the north central and northern part of the country except for the area near the Scottish border, where *saw* is the only form reported. Over most of this area, *seed* is the only non-standard form reported; in part of the Southwest it is the only form, and in the North it varies with the standard *saw*.

Map 2.6, which is based on the data of the Linguistic Atlas of the U.S. as interpreted by Atwood (1953, Fig. 17), shows that the situation in the eastern United States is also complex. Atwood comments as follows:

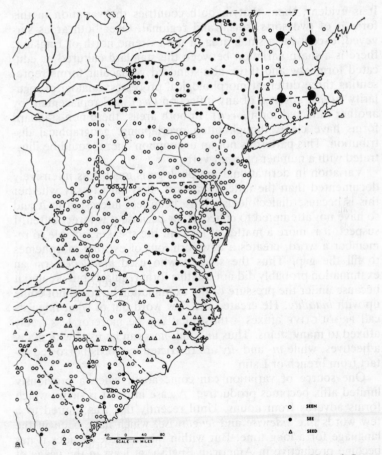

○	SEEN
●	SEE
△	SEED

SCALE IN MILES
40 0 40 80

MAP 2.6. Irregular past tense forms of *see* in eastern United States (from Atwood 1953).

The standard *saw* /sɔ/ is practically universal in cultured speech; in other types it is universally recorded only in central Massachusetts and in a small area around New York City.... The uninflected preterite *see* /si/ ... is by far the most common variant form in New England.... [It] also prevails in New York and the northernmost edge of Pennsylvania.... It predominates over other variants in the Piedmont area of Virginia and part of the Tidewater area, as well as in parts of northeast North Carolina.... The form *seen* /sin/ ... strongly predominates in the Midland area.... The weak preterite *seed* /sid/ ... extends more or less all across North Carolina, in some areas being the only preterite form in use other than *saw*. [It] also occurs in a rather scattered way in South Carolina and Eastern Georgia.

(Atwood 1953, *p* 20; geographical abbreviations have been expanded)

It is evident, then, that in both countries the variation in this form is of two sorts, social and regional. Over both areas surveyed, except for a small area in the extreme north of England, there is a sharp variation between the standard cultured or educated form *saw* and three non-standard vernacular forms representing three different morphological processes: analogical regularity (*seed*), absence of any inflection (*see*), and replacement by another inflected form (*seen*). In both areas, these non-standard forms have clear, though often overlapping, geographical distribution. This pattern is not an uncommon one; it could be illustrated with a number of other verbs.

Variation in derivational morphology is much less intensively documented than the inflectional sort. It is hard to say whether this is because dialectologists have been less interested in it and so have not attempted to collect it, or because it is rarer. Often, I suspect, it is more a matter of lexicon: the speaker, unable to remember a word, creates a new form out of existing morphemes to fill the gap. Thus the student who used *unableness* on an examination probably did not use this form regularly but created it because under the pressure of the examination he could not come up with *inability*. He created the new word out of what linguists call PRODUCTIVE affixes – those that can be more or less freely affixed to many stems. Thus *un-* and *-ness* can be used with many adjectives, while *in-* and *-ity* are restricted to words borrowed intact from French or Latin.

One source of variation can come about when a previously limited affix becomes productive. A case in point is *-wise*, which forms adverbs from nouns. Until recently this was limited to a few words like *sidewise* and *lengthwise*, which have been in the language for a long time. But within the last few decades it has become productive in American English, at least in the usage of some speakers. This has produced new synonyms or near-synonyms for words already in the language like *job-wise* (*occu-pationally*), as well as some new adverbs which have no easy equivalent except a rather cumbersome phrase, such as *price-wise* (*with regard to price*, or *as far as price is concerned*). Many con-servative speakers object strenuously to this innovation.

Syntax

Variation in syntax has been very little studied by dialectologists, for two reasons. In the first place, syntax as a branch of linguistics has not been given much attention until fairly recently. Secondly, most significant syntactic variation requires larger samples of a language than it has been convenient or even possible to collect by the usual methods. Usually a complete sentence, often a quite long one, is needed to display a variant syntactic construction. The fieldworker collecting material with notebook and pencil finds it very difficult to record long sentences without asking the informant to repeat what he has said, a procedure which is dif-ficult and unsatisfactory for both. As a result, the syntactic mate-rial which has been collected more or less systematically is limited to those variations which can be displayed in a short sample. Among these are such matters as subject – verb agreement, the formation of negatives, pronoun reference and case, and question formation. The systematic study of larger forms of syntactic vari-ation is only now becoming possible because of the accumulation of larger samples of speech by tape-recording. This is one of the challenging areas of dialectology today.

One field in which there has been considerable study of syntac-tic variation is the kind of English called Black English Vernacu-lar (or BEV for short). This has been defined as 'the variety most typically spoken by working-class [American] blacks' (Wolfram and Fasold 1974, *p* 11, n. 4). It is thus a rather vague term used to describe the variety or varieties of English spoken and to some extent written by those Black Americans who do not customarily use standard English, either as native speakers or as a result of education. This variety of English, southern in origin, has been spread over the country by the movement of Black people. It ex-hibits considerable syntactic variation, which has been quite ex-tensively studied and analyzed during the last twenty years or so (*eg* Labov 1973).

The incidence of variation in the community

So far, the discussion has dealt primarily with the incidence of variation in the language: the particular sections of the overall linguistic system where variation occurs. It remains to discuss the incidence of variation in the speech community: the particular groups or individuals in the total community of speakers of a language who exhibit the kinds of variation we have been discussing. To a certain degree this has been implied or even explicit in the illustrations so far given. Insofar as it is possible to make maps of the kind appearing earlier in this chapter, it is assumed that such variation exists at least on a geographical basis. But the incidence of variation in the community requires a closer and more detailed examination.

At the outset, it can be observed that this variation can be of three principal sorts: (1) between groups of speakers, (2) between individual speakers, and (3) within the performance of the individual speaker. The first of these can be called DIALECTAL variation proper, the second IDIOLECTAL, and the third STYLISTIC. There are difficulties with all of these terms; we have already seen those surrounding the term *dialect*. Because of these difficulties, one recent student of linguistic variation has recommended abandonment of the term *dialect* altogether, in favor of LECT, which he describes as 'a completely non-committal term for any bundling together of linguistic phenomena' (Bailey 1973a, *p* 11). It thus becomes a comprehensive term which includes the three kinds of variation mentioned above. If we wish to use it to refine the terms used above, we can define a *dialect* as 'a lect characterizing a group of speakers', an *idiolect* as 'a lect characterizing a single speaker', and a *style* as 'a lect constituting one mode or phase of an idiolect'.

Dialectal variation

Any community of speakers of a language, with the possible exception of very small ones, will be found to be subdivided into groups according to various parameters, each of which will exhibit some linguistic features different from those of other groups. There are five such parameters which are important and general; others may occur within special linguistic communities. These five are geography, class, racial or ethnic identity, sex, and age.

Geographic variation

By the necessity of occupying a particular place of abode, a group sets itself off from other groups. Particularly before the explosive technological advances in modes of transportation and communication which have occurred in the twentieth century, it simply was very difficult or actually impossible for most speakers to converse with other speakers who lived more than a few miles away. Thus, even without the intervention of some sort of group loyalty or identity, speakers were limited to a speech community consisting of a relatively small number of the total population using the language. The single village or tribe of a few hundred people has traditionally been assumed by dialectologists to be the first place to look for distinctive linguistic variation. Larger geographical subdivisions, set apart by political, economic, or geographical barriers, are characterized by their own dialectal variation, which may be considered either the sum of the variations among the smaller communities or their common core. Density or sparseness of population and ease or difficulty of travel further influence the size and diversity of local dialects, as may the degree of mobility of the population. From farmstead to village, to market town, to city is a scale which may ultimately extend to nation – references have been made earlier in this book to differences between American and British English, or between the Flemish of Belgium and the Dutch of the Netherlands. It is this kind of regional variation which has been most commonly the subject of dialectological study, at least until recently.

Class or social variation

Virtually all human societies exhibit other kinds of grouping, within the larger group of those living in the same geographical area. A most important one is based on the social class structure of the community. No matter how equalitarian or democratic they may be in theory, all societies – even the idealistic 'classless' societies based on religious or political ideology – exhibit some form of class structure. There are laborers, farmers, craftsmen, governors, judges, teachers, usually priests, not to mention entertainers, idlers, criminals, and vagabonds. The society may not officially recognize all these classes to the point of spelling out their particular duties, responsibilities, privileges, and constraints, but their members will tend to associate with one another more closely than with members of other classes. As the old adage has it: 'Birds of a feather flock together.' In turn, this selectiveness of association will foster linguistic variation. The term SOCIAL DIALECT is often used as a cover term for diverse forms of class-based linguistic variation.

Racial or ethnic variation

The tendency for members of a community to be set apart from the rest by hereditary racial or ethnic qualities is also widespread in human societies. Such separation may be imposed by the over-

all community, as in the confinement of Jews in ghettos in some
European cities, or the segregation of American Negroes in their
own churches, schools, and residential areas in some parts of the
United States. It may also be by the more or less free choice of
the members of the group, as in the case of ethnic communities
within cities. Many American cities have Italian, Polish, Chinese,
and other districts where people of those national heritages
choose to live, though under no overt compulsion to do so.
Usually it is a combination of outside social pressure and internal
ethnic pride and social ease which creates and preserves these
ethnic subcommunities. In any case they are strong breeding-
grounds for linguistic variation.

Sexual variation

In most societies, individuals tend to associate more with members of their own sex than with those of the opposite sex. In more
primitive societies this may be an inevitable consequence of the
way in which the community supports itself. The men act as hun-
ters, often of large game which must be captured by group cooperation, and the women maintain gardens, cook the food, and
make the clothing, which are also cooperative tasks. The same
type of division may perpetuate itself in more 'civilized' societies.
The men leave the home for the work-place or office, lunch
together at restaurants or clubs, and seek recreation of various
forms from which women are often barred, from cock-fighting to
bowling or poker-playing. The result of the combination of economic, social, and to some extent physical segregation by sex
leads to various degrees of linguistic variation. One of the many
consequences of the recent women's liberation movement in
American society is the degree to which younger women avoid
the more clearly marked feminine linguistic traits of their mothers
and grandmothers. Other societies, on the other hand, may en-
force the separation to the point where there is a special women's
language, differing quite widely in many respects from that of
men.

Age variation

Every child learns – or, rather, teaches himself – the language of
the community in which he grows up. In many communities, as
soon as the child is beyond infancy his principal associates are
other children of his own age or somewhat older. This community
of the very young often has marked language variations of its
own, which are passed down from child to child, along with other
aspects of culture like games, rimes, and songs. In a culture as

strongly stratified by age as that of modern America, the individual may pass through several age-groups before attaining social (and linguistic) maturity. Teenage slang is a notorious locus of innovation and rapidly changing variation in our society.

There are, of course, other kinds of groups besides these which may lead to linguistic variation. Occupation is one common form of class grouping which leads to the special kind of linguistic variation, primarily lexical, called CANT or JARGON. Recreation is another: every hobby or sport has its own vocabulary, the mastery of which marks one as belonging to the group of golfers, sailors, tennis players, or whatever; once again the variation is primarily lexical. A person's vocabulary beyond the basic core is the product of all the groups which his special interests lead him to belong to.

Idiolectal variation

The last sentence reminds us that not all the subgroups within a community are self-contained and mutually exclusive. Some are, of course. One person cannot be both male and female, old and young, black and white, educated and uneducated. But he can be at the same time a middle-aged white male, a salesman, a golfer, a freemason, a high-school graduate, and a stamp-collector, each of which places him in a more or less tightly structured group evincing its own linguistic variation, at least in lexicon. The particular combination of overlapping groups to which he belongs helps mold his own vocabulary, and to some degree grammar and pronunciation as well.

Other factors beside group affiliation will also affect the individual's knowledge and use of language. There is, for example, the degree to which he feels comfortable and secure, whether by hereditary position or by personal achievement, within the overall community. Language is in most societies a carefully watched index to social position, and the individual who is insecure socially often is insecure linguistically. On the other hand, the secure person usually does not worry too much about the 'correctness' of his language; he has a deeply ingrained feeling that the way he uses language is the right way.

Another factor is that complex of individual traits we commonly call 'personality', especially as it relates to language. Some people enjoy language the way others enjoy food; they relish neat turns of phrase, picturesque figures of speech, puns, riddles, and word games. Others look upon it as a necessary evil, something we have to use for communication, the more's the pity. Perhaps related to this difference is the great range of variation among individuals in the skill with which they use language. This is a matter which has not been given much attention by theoretical linguists, who tend to think of linguistic competence as more or less uniform among the members of a speech community. Nothing could be further from the truth. The range of skill from a Winston Churchill, Martin Luther King, Jr, or Adlai Stevenson to the inarticulate speaker who gropes for words, mixes up his sentence structure, and interlards his phrases with 'you know', 'I mean' and 'actually' is as great as the range of skill in any other common occupation. Literary critics speak of a writer's STYLE in this sense; the linguistic virtuosity of Shakespeare, Goethe, or Voltaire is apparent in every sentence they wrote. It is, of course, possible to increase one's individual skill in handling language by study, much practice, and hard work under good instruction, but only within limits. Individual talent plays a part here as it does in all the more difficult things we humans try to do. No amount of hard work and dedication can turn a mediocre pianist into a Rubinstein, and no amount of instruction and writing under criticism can make a Shakespeare out of someone with no flair for language. He may become a competent writer and speaker (in the usual sense of the word), but his abilities impose limitations beyond which he cannot go.

Stylistic variation
Finally, we must take account of the fact that considerable variety exists within the language use of virtually every individual speaker. The adult adjusts his usage to the circumstances: the time and place, the nature and size of the audience, the subject matter, and the medium (speech or writing). Sociolinguists call this CODE-SWITCHING. The range of variation depends to a considerable extent on the occupation and education of the speaker, but personality enters in here as well. There are those who enjoy and use a wide range of styles, from the most formal to the most colloquial, while others feel safer staying within a narrower range. But nobody always talks or writes the same way. Lexicon, pronunciation, and grammar all shift as the occasion and audience change.

This is another area of linguistic variation which until recently has been little studied by dialectologists. The traditional dialect studies have on the whole dealt with less educated informants, whose range of styles may be relatively narrow. Furthermore, the very nature of the dialect interview – usually a single informant being questioned by a single interviewer, who cannot help revealing his superior education and social status – almost inevitably encourages a more formal style than the informant uses among his peers. Fieldworkers are, of course, aware of this, and make an effort to alleviate the unnaturalness of the situation. Intelligent informants as well, as soon as they are sure of what the interviewer is after, may relax their cautious formality and revert to their more 'natural' colloquial style. Commonly differences appear between the forms produced consciously in answer to questions and those used unconsciously in rapid speech. This is particularly true of items like the noun and verb morphology discussed earlier in this chapter. Many of the English informants who produced *saw* in response to the question eliciting the past of *see* were recorded as using one or another of the non-standard forms in conversation. The same is true in phonology. In a one-word answer to a question, producing what linguists call a CITATION FORM, pronunciation is always more careful than it is in ordinary speech, where contractions, vowel reductions or deletions, and simplification of consonant clusters occur frequently in all varieties of speech. In this sense, it is inaccurate to speak of *the* phonology of a given dialect or idiolect; there are as many variant phonologies as there are oral styles. Once again this is an area of language variation which has been little studied by traditional dialectologists. As we shall see in Chapter 8, this deficiency is being remedied by current emphasis on sociolinguistic dialectology.

Note

1. The system of distinctive features used in this book is given in Appendix A.

Chapter 3

Sampling the language

Although interest in language variation, especially as it is manifested in regional dialect, is presumably as widespread and as old as interest in language itself, the formal, more or less scientific, study of the subject – dialectology as an intellectual and academic discipline – is a product of the last century and a half. It is a natural outgrowth of the comparative study of language differences and similarities across both space and time which may be said to begin with the work of Jones, Rask, Grimm, and others in the early nineteenth century and to culminate in the remarkable accomplishments of the Indo-Europeanists through the century. These scholars were able to demonstrate that languages which seem at first to be so different as to be totally unrelated are actually members of a LANGUAGE FAMILY, sharing large numbers of features which can most rationally be accounted for by divergence over a long period of time from a common original. They showed that language change, particularly in phonology, proceeds according to regular and systematic patterns, so that the trained linguist can work backward from existing variation toward a reconstructed original or PROTO-LANGUAGE. They established the fact that the diversity of languages in the world came about not by some instantaneous 'confusion of tongues', as in the Old Testament myth of the Tower of Babel, but by natural evolutionary processes. Their work is thus parallel to that of contemporary biologists such as Darwin, who were attributing the diversity of living forms to natural processes of change and selection. In linguistics, as in biology, geology, and other sciences, the nineteenth century was the period when theories of orderly evolution replaced the old views of instantaneous creation by supernatural intervention.[1]

The science of comparative linguistics thus established the view that the members of a linguistic family reached their present wide differences, amounting to total lack of mutual intelligibility, by orderly processes of change over several millennia. A logical conclusion from this view is that the further back in time the re-constructing process is pushed, the more alike the so-called daughter languages become. Ultimately there must have been a time when they were not separate languages at all, but mutually intelligible dialects of the proto-language. The study of dialects thus fits neatly into position in the overall study of language; dia-lectology becomes a part of historical and comparative linguis-tics. And since that discipline was attempting to form general, hopefully universal, theories of language change and evolution, it was seen that the study of contemporary dialects should cast light on the early stages of the development of a proto-language into a family of related but divergent daughter languages.

The corpus

In order to study a language or languages of which he is not a na-tive speaker, a linguist must have access to a large sampling or CORPUS. The historical linguist's corpus consists of those written samples or TEXTS which historical chance has allowed to survive. As he pushes his study backward in time, he eventually reaches the point where the texts run out, either because of natural de-struction and decay or because the language had not yet acquired a writing system. From there on, he must proceed by difficult and complicated methods of hypothetical reconstruction. The dialec-tologist studying current language variation is more fortunate. He may, at the cost of at most some physical inconvenience, sur-round himself with speakers of the dialects he is studying, who constitute a living and inexhaustible corpus. The comparative linguist is like the paleontologist, reconstructing earlier forms on the basis of the fossil forms which chance has preserved. The dia-lectologist is like the naturalist, who need only venture into the jungle, the desert, or the sea to make his observations. The com-parative linguist, like the paleontologist, must make the most of what he has; the dialectologist, like the naturalist, must make cer-tain crucial decisions to impose systematic limits on the corpus with which he chooses to work.

The simplest form of dialect corpus is a random sample. The collector, armed with notebook, or, in these days, tape recorder, simply records whatever dialect materials come his way. This is the method of the amateur – and until 150 years ago or so all dialect collectors were amateurs. Typically an educated man, often a clergyman or schoolmaster, who found himself among speakers of a dialect which he considered interesting or picturesque, would make a hobby of collecting dialect words and expressions. Many such collections were published, some of them by local or national dialect societies.[2] They consisted mostly of lexical items which the collector, on the basis of comparison with his own educated standard, considered to be localisms. Pronunciation was sometimes suggested or discussed, but in a period before the development of precise phonetic writing systems, this could only be done by applying the standard writing system. There is little attempt in these amateur studies at systematic description of dialect phonology. Nor is much attention paid to syntax. Samplings of this sort, which are still being made by amateurs, are of some value for the study of the distribution of dialect words,[3] but they are far from adequate for the purposes of the modern dialectologist. He requires that the corpus he uses be collected by more carefully controlled methods.

In the first place, the dialectologist planning a survey of the dialects of a given country or region must decide what aspect or aspects of the dialects he is to be concerned with. If his aim is to study lexical variation, leading ultimately to some sort of word geography or dialect dictionary, his sample must cover a wide range of subject matter, in order to elicit as many regional phrases and words as possible. If on the other hand he is interested in phonological variation across his territory, he will structure his sample in such a way as to supply evidence of the complete phonological system of each locality within the region to be investigated. Rather than strive for as much lexical variety as possible, he will attempt to restrict his corpus to common words known over the whole area, in order to facilitate systematic analysis and comparison. A corpus intended to uncover grammatical variation – a difficult problem – will have to be structured to include whole sentences or longer passages of as much variety as possible.

Another preliminary decision that must be made is the scope of the desired sample. Both the patience of informants and the time of collectors are limited, so that a sampling procedure should be designed to elicit just the material wanted in the most economical way. The lexicologist may be interested in a special subset of the dialect vocabulary, the terminology of a particular trade or occupation, for example. The phonologist may be investigating vowel systems, or the grammarian inflectional morphology. In each case the sampling procedure can be structured to produce the relevant data with a minimum of dilution of extraneous material. An amusing example is the technique devised by William Labov to acquire evidence on the treatment of postvocalic /r/ after low back vowels in New York City. The informants were salespersons and other employees of three large department stores.

> The interviewer approached the informant in the role of a customer asking for directions to a particular department. The department was one which was located on the fourth floor. When the interviewer asked, 'Excuse me, where are the women's shoes?' the answer would normally be, 'Fourth floor.'
>
> The interviewer then leaned forward and said, 'Excuse me?' He would usually then obtain another utterance, *'Fourth floor'*, spoken in careful style under emphatic stress. . . . The dependent variable is the use of (r) in four occurrences:
>
> | (casual) | (emphatic) |
> |---|---|
> | fourth floor | *fourth floor* |
>
> Thus we have preconsonantal and final position, in both casual and emphatic styles of speech. (Labov 1966, *pp* 70–1)

Since the three stores were chosen to represent three different social and socio-economic levels of customer, and hence presumably of employees, another variable was introduced and controlled. Using this method, including what must be the shortest dialect questionnaire on record, Labov obtained the desired data from 264 informants in approximately six and a half hours.

Finally, the sampling plan must be directed toward the stylistic level of the dialect sample to be elicited. The older view, and still the view of the linguistically naïve amateur, was that 'dialect speakers' are a distinct class from 'standard speakers', and that the true dialect speaker has only one kind of language, his local and class dialect. But, as was pointed out in Chapter 2 above, linguists now recognize that all users of language have different styles, varying according to the subject matter, the social circumstances, and the person or persons spoken with or addressed. The dialectologist may decide to investigate a single style – informal friendly conversation, for example – or he may want to study the stylistic variations within the speech of individuals. In either case, he must plan the sampling procedures to elicit the kind or kinds of language he wants from his informants without overloading the sample with extraneous material.

All these decisions must be made during the planning stage before actual collecting begins, and they may not be altered once it is under way. Only thus can the collector be sure of COMPARABIL-ITY across his corpus; that is, that the material collected from each informant or each locality is as near as possible to being exactly parallel to that from other informants and localities. Otherwise valid comparisons would not be possible. The qualities of a well-planned dialect sample, then, are economy, relevance (precise control of the aspect or aspects of language covered), and comparability of content, social level, and style. Paradoxically, in order to insure this, the investigator must know a good deal about the dialects he wishes to sample before he can plan the sample. It is no wonder that the famous French dialectologist Gilliéron wryly observed that 'the questionnaire, in order to be clearly the best, ought to be made after the survey' (Gilliéron 1915, quoted by Mather and Speitel 1975, *p* 10).

The questionnaire

The central instrument used in the systematic collection of dialect is the QUESTIONNAIRE. This may take many forms, but in all cases it amounts to a more or less structured program of questions to be put to a number of informants so that their responses can be recorded and studied. It is essential that any serious effort at collecting dialect make use of a questionnaire to insure that precious interviewing time is not wasted on trivial or irrelevant material. For this reason, all modern dialect surveys devote a great deal of attention to the preparation of the questionnaire. The typical questionnaire goes through several preliminary stages – five in the case of the SED – each of which is tried out in the field. After each trial, difficult, irrelevant, and unproductive questions are amended or deleted; new questions are devised; the order of material is altered; and other changes are made to increase the productivity and efficiency of the instrument. There is no way to be sure that it is finally perfected, since each interview has its surprises and reveals flaws in the questionnaire. But at some point it becomes apparent that it must be frozen so that the survey may go forward. Once this point has been reached, only minor changes are permissible.

Format

The form of the questionnaire depends, of course on the objectives and methods of the survey. Most large-scale surveys attempt to cover a large geographic area – usually a whole country or major region – and a wide variety of aspects of language: lexicon, phonology, morphology, and to some extent at least, syntax and semantics. It is general questionnaires directed at these broad goals which will be discussed here. Questionnaires of smaller geographic or linguistic scope are, after all, simply reduced forms of the general questionnaire, subject to the same restrictions but capable of sharper definition because of their narrower scope.

Karl Jaberg and Jakob Jud, editors of the linguistic atlas of Italy and southern Switzerland (AIS), state the requirements of a good questionnaire in these terms:

(a) It should include as rich and characteristic a selection as possible of the linguistic peculiarities of the dialect region to be studied.
(b) It should represent the cultural circumstances of the dialect region to be studied.
(c) It should guarantee at the same time the spontaneity and indigenousness of the answers on the one hand, and their comparability on the other. (Jaberg and Jud 1928, p 175)

It is apparent that there are conflicting requirements implied here, which must somehow be reconciled or compromised. These may be reduced to two major sorts:

1. Regional and individual. Each region – in fact each village within the region and ultimately each potential informant in the village – is different in culture, occupation, education, and many other ways from every other.
2. Linguistic. The kind of material elicited for lexical studies – word geography – is different from, in fact diametrically opposed to, what is required for phonology and morphology.

Regional and cultural differences

These affect lexicon more than other aspects of language. Even in a small country such as the Netherlands, which appears superficially quite homogeneous to the outside observer, there are great differences between the life of the city dweller, the farmer, and the fisherman. And when it is a matter of a large geographical area such as France or the United States, with many kinds of geographical conditions profoundly influencing the life of the people, the range of variety in vocabulary becomes great. Since the essence of dialect study is comparability, the same kinds of linguistic forms must be elicited in each locality in order to chart the range of systematic variation. Yet the day-to-day preoccupations, and hence the commonly used working vocabulary of the Breton fisherman is very different from that of the mountaineer of the Massif Central, not to mention the Paris taxi-driver. A lexical questionnaire that would do justice to all is an impossibility; some compromise must be sought. Jaberg and Jud point out in vivid terms the difficulties caused by the geographical and cultural differences between the two main regions of their survey:

The circumstances of life and the cultural forms of southern Switzerland and northern Italy are very varied and differ strongly from one another. One thinks simply of the contrast between the aristocratic farmers of the [Swiss] republic and the partially proletarianized agricultural work-force of the [Italian] plain, especially the Venetic region; between the alpine-economy oriented smallholders of the Piedmontese, Lombardic, Swiss, Trentinian, and Friulian alps and the large-scale enterprises of the lowlands; between the sub-alpine fruit and vine culture of the north Italian lakes and the rice and maize culture of the Novaresian plain or the pasture culture of the Lombardian plain; between the terrace-agriculture of Liguria and the wide uniform fields of Emilia.

If the Atlas was not to fall into a set of provincial individual atlases, it was necessary for a single uniform questionnaire to be retained. It was, therefore, a matter of working out the cultural unity of the area to be investigated, of separating the different, so far as it had purely provincial character, but not pushing it wholly aside.... A complete cutting out of all peculiarities would have leveled off the lexical relief-map of Italy. (Jaberg and Jud 1928, *p* 178)

This kind of compromise suggested in the last paragraph of this quotation means that the lexical phase of the questionnaire will strive to have a majority of items which can be responded to meaningfully by all or most informants, while preserving some that may be relevant only to certain subregions or types of informants. Such matters as the parts of the body, the calendar, the weather, and to a lesser degree the management of the home, the school, the church, and the government constitute a core vocabulary; they are universal enough to elicit responses from all informants, while particular occupational, topographical, even social terminology is limited in distribution. The investigator must decide how much of the latter kind of material he wishes to include at the risk of losing a measure of comparability across the whole area. The kind of compromise between language-wide generality and local particularity which a good lexical questionnaire should seek is aptly summarized by Pierre Nauton, editor of one of the excellent regional atlases of France. The basic principles, he claims, are:

– to adopt as base a detailed schema, arranged according to subject matter, dealing with *nature, man*, and *human activity*, which will supply a common body of lexicon;
– to insert various particular items conditioned by diverse factors: geography for nature, psychology and sociology for man, ethnography for human activity;
– to present the whole, coordinated as carefully as possible so as to give the general and particular linguistic physiognomy of the region. (Nauton 1963, *p* 57)

Obviously the larger and more diverse the region, the less likely will it be to present a single 'linguistic physiognomy'. It then becomes incumbent on the dialectologist to decide to what degree he is willing to sacrifice comparability in the interest of collecting what may be the most unusual and interesting components of the local dialect vocabulary, the words associated with particular local aspects of nature and of human activity.

One mode of procedure that has been suggested is to divide the lexical part of the questionnaire into two parts: one general for the area and the other a series of particular questionnaires for various subregions.[4] This would, in effect, subject half the questionnaire to government by the principle of comparability, and the other half by the principle of inclusiveness and 'indigenousness'. Though this suggestion has not been widely followed, it is particularly adaptable to surveys like the *Dictionary of American Regional English* (DARE), whose goal is an exhaustive collection of dialect words across the whole United States.

Linguistic differences

As was stated above, the kind of material to be elicited for lexical purposes is directly opposed to that required for phonology and morphology. The aim of the phonological collection is to accumulate sufficient material from each locality surveyed to make possible an adequate, if not completely detailed, phonological description of the speech of that locality. As we saw in Chapter 2, this necessitates phonological and phonetic information of four sorts:

1. the number of phonemes in the system;
2. the feature constituency of the phonemes;
3. the phonetic (allophonic) realization of the phonemes;
4. the incidence of the phonemes, *ie* their distribution through the lexicon.

It is obvious that this information can be supplied only by a sizeable body of phonetically recorded material, expressed, either at the time of recording or by later transcription of tape-recordings, in a sensitive phonetic alphabet. It is also obvious that if the phonology of one locality is to be compared with that of another, a large part of the material collected must be, in other aspects than pronunciation, the same in both localities. Here comparability takes on a new aspect. In lexicon it required that one aspect of a word – usually the meaning – be held constant while the other – usually the form – is allowed to vary. Thus one is interested, for example, either in the different words used to describe the meaning 'midday meal' or in the different meanings given to the word *dinner*. But phonological comparability requires that the words themselves be held constant in both meaning and general form while the pronunciation varies. Therefore the phonological part of the questionnaire must deal with vocabulary items which it is expected will be universally distributed through the region, varying only in pronunciation. Lexical variety and interest must be sacrificed in the interest of phonological precision. Here again a subdivision of the questionnaire seems both reasonable and efficient. Even the methods of elicitation may be different, as we shall see in Chapter 5. Lexical collection requires precision of semantic identification of the words solicited, but only a general record of pronunciation. Phonological collection requires phonetic precision but only enough semantic care to assure that we are dealing with 'the same word'.

It may be asked how the investigator is to know in advance what words are universal across the whole region under investigation. The answer is, of course, that he cannot. He must depend upon prior studies, earlier collections, even amateur ones of the sort described early in this chapter. As a native speaker (usually) and a student of the language, he will, of course, have a great knowledge of the language as well as a store of informed guesses as to what parts of the lexicon – numbers, for example, or days of the week – are most likely to be stable and generally distributed. In the end he may well have to resort to systematic advance sampling. In any case, he will do well to build a certain amount of redundancy into the phonological part of the questionnaire. Costly and time-consuming revision might result if important phonological items were based on single words which might turn out to be unknown to some of the informants.

Morphological information collected in dialect surveys is commonly limited to inflectional paradigms: noun plurals and cases, pronoun forms, verb conjugations. The requirements here are similar to those for phonology: comparability depends on selecting words distributed generally across the area under investigation. A typical example is the past tense of *see* in English, as illustrated in Chapter 2. The dialectal interest here is in the fact that a verb universal in the language has variant past tense forms with clear-cut regional as well as social distribution.

So far as content goes, then, the general questionnaire should include a sample of common words sufficient to allow at least a broad characterization of each informant's phonology and morphology, and a broad enough collection of lexical items to give an idea as to the regional peculiarities of his lexicon. Syntactic items are difficult to incorporate into a questionnaire, except perhaps for lesser details like noun–adjective ordering or subject–verb concord. The total number of items depends on many factors, some of them non-linguistic, such as the amount of time the field-worker can be allowed to devote to each interview, and, conversely, the amount of time the informant may be expected to be willing and able to give to the interview. In the end it is usually a compromise between the dialectologist's desire for completeness and the practical limitations imposed on the collection process.

Contents

The contents of the questionnaire thus consist of at least four kinds of items:

1. A sufficient number of common and universal words to illustrate the phonemic inventory and principal phonetic rules which the investigator expects to encounter. In order to make the work of comparison simpler, these are commonly short words, with all possible vowel nuclei in at least a representative selection of consonantal environments. Such matters as the types and restrictions on consonant clusters, allophonic differences between vowels in open and closed syllables, and morphophonemic changes accompanying shifts of stress should all be provided for. For a full phonological inventory as many as a thousand such items may be needed,[5] though practical considerations of time, cost, and informant's patience may indicate some reduction.

2. Several hundred items from the core vocabulary: nouns for body parts, days of the week, numbers, common holidays, tools and utensils used about the house, articles of dress, trades and occupations; verbs describing common activities; adjectives dealing with common qualities such as size, shape, color, temperature, consistency, etc. Most of these will be naming or ONOMA-SIOLOGICAL questions, in which the referent is indicated or described and the informant is to supply the word. But some may be defining or SEMASIOLOGICAL questions; that is, the word may be given (*eg barn*) and the informant asked to supply a description of the referent (how large? what made of? what used for? etc.). This latter type of question is likely to be harder to get a satisfactory answer to; the informant, especially if he has not traveled beyond his local region or received much education, may not have considered that common words in his vocabulary may refer to different things in different places. For him a barn is a barn, and the interviewer who asks bluntly 'What do you mean by *barn* around here?' is likely to be marked down as hopelessly stupid or ignorant. Yet some questions of this sort are necessary to uncover the complicated interrelationships between cultural and linguistic variation which may mark a diverse area such as

that described by Jaberg and Jud in the passage quoted above. If they become predominant, the questionnaire is in danger of sliding over from the domain of linguistics to that of popular culture and ethnography. When dealing with a complicated process – such as thatching a house or hauling a purse seine, for instance – the dialectologist is primarily interested in the words used to designate the materials, tools, and actions involved, while the anthropologist or ethnographer is interested in the objects and processes themselves and how they differ from place to place. One school of investigators – the *Wörter und Sachen* ('words and things') school – attempts to balance the two. Jaberg and Jud called their atlas of Italy and southern Switzerland a *Wort- und Sachatlas*, and one of its by-products is two large volumes illustrated with many photographs, dealing with the work of the farm in all its differing details across the countryside (Scheuermeier 1943–56).

3. A number of sets of lexical items more specialized in use and application, which will elicit answers from special subsets of the population and may be omitted when dealing with others. It is of no use to ask town-dwellers about agricultural details or mountaineers about offshore fishing terminology. Yet a prominent part of the vocabulary of the relevant group may be made up of such terminology, so that especially in a wide survey of a large and diverse area, some material of this sort must be included, along with a carefully thought-out rationale as to when to use it and when to omit it in an individual interview. Otherwise, as Jaberg and Jud put it, the relief map of the language will be reduced to one level.

4. A selection from the morphologically variant part of the language. The type of items included here will, of course, depend on the structure of the language. Verb inflection is a common kind of morphological variation, and one where there is likely to be variation from point to point. In English, common irregular verbs like *be, do, have, see* show great variety in the folk speech, and some even in local standards. The same is true of German and French. Pronouns often show considerable formal variation as well. Since questions intended to elicit this kind of material are difficult to make clear and may be boring to informants, in contrast to the ever-fascinating variety of names for things, this material must be especially carefully selected and prepared.

Size of the questionnaire

The problem of how long to make the questionnaire, how many individual items to attempt to elicit from each informant or in each locality, must depend upon the circumstances and limitations of the survey. Given a finite amount of time, energy, and money to be spent in the collecting phase, this question must be answered in relation to others, particularly the breadth and desired density of the survey. Is the time to be spent asking a large number of questions of relatively few and hence more widely scattered informants, or the reverse? The more informants, the shorter the questionnaire; the more questions, the fewer the informants. In practice, questionnaires used for fairly broad national or regional surveys have ranged from about 700 items to more than 2,000. Some typical examples:

Linguistic Atlas of New England (LANE)	711
Linguistic Geography of Wales (LGW)	750
Survey of English Dialects (SED)	1,322
Atlas linguistique de la France (ALF)	1,920
Wort- and Sachatlas Italiens und der Südschweiz (AIS)[6]	2,000
Atlas linguistique et ethnographique du Massif Central (AMC)	
	4,000

The experience of collectors has shown that the number of items that can be obtained comfortably from an informant in a single day's interview is somewhere between 500 and 1,000. Thus a questionnaire of 2,000 or so items will probably occupy the better part of a week.

Arrangement of the questionnaire

In overall format, most modern questionnaires arrange the material topically, including in each section the names of relevant objects and processes, as well as verbs describing acts, functions, etc.[7] The emphasis is on the concrete; many dialectologists have commented on the difficulty of eliciting affective, subjective, emotional, and abstract vocabulary by direct questioning. As Jaberg and Jud point out:

> The range of adjectives referring to moral qualities is, in lively conversation, remarkably varied and subtle . . . ; when one sits down with the village people in the tavern of an evening, one can get to hear a very juicy collection, and yet it is very difficult to bring out by questions a few local expressions for 'miserly', 'lazy', and 'timid'. (Jaberg and Jud 1928, *p* 180)

The more subjective part of the dialect lexicon, if collected at all, is more likely to be derived from tape-recorded free conversation or narrative rather than direct questioning.

To illustrate the content, format, and bias of a questionnaire used in a predominantly rural, agricultural area (as in the past most have been), we may take that prepared by Pierre Gardette for the *Atlas linguistique et ethnographique du Lyonnais* (ALLy), one of the more recent in the series of regional atlases of France (Gardette 1968). It consists of 1,875 lexical questions, divided

TABLE 3.1   Questionnaire for *Atlas linguistique et ethnographique du Lyonnais*

Section	Number of questions
1. Meadow, hay, rake, fork	57
2. Grain, sowing, harvest	58
3. Threshing, the flail	57
4. Yoke, goad	39
5. Plows and working the land	55
6. Carts and wagons	66
7. The vineyard	89
8. The wood	54
9. The garden, potatoes, root vegetables	36
10. Cattle, horses, donkeys	63
11. Sheep, goats, swine	62
12. The barnyard	50
13. The barnyard (concluded), bees, dog, cat	43
14. Milk, butter, cheese	64
15. Bread	43
16. Trees (other than fruit-trees)	59
17. Fruit-trees	59
18. Birds, flies, parasites	58
19. Harmful animals, snakes, water creatures, insects	48
20. Women's life: 1. the bed, housekeeping, meals	59
21. Women's life: 2. washing, sewing	52
22. The house: 1. generalities, doors and windows, kitchen	61
23. The house: 2. lamps, fireplace, bedroom, outbuildings	56
24. Weather: winds, rain, snow, sun	70
25. The stars, landscape	45
26. The calendar	44
27. The day, kinship	48
28. From cradle to grave	107
29. The body	85
30. Clothing; manure; occupations	50
31. Hemp	31
Total lexical items	1,875
Morphological items	68

among 31 sections, with an additional section of 68 questions on morphology, most of them multiple (one calls for six complete retellings of the parable of the Prodigal Son!). The titles of the sections and the distribution of the questions among them are presented in Table 3.1.

As will be seen, about half of the questionnaire is devoted to the farm and countryside, and the remainder to common daily concerns. Within each section, the questions are arranged to lead easily from one to the next, thus easing the task of the interviewer and sparing the informant rapid and discontinuous transitions from one to another. The section on the calendar, for example, runs through the seasons, the months, the days of the week, then the important holidays, and by an easy transition, goes to the church, the market-place, and the fair. In many cases the order is so obvious that the informant might well volunteer the next answer without waiting for the question. The division into groups of around fifty questions allows for breaks in the interview, providing relief from questioning sessions, and permitting, as the author points out, opportunity for casual chat or for going to look at some of the objects discussed. 'Thus the informant gets less tired and has the comforting impression of having covered a subject, of having told about one chapter of his life.' (Gardette 1968, p 33)

The section of this questionnaire dealing with morphology elicits paradigms for pronouns, demonstratives, regular and irregular verbs, adverbs and adverbial phrases. The parable is used to elicit verb forms in context: the informant is asked to repeat the story six times, in various persons, numbers, and tenses. This is the nearest the questionnaire comes to syntactic information.

This questionnaire, then, is entirely lexical and morphological. It contains no questions designed primarily to elicit material of phonological interest. The author claims, however, that in a questionnaire of this length there is bound to be enough phonological material indirectly derived:

> It is indeed evident that these lexicological records also have phonetic value, since the words have phonetic form; it will be possible to do the phonetics with the help of these records. (p 35)

Beyond that, he maintains that a phonological inquiry should make use of a separate, specialized questionnaire, which is not included in the particular survey in hand.

The form of the questions
There has been considerable discussion and disagreement among dialectologists as to the form in which the questions should be recorded in the questionnaire and presented to the informant. Two

opposing views emphasize on the one hand strict comparability, and on the other ease of interviewing. The first, followed, for example, in SED, maintains that the questions must be formulated in detail and presented to each informant exactly as formulated. Only so, it is contended, will strict comparability be preserved. The second, used by the American surveys and to a large extent in the continental European ones, simply lists the items to be obtained and leaves it to the interviewer to elicit them in whatever way he thinks best. The contention here is that this allows the interviewer to adapt his methods to the particular situation – the intelligence and alertness of the informant, the presence or absence of relevant objects or circumstances at the scene of the interview, and the possibility of leading the informant into a discussion in which many of the items wanted will occur spontaneously without formal questioning. There are valid arguments on both sides. Perhaps the best solution is a mixture of the two types, as is done in some of the French surveys, including the ALLy described above.

Whether formulated in advance or developed individually by the fieldworker, the questions, especially the lexical ones, which constitute the largest part of most questionnaires, can be of six different types.

1. Naming in the presence of an object or picture

Here the typical form of the question is 'What do you call this?' spoken while the interviewer displays or points to an object or picture. The advantage of this type, of course, is that the referent is definite and specific, leaving the word as the only variable. The opportunity it affords to ask as many questions of this type as possible is the reason for recommending strongly that the interview be conducted in the informant's home or workplace.

2. Naming by definition

Here a typical question might be 'What do you call the creatures that give you honey?' Such questions must be carefully phrased to insure that the referent is unambiguously indicated. They often are more difficult for the informant, who is required to go through a mental process, however simple, to arrive at the referential notion, and then to supply the correct word for the notion. There is always danger that he will misunderstand the question. Furthermore, the creator of the questionnaire – or the interviewer – may not be aware of some cultural circumstance that produces a shift in the referent. A question like 'What do you call the animals that give you milk?' to elicit the word for 'cows' might get the word for 'goats' instead. This is one of the strongest reasons for allowing the interviewer to phrase the question himself, in the light of his knowledge or observation of the local scene.

3. Supplying the meaning for a specific word

This is what the French dialectologists call a semasiological question. Here the question might take the form 'What do you mean by *corn* here in these parts?' (question II.5.1 from SED). This kind of question is useful particularly for tracing local variation in meaning of words of widespread distribution; recall the variations in *shaft* and *shank* illustrated in Chapter 2. They are often more ethnological than linguistic, especially if they lead to extended discussions of such things as the construction and parts of plows or fish-nets. For that reason, they are not extensively used in primarily linguistic surveys, though of importance in those of the *Wörter und Sachen* type.

4. Completion questions

Here the interviewer sets up a context requiring a specific word and hesitates or stops at the point where the word should occur, expecting the informant to supply it. For example, 'When you have done the laundry, you hang it on the line to ———.' These questions must also be carefully phrased so that there is no uncertainty or ambiguity about the word wanted. Intelligent informants often enjoy them for their game-like quality; the less intelligent are sometimes confused to the point of becoming tongue-tied.

5. Conversion questions

These are useful in eliciting morphological information. They require that the informant supply a morphological variant on the basis of context. For example, the questionnaire may give the basic question in completion form, 'I have my troubles and you have ———' with further instructions to the fieldworker, 'Convert for *mine, his, hers, ours, yours, theirs*' (question IX.8.5 of SED). These go well with intelligent informants, who will often quickly perceive what is wanted and rattle off the whole paradigm without further prodding. Again, however, the less intelligent may become confused. The difficulty of this type of question is one reason that many questionnaires put the morphological questions at the end (as in the ALLy discussed above), by which time the informant is likely to have become used to being questioned and is more ready to supply answers. Also, if because of confusion or boredom he gives up, the lexical part of the interview is not lost.

6. *Translation questions*

Here the informant is given the standard word and asked to supply the dialectal equivalent, as in 'What is your word for *brook*?'
This kind of question makes the basic assumptions that the informant is bilingual (or bidialectal), that he has a clear understanding of the difference between standard and dialect, that he is not
ashamed to identify himself as a dialect speaker, and that he will
make the effort to recall the dialect word rather than parrot the
standard word back to the interviewer. Such questions can only
be used when these assumptions can be safely made – normally in
an area where the two varieties of language are distinct and recognized. They are used extensively, for example, in France –
almost exclusively in the ALF and frequently in the more recent
regional surveys – because there the distinction between 'French'
and 'patois' is accepted and widely recognized. They are, however, avoided entirely in the SED, since most English speakers are
inclined to look down on 'dialect' as an inferior form of language
and even to refuse to acknowledge that they speak it. An extreme
case of the use of this question is in bilingual areas, where the
keyword is given in one language to be translated into the other,
as was done in the Linguistic Survey of Wales and the Gaelic
areas of the Linguistic Survey of Scotland.

Phonological questions present a special problem, since the interviewer is required to elicit the exact word, varying only in pronunciation, preferably without saying it himself. The most direct
way to do this is to give the informant a list of words to read
aloud, the result to be tape-recorded and/or taken down in
phonetic notation. In this way, even if a word is not in the informant's vocabulary, he can pronounce it more or less according to
the spelling equivalents in his dialect. This is the method used in
the phonological section of the LAS, where a lexical questionnaire of about 500 items, collected by post, is supplemented by a
list of 975 words, mostly of one syllable, collected directly by a
fieldworker. The assumption here, of course, is that all informants will be literate – a safe assumption in Scotland. In the
SED, on the other hand, 387 out of 1,322 items to be collected
are marked in the questionnaire to be obtained for phonological
purposes, which means that the exact word, not a dialectal
equivalent, must be elicited, even though it is not the informant's
first response to the question. On the whole this was successful,
though in some cases words chosen were not known to informants
and therefore could not be elicited and recorded.

The danger of the list-reading method is fairly obvious: the informant, not used to reading aloud naturally, may pronounce the

words in an artificial and stilted manner, perhaps using spelling pronunciations in which letters are pronounced that are 'silent' in his normal pronunciation. As has been pointed out, such lists 'do not correspond to linguistic reality, since a speaker normally never has his whole concentration fixed on his pronunciation' (Löffler 1974, *p* 52). Also, a list of single short words gives no information about intonation, vowel reduction due to sentence stress, and other discourse phenomena. Therefore any survey using the word-list method should supplement it with recordings of connected speech, as was done in the Scottish survey.

We may conclude, then, that the preparation of the questionnaire is a very important stage in any dialect survey, especially a general one, to which much care and attention must be devoted. It is always a compromise between what the investigator would like to obtain and what he can reasonably hope for, given the constraints of time and money to which he is subject. It is the responsibility of the investigator who prepares the questionnaire to know as much as possible in advance about the dialectal phenomena of the region to be studied, and to establish and maintain explicit and realistic goals for the survey. Finally, the completed questionnaire must be tried out in the field and revised in the light of the results until the investigator is reasonably well convinced that it is a realistic and efficient instrument.

Notes

1. The parallel with Darwin was recognized by August Schleicher, in his 1863 paper *Die Darwinsche Theorie und die Sprachwissenschaft.*
2. The English Dialect Society was founded in 1873 and the American Dialect Society in 1889. Both have issued many word-lists, monographs, and other dialect publications.
3. They formed valuable sources of material for the monumental *English Dialect Dictionary* of Joseph Wright, 1896–1905.
4. Nauton cites Jaberg 1955 and Alvar López 1960 as advocating this course (Nauton 1963, *p* 51).
5. The phonological word-list of the *Linguistic Atlas of Scotland* has 975.
6. Actually AIS used three questionnaires: the normal one of 2,000 items, the reduced, of about 800, and the expanded, of about 4,000. These were used respectively in 354, 28, and 29 localities.
7. A notable example is the German questionnaire deriving from Wenker's original one, which consisted of forty sentences to be 'translated' into the dialect. Its orientation was principally phonological, in spite of the fact that the data were collected by post (see Mitzka 1952, *pp* 13–27).

Chapter 4

Sampling the speakers

A dialectologist who plans a study in depth of the dialect of a single locality, resulting in a detailed monograph, must live there long enough to steep himself in the local speech virtually to the point where he becomes a competent speaker himself. In the course of his research he may speak at some time or other with every inhabitant, so that he can truly claim to know the local speech. This is, of course, not possible in a general survey. Then the investigator must deal with a quite small sample of the population – a sample which he must be reasonably certain is representative of the variety or varieties of the language which he wishes to study. This is by no means an easy task, and a great deal of discussion and controversy has occurred over the question of finding and choosing informants.

Sampling the speakers is actually a two-stage process. First a NETWORK of localities to be investigated is established, based on the distribution of the population and what is already known about particularly important areas of dialect variation. Then procedures are set up for discovering and testing potential informants. Both these processes are controlled by two factors: the size and type of language sample desired and the resources of time, money, and skilled investigators available.

Direct versus indirect surveys

A decision of great importance for the sampling process is whether the survey is to be carried out by the DIRECT or the INDIRECT method of collection. The direct method involves the face-to-face contact of investigator and informant in an interview normally conducted in the home locality of the informant, usually in his residence or workplace. The indirect method, on the other hand, involves the use of an intermediary – often a student, schoolmaster, or priest – who reports on the local speech by means of a POSTAL QUESTIONNAIRE. Each of these methods has its advantages and disadvantages; each has been used with varying success in major surveys.

The indirect method
This has the major advantage of allowing a very large sampling of the population. The first broad survey of a whole language community, the *Deutscher Sprachatlas*, begun in the 1870s by Georg Wenker, ultimately collected responses to its questionnaire from nearly 50,000 localities in German-speaking Europe. The method, originated by Wenker and carried on by his successors, Ferdinand Wrede and Walther Mitzka, was to send the questionnaire to every village school, to be 'translated' into the local dialect. Unlike the questionnaires used in most other surveys, Wenker's questionnaire consisted of forty complete sentences, which were later supplemented by a list of individual words. As Mitzka describes the process:

> In the villages which have a single school and where only one teacher is employed, the teacher translated the 40 sentences into the local dialect, with the help of the pupils or of local adults. How widely he sought out from among the schoolchildren the best dialect speakers, and whether he also questioned local adults, depends on his willingness to accept responsibility. Important for evaluating the dialect text is the requested statement about the teacher's birthplace. Where there were several schools available, the headmaster or his superior selected the one with a master most conversant with the local dialect. The response is in every case *voluntary*. For that reason, not every school-locality is represented in the Atlas. (Mitzka 1952, *p* 36)

In spite of the reservation in the last sentence, this is undoubtedly the densest survey ever conducted, which is certainly in its favor. But it has the obvious disadvantage that the selection of the informants from among schoolchildren or 'local adults' is conducted by local teachers, with a minimum of control by the director of the survey. A great deal of dependence is placed on the individual teacher's 'willingness to accept responsibility' (*Verantwortungsfreudigkeit*), as well as on his familiarity with the local dialect. It says a good deal for the devotion of village schoolmasters in Germany during the period from 1880 to 1925 that so many completed questionnaires were received and that their reliability was, on the whole, quite high. But it still was necessary for the editors to reject many responses which were, for one reason or another, obviously inadequate. So dense was the coverage, however, that missing or rejected responses did not leave serious gaps in the network.

The indirect method has been used in other surveys, none with such extensive coverage as the German one, and usually with modifications correcting to some extent the shortcomings of Wenker's total reliance on village schoolmasters. For the lexical part of the Linguistic Survey of Scotland, a questionnaire of around 500 items was sent in two instalments to 3,000 elementary schools (two copies, one for each language, were sent to bilingual Gaelic-speaking areas), with a request that the schoolmaster put it into the hands of 'a local person who is willing and competent to undertake this work' (Mather and Speitel 1975, p 14). Ultimately about 60 per cent of these were satisfactorily completed and returned, and used for the Atlas. In this case, detailed instructions were furnished, and the responses were reported in a carefully prepared book which was later cut up into cards for filing. Likewise, biographical information about the informants was sought, in contrast to the anonymity of the German informants. Normally a single informant represented each locality, in contrast again to the German procedure, where the schoolmaster was simply entrusted with the task of translating the sentences with whatever help he could get from schoolchildren and local adults. There was thus more control over informants in the Scottish survey. Nevertheless, the editors recognize the sampling deficiencies of this method:

> ... our enquiry is directed to a numerical minority of speakers of a socially restricted speech variety in Scotland; our atlas reflects a potential of dialect available in the early 1950s but it does not tell the reader how many people in a locality would use it and in which specific situations. Our questionnaire techniques were not powerful enough to deal with these important questions. It remains to be seen, whether a postal questionnaire could be developed which might handle problems of this kind. (Mather and Speitel 1975, pp 14f)

In both the German and Scottish surveys, the establishment of the network was largely a matter of chance; only those localities were represented from which suitable completed questionnaires were returned. Likewise the selection of the informants was left to the judgement of the intermediaries, with only general instructions to guide them. In contrast, the Linguistic Survey of Wales, which also used the indirect method, made an effort to control both of these factors. For the network, a predetermined selection of points of inquiry was made, distributed through the country in proportion to the Welsh-speaking population. The intermediaries were also selected and instructed. 'At each point of inquiry, contact was established with a person of educated background who undertook to receive the questionnaires, and to supervise their completion by a suitable informant.' (Thomas 1973, *p* 9) As a result, 180 completed questionnaires, distributed by plan through the population, were ultimately received. Their validity was checked in various ways, primarily by examining their self-consistency and conformity to expectations based on the general distributions of variant forms and the previous knowledge of the investigator.

A modification of the indirect method makes use of a CHECK-LIST, in the hands of an untrained but willing fieldworker. The checklist differs from other questionnaires in supplying a list of possible answers to each question, with provision for the interrogator to check the one used by the informant. This method is rapid and has the advantage of some personal contact with the informant; otherwise it is subject to the same weaknesses as the postal indirect method. Obviously the investigator who prepares the checklist must know a good deal in advance about the regional dialect, in order to include all the expected variants. It has been used, in the United States particularly, as a supplement or preliminary to direct field interviewing. The checklist is used principally for lexical material – as is the indirect method generally – though some phonological material has been collected this way. It was used successfully by Atwood in his survey of the regional vocabulary of Texas (Atwood 1962). He supplied the checklists to students at the University of Texas, asking them to fill them out with an elderly relative or other inhabitant of their home town. In this way he collected 273 completed lists from all counties of Texas and parts of Louisiana and Oklahoma.

The direct method
In contrast to the large amount of chance in the indirect method, the direct method permits much closer control of the selection of localities and of informants, as well as of the actual interview. Typically a network of localities is selected on the basis of population density and distribution, known linguistic history, and the particular type of language to be sampled: rural, town, or urban, educated or uneducated, etc. Usually some discretion is given to the fieldworker to make substitutions in the network if he finds some localities totally unsuitable, but he is expected to preserve the overall distribution of localities as closely as possible. It is also the responsibility of the fieldworker to find and re-

cruit informants who conform to the specifications of the survey. In most traditional surveys, this has been a matter of subjective judgement rather than scientific sampling, for reasons that will be discussed shortly. Unlike the intermediaries of the indirect method, who are at least residents if not natives of the community, the fieldworker is a stranger, with limited time and relatively little local knowledge. He must locate potential informants rapidly, make sure of their qualifications, and ingratiate himself with them to the point where they are willing to spend many hours answering questions. It is no wonder that many experienced fieldworkers consider this the hardest part of their work.

The selection of informants is often heavily constrained by the type of dialect which is being sought. Theoretically, one might suppose that 'the dialect' of a locality would be the language used by all the inhabitants – or at least the common core which they all share. If this were the case, a truly random sample across age-groups, educational levels, social classes, and perhaps occupations should supply satisfactory informants. But it is only the more recent surveys in cities like New York, Chicago, and Detroit in the United States and Norwich, Leeds, and Newcastle upon Tyne in England that have followed this approach. The traditional surveys have proceeded on another assumption: that there is an indigenous local dialect of a village or town, which has been established there for a long time, which may be used by only a fraction of the population and by them only in limited contexts, and which is in process of being contaminated by incursions from the standard language, by newcomers to the region with different dialect background, or by a younger generation subject to social and educational influences which turn them away from the old-time local speech. This view is particularly strong in a country like France, where the distinction between 'French' and 'patois' is clearly recognized by everybody, and where the local patois are undergoing rapid decay and extinction. In such a case, the dialectologist may feel like the naturalist in the presence of a rare and endangered species; he must work fast to collect what he can before it is too late.

Under such circumstances, the number of suitable informants is much reduced, and the task of finding them and enlisting their help much more difficult. The requirements established for informants in the SED are typical:

> Great care was taken in choosing the informants. Very rarely were they below the age of sixty. They were mostly men: in this country men speak vernacular more frequently, more consistently, and more genuinely than women. Bilingual speakers could not be shunned: as a

result of our educational system, the inhabitants of the English coun-
try-side can readily adjust their natural speech to the social situation in
which they may find themselves. But dialect-speakers whose residence
in the locality had been interrupted by significant absences were constantly regarded with suspicion. Informants with any speech handicaps
were always avoided. In no case was an informant paid for his ser-
vices. (Orton 1962, *pp* 15–16)

Though not stated here, it was assumed that the informant should
be a native of the locality which he represented, and preferably
that his parents were as well.

In addition to these requirements of age, local birth and residence, and availability, certain qualities of mind and personality
are needed in a good informant, as Pierre Nauton points out:

The informant must also show certain psychological qualities: if he
seems timid or distrustful or reticent because of an inferiority complex,
and if he can't be set free from such feelings, he should not be used in
such a long interview. He must also have good intelligence and a good
memory, which is not rare among peasants, for even if they have never
had much education, they often have remarkable knowledge, which
has enabled them to 'understand dialectal facts, country facts, which
the majority of linguists are not capable of doing'. (Nauton 1963, *p* 94;
quote from Roques 1957)

Given these restrictions – not to mention that the informant
must not be deaf or in delicate health – it is understandable that
the task of finding and recruiting one or more in a village of 500–
1,000 inhabitants may be very difficult. Every field dialectologist
can tell tales of his frustrations and successes in the search for informants, many of whom may become close friends after a week
or so of intensive interviewing. It is apparent that for surveys of
the traditional type, good informants are rare and must be sought
out and cajoled. This aspect of traditional dialect-collecting has
been criticized (Pickford 1956), but so long as the type of dialect
sought remained the historic local patois in its purest form, no
more scientific method of sampling could be successful.

One major shortcoming of this informal sampling procedure is
that it gives no indication of how representative the informants
selected are of the total population. If the fieldworker approaches
a village of 1,000 people under the restrictions cited above, he may
be lucky enough to find a suitable informant almost at once, or he
may have to spend a day or more tracking down and interviewing
recommended informants only to find all of them unsatisfactory
for one reason or another. In either case he will have no way of
knowing how many inhabitants of the village speak essentially the
same dialect as the informant he ultimately selects. He may, of

course, gather a general impression on the basis of informal contacts with other villagers, an impression which can be surprisingly accurate if he is an experienced and successful observer of dialect. Since the kind of survey which makes use of these informal methods is, as we have said, one which is directed at eliciting the older, indigenous, 'pure' form of local speech – sometimes called the BASILECT – it is, of course, not necessary that the number of suitable speakers be a majority or even a sizeable proportion of the total population. But if the survey is to present information of any value as to the status of the basilect in the locality in question, it should attempt to determine what proportion of the population speak it, and how they are distributed according to age, sex, occupation, education, economic status, and other social variables. It is this kind of information that more recent surveys have attempted to discover and present. Accordingly, their sampling techniques must be more objective and formal.

Sociological sampling

As examples of recent surveys in which much care and planning is devoted to the identification and recruiting of a representative cross-section of the population, we may cite that of William Labov on the Lower East Side of New York City (Labov 1966), that of Peter Trudgill in the city of Norwich (Trudgill 1974a), and that of Barbara Strang, John Pellowe, and others in the Tyneside area of northeastern England (Pellowe et al. 1972). Unlike most previous surveys, all three of these are involved with an urban population, more subject to variation and to flux and change than the rural villages of traditional surveys. The investigators were prepared to accept – and, in fact, were actually looking for – variation of dialect within the local sample as well as a common denominator or basilect, if indeed it existed. They represent primarily a sociolinguistic approach to the problem, though Labov and Trudgill at least also have the historical linguist's interest in the origins and progress of language change. By extending their surveys across a wide range of ages, they hoped to catch synchronic evidence of diachronic change in the contrast between conservative elders and innovative youth, on the assumption (yet to be proved) that older speakers continue throughout life to use basically the same language they learned in youth.

The Lower East Side
The area which Labov chose to investigate is the Lower East Side of New York City, which was for a long time the place of first set-

tlement of immigrants and which is still characterized by 'rapid social movement, with second and third generation citizens moving out and upward in a continuous stream, while new groups take their place from outside. Those who do remain are often marked by either a strong sense of local tradition, or total inertia.' (Labov 1966, *p* 157) The population of the area when the survey was undertaken was about 107,000, including a quite large proportion of non-native speakers, who had to be excluded as not representative of the English of the area. (Labov extended the definition of native speaker to include those who had come to the United States before the age of eight.) He was fortunate in being able to make use of the previous work of an exhaustive sociological survey of the area, which had selected by carefully objective methods a sample of about 1,000, representing an accurate cross-section of the population, constituting about 1 per cent of the whole. When non-native speakers, those who had moved away, and those who had lived less than two years in the area were eliminated, Labov was left with a group of 195 selected informants, chosen, it should be noted, according to predetermined principles rather than by chance encounter or casual recommendation. A determined effort was made to interview all of these, but as may be suspected some could not be pinned down and others refused to be interviewed. In the end, 122 were interviewed with a standard questionnaire and 33 more with a shorter one, for a total of about 80 per cent of the preselected sample.

As Labov points out, the choice of a mobile area like the Lower East Side, and the selection within that area of a careful cross-section of the target group (native speakers of at least two years' residence) 'did not represent a retreat from the problem of variability among New York speakers' (*p* 176). Quite the opposite; it faced the question as to whether there could be such a thing as a common speech pattern among such a disparate group. The approach is thus very different from that of traditional rural surveys, where it is assumed that an indigenous dialect exists, though spoken perhaps by only a small part of the population, and where the goal is to record that indigenous dialect by seeking out as informants only those members of the population who can be considered authentic dialect speakers.

Norwich

Peter Trudgill calls his work on the dialect of Norwich 'a study in sociological urban dialectology' (Trudgill 1974a, *p* 1). He goes on to claim that 'in the application of sampling techniques to linguistic problems and in the handling of problems connected with the concept of social class we shall be making use of the methods and findings of sociology'. Thus, like Labov (whose influence he acknowledges), while keeping his focus on language and therefore remaining within the domain of linguistics, he recognizes the usefulness and value of sampling techniques developed by a sister discipline. A salient characteristic of urban speech is the presence of considerable variation on the vertical dimension of social class as well as on the horizontal geographical dimension. In fact, as Trudgill points out, in urban dialectology 'sociological factors are more important from the point of view of linguistic differentiation than geographical factors; and the social structure is of a complexity that makes close individual knowledge of the area impossible, and person-to-person contact as a means of selecting informants useless' (*p* 20).

The urban area of Norwich, the field of Trudgill's investigation, has a population of about 160,000 – somewhat larger than Labov's but in the same general order of magnitude. Since he felt that the maximum number of informants that could be interviewed within the time and resources available was 50, Trudgill's sample was one in 3,200, or 0.03 per cent, compared with Labov's one in 690, or 0.14 per cent. The first selection was to pick five subareas (out of seventeen) from different parts of the total geographic area, chosen so as to preserve the sociological characterisics of the total population. From this point on, the selection was done by random methods, using the voting lists as the population. Twenty-five names were first selected from each area, with the ultimate goal of recruiting ten from each. A preliminary letter was sent to the first ten from each area, intending 'to secure the goodwill of the informant, to explain the purpose of the interview, to allay any suspicions concerning the integrity and honesty of the interviewer and the non-commercial nature of the study, and to warn the informant that he was to be called on' (*p* 24). Ultimately, because of refusals or failure of individuals selected to meet basic requirements, it was necessary to contact ninety-five before the quota of fifty was obtained. In addition, a sample of ten schoolchildren between the ages of ten and twenty was added, since the voting lists do not contain minors.

In order to verify that his sample of fifty adults was a true cross-section, Trudgill subjected them to sociological analysis, establishing a 'social index' for each. This index was derived from six indicators to which numerical scores were given: occupation, income, education, housing, locality, and father's occupation. On the basis of this information, obtained from the informants themselves, he gave each informant a number, the total of his scores on the six individual scales. The range of these numbers satisfied Trudgill that his sample 'accurately represents the whole range of class differences, from the lowest to the highest' (*p* 41). It also appeared that the distribution by age and sex was representative, at least to the point that the sample included informants of each sex within each five-year age interval from twenty-five to sixty-five. Later, after the informants had been interviewed, Trudgill added some linguistic criteria to help in dividing the social con-tinuum into five social groups recognized as classes, ranging from 'middle-middle class' to 'lower working class'. Seventy-five per cent of the group were in the upper and middle working class, with the remainder distributed evenly among the other three. This seemed a reasonable distribution, though in the absence of a complete sociological analysis of the whole population, the accuracy of its representativeness could not be precisely checked.

Tyneside

The objective of the Tyneside Linguistic Survey (Strang 1968) is to answer the question 'How can we determine the ecology of varieties of spoken English in urban areas?' (Pellowe et al. 1972, *p* 1). The term ECOLOGY, taken over from biological and socio-logical studies, is defined as the attempt 'having identified the speech varieties themselves, to determine the relative common-ness or rarity of each and to define their distribution across social attributes' (*p* 1). This is, therefore, an attempt to answer the kind of questions we have seen to be either avoided or left unanswered by traditional surveys. Former surveys, as we have seen, either identified a single social group of 'dialect speakers', representing a minority (often a small minority) of the population, as the target for investigation (*eg* Orton 1962) or subdivided the popula-tion into a small number of social classes on the basis of relatively few criteria (*eg* Labov and Trudgill, also Kurath et al. 1939) and attempted to measure linguistic variables among them. The Tyneside Survey attempts a double statistical survey, using the methods of numerical classification. These methods call for the use of large numbers of criteria, which are studied statistically in order to see how they cluster into natural groups. The methods are to be applied to a set of over 300 linguistic features to deter-mine how they cluster into what may be recognized as linguistic varieties, and they are also to be applied to some 60 social attri-butes to determine how these cluster into markers of social classes. The former is a linguistic exercise; the latter a sociologi-cal one. The ultimate aim is to attempt to match the language varieties thus discovered with the social groups, thereby demonstrating, among other things, how it is that residents of a complex urban area can place others by their speech, swiftly and accurately, within the area, both socially and geographically. This survey thus represents the most intimate joining of the two disciplines yet attempted.[1]

Three separate samples of the Tyneside population were selected, to be used in three successive phases of the work. The first sample included three groups:

(a) 40 speakers, individually picked as *known* speakers of NL [non-localized] varieties, (b) 60 speakers, being all the residents available for interview, in a 'middle-class-street' which was chosen on subjective criteria..., (c) 150 speakers chosen randomly from the Electoral Register. The random subsample is a two stage nonstratified one (wards, polling districts), with probability of selection proportional to size (giving every individual an identical calculable probability of selection). (Pellowe et al. 1972, *p* 22)

The second sample was another random group of 150, and the third was a stratified sample of 150 from another section of the area, based on the single criterion of the taxable value of homes. One of the aims of the survey is to test the relative validity of these three methods of selection.

Traditional versus sociological surveys

Reviewing what we have discussed about methods of selecting informants for dialect surveys, we can see that, in spite of their great diversity, the surveys fall into two groups, differentiated by their aims. The older surveys – and some recent ones – which we have called 'traditional' have as their objective the discovery and recording of a 'local dialect'. This is thought of not as the common mode of speaking of all inhabitants of a locality, but as an indigenous variety of language, historically of long standing in the locality, preserved perhaps by a small segment of the population, and in danger of being exterminated by such forces as education, with its emphasis on the standard or prestige language; population flux and mixture, with resulting dialect mixture; and the influence of media such as cinema, radio, television, and the press. The investigator's task is to identify the authentic users of this dialect and to seek them out and record the dialect in its pure form, before it is further contaminated and weakened or totally lost. It is clear that with such an aim the selection of informants cannot be left to chance or to the mechanical working of a scientific sampling procedure. Instead, it becomes part of the duty of the fieldworker to know in advance what kind of speaker he is looking for and to recognize one when he finds him.

The sociologically oriented survey, on the other hand, is interested in the total linguistic situation of a locality in all its complexity. It does not assume that there is a local dialect, but attempts to discover whether a common denominator can be found in the language of all social groups. Rather than excluding heterogeneous variations as corruptions of the pure local dialect, it attempts to measure them and fit them into an overall picture of the linguistic situation in the total community. With such an aim, it is clear that the investigator must be as objective as possible; if he cannot interview all the inhabitants of a locality – which is nearly always impossible – he must make use of a statistically valid sampling procedure to identify potential informants in advance, and then make every effort to adhere to the sample thus selected. Only so can he be sure that he is dealing with a representative cross-section of local speech.

Both types of survey have their value. The traditional survey is of particular value to the historical linguist, interested in reconstructing the history of the language as a whole, and in pinpointing the points of origin of language change and tracing their diffusion across space and through time. The sociolinguistic survey reveals much about the uses of language as a marker of social status and interrelationships and its integration into the general social fabric of a community. There is room for both emphases in the discipline of dialectology.

Note

1. Since this was written, a doctoral thesis presenting in detail the methods of analysis of the Tyneside Survey, with some significant results, has become available (Jones, 1979). Jones describes the aims and theoretical basis of the study in some detail and goes on to demonstrate them in a model study limited to 51 phonological variables and 52 informants. Using sophisticated computer techniques, she shows how clusters of sociological characteristics may be matched with clusters of linguistic features. The results show great complexity. As she concludes: 'The relationships between linguistic behaviour and social group membership are not simple. . . . Therefore to seek relationships between single linguistic features and single social factors (or social indices based on a small number of sociological variables) bypasses completely the complexity of sociolinguistic differentiation.' (p 291)

    In its use of a full spectrum of phonological data together with a set of 38 social variables, this study marks a significant advance over the more limited and selective criteria used by Labov and Trudgill. Dr Jones has 'begun to tackle' syntactic, prosodic, and paralinguistic variables, which are more difficult to handle than the phonological ones (personal communication, 13 May 1982).

Chapter 5

Collecting the data

Once the questionnaire for a dialect survey has been prepared and tested, the localities comprising the network at least tentatively identified, and the number and type of informants decided upon, the actual collection of data can begin. This is the most important and in some ways the most difficult phase of the survey. If it is done with forethought and care, a corpus of data will be produced which is a permanent record of the dialect under investigation, available for analysis not only by the conductors of the survey themselves, but by future scholars as well. On the other hand, if it is done unskillfully, carelessly, or amateurishly, the data produced will be inconsistent, unreliable, possibly totally worthless. As in any collection of materials for scientific investigation, careful records must be kept of time, place, source, and circumstance. In addition, a substance so flexible, variable, and ephemeral as spoken language, so intimate a part of the personalities of those who use it, poses unique problems of elicitation, identification, and preservation. As might be expected, though there is agreement on fundamentals, there is considerable controversy over details of method. It cannot be said that there is a single standard procedure; instead, we will see that methods vary greatly from one survey to another, depending not only on the particular conditions involved but also on the convictions of dialectologists concerning the effectiveness and reliability of their own procedures. In what follows, the attempt will be made to present the conflicting views as objectively as possible.

The first important decision that must be made is whether the collecting is to be done by the direct method, the indirect, or a combination of the two. This distinction, as well as the advantages and disadvantages of each, was discussed in the last chap-

ter. In brief, the direct method involves the use of the questionnaire as the guiding instrument of an interview, in which the
FIELDWORKER attempts to get the dialect speaker or INFORMANT
to produce the desired sample of his dialect. The indirect
method, on the other hand, involves delivering the questionnaire,
usually by post, either directly to a previously identified informant, or, more often, to some INTERMEDIARY, who in turn finds
an appropriate informant who fills it in and returns it. The differences between the two methods are so fundamental that they
must be discussed separately.

The direct method

The case for the direct method has been strongly put by Pierre
Gardette, the director of ALLy. He claims that to have used the
postal questionnaire in his survey would have been 'disastrous'.
After citing the precedents of ALF and AIS, he goes on:

> As for us, it was on the scene, in the barn or under the hangar or in
> the open field that we interviewed our informants, where they gave us
> the names of the tools that we touched or of the parts of the structure
> that we pointed out, where they described the harvest which they had
> just completed, and so on. *Patois* is, as it were, attached to the reali-
> ties of rural life; one should not upset the dialect-speaker by getting
> him to write and to find an orthography which he has never learned.
> When we forgot to ask certain questions, we never considered writing
> to one of our informants to ask for the answer; we went back to the
> place in order to carry out a supplementary interview. There have
> been times when I had to go back twice after the actual interview to
> some villages in this way. (Gardette 1968, *p* 47)

The virtue of the direct method is thus the face-to-face contact
between the fieldworker and the informant in an environment
conducive to natural use of the dialect.

The fieldworker
The key figure in the direct method is thus the fieldworker. There
may be a single one, usually the dialectologist conducting the survey; if the number of informants to be interviewed is small or the
questionnaire is short, this is possible. More often, a group of
fieldworkers is assembled, often students of the director. This immediately raises the question of comparability. If the data are to
be consistent enough for comparisons to be meaningful, the various fieldworkers must use essentially the same methods. On the
other hand, differences in personality and temperament between
individuals will lead them to carry out their common task in

somewhat different ways. In some cases, such as LANE, the fieldworkers have all been selected at the same time and trained as a group. In others, such as SED, they have been recruited over a period of time, and consistency of training and practice has become the responsibility of the director of the survey. In any case, it is essential that an exact record be kept of which localities are visited by which fieldworkers in what order, and that this information be published with the records. In this way, any discrepancies due to differences of field methods can be taken into account when the data are used. Allowance can be made not only for differences between individuals, but for differences, conscious or unconscious, in the work of the same individual as he becomes more familiar with the dialect and more skilful at elicitation. Those who have studied the field records of Edmond Edmont, who investigated all 639 localities of the ALF over a period of 4 years, have observed this kind of change in his work.

The qualities that make a good fieldworker are many and diverse. They are of three kinds: social, regional, and linguistic background; amount and type of training; and qualities of temperament and personality. This ordering is intended to be climactic; in my view, at least, the personal qualities outweigh background and training. But all are important.

The principal questions relating to background are (1) Should the fieldworker be a native of the area under investigation? (2) Should he be directly familiar with the way of life of his informants? (3) Should he be a dialect speaker himself? All of these points have been discussed by the directors of dialect surveys, particularly those from continental Europe. In general, the consensus seems to be that these qualities are not essential, but they might help. A fieldworker working in his own region starts with many advantages, especially in the logistic aspects of his work and the identification of informants. He can proceed more directly to work, without having to spend time familiarizing himself with local culture. He is more likely to achieve ready acceptance and less likely to make the kind of social errors that cause the stranger to be looked on with suspicion or ridicule. On the other hand, many excellent surveys have been carried out by strangers, even foreigners. The Swiss Eugen Dieth, co-founder with Harold Orton of the SED, produced an excellent monograph on a Scottish dialect (Dieth 1932). The fieldworkers who surveyed Italy for AIS – Scheuermeier, Rohlfs, and Wagner – were all from German-speaking Switzerland, as were the two directors, Jaberg and Jud. I can testify from my own experience as a fieldworker for SED that a city-bred American could perform effectively in rural England.

The same is true about the social background of the field-worker. If he has a working-class background which shows through his educated surface, he may be more readily accepted by informants who are themselves working people. But the reverse may be true as well – he may be felt to be acting above himself. In a class-conscious society, an inevitable gulf separates the university professor or student from the artisan or peasant. This gulf is more likely to be bridged by basic human qualities of understanding, sympathy, and friendliness than by the accident of common background. After all, the scholar who takes to the field has already departed a long way from the sheltered life of library and common room; if he does not have the native ability to immerse himself in the life of the countryside and adjust to its ways, he will be both miserable and unsuccessful as a fieldworker.

Whether the fieldworker should be a native speaker of the regional dialect where he is working has been discussed *pro* and *con* by dialectologists. On the one hand, the ability to understand and even speak a version of the dialect being investigated has obvious advantages in communicating easily with informants. On the other hand, his very familiarity may lead him astray – in effect to rely on himself as an informant rather than the person he is interviewing. As Gardette puts it:

> A fieldworker who speaks his dialect fluently, who can therefore carry on the interview without speaking [standard] French, has several advantages; he. puts the informant at ease from the beginning, he distracts him as little as possible from the dialect, he does not impose on him the wearying task of hearing a question in French and answering in dialect. He thus avoids French loan-words. Let us add, however, that such an interviewer should guard against one danger: that of thinking he hears in other varieties the sounds of his own dialect. (Gardette 1968, *p* 45)

In a broad-ranging survey, it is, of course, not possible in any case for the fieldworker to command all the local dialects he will encounter. There does seem to be some advantage, however, in his having familiarity with one form of local speech, usually that of his native region, into which he can lapse when the situation seems to require it. Stanley Ellis, who did more than half the fieldwork for SED, covering many different dialect areas, found it advantageous on occasion to use his native Yorkshire speech, more to establish an easy rapport with informants than to insure better communication. Exclusive use of the standard language by the interviewer may lead to imperfect communication, even if the informant is at least receptively bidialectal, as most informants are in these days of radio and television. On the other hand, if the interviewer attempts to use a version of the dialect under investigation, there is the danger of the informant simply giving back the forms which he hears. As Jaberg and Jud point out: 'Accommodating informants are always ready to pronounce a word in their dialect as it was in the question. "É l'istess" [it's the same] is one of their favorite responses.' (Jaberg and Jud 1928, p 181) As they point out, the decision as to how far to go in adapting the questions to the informant's dialect is a matter for 'the linguistic sensitivity, the experience, and the painstaking discrimination of the interviewer' (p 182).

The question as to the amount of linguistic training necessary for a fieldworker is another point on which there has been disagreement. Opinions have varied from the extreme position of Gilliéron, who argued with characteristic vigor that the fieldworker should not be a linguist at all, to the more common view, that he or she should have considerable linguistic training in order to be able to understand the objectives of the survey and recognize valuable responses when they occur. On one point there is no question: the fieldworker should be well trained in articulatory phonetics and narrow phonetic transcription. This is true even in the age of the easily portable tape recorder. Fine distinctions can often be made based on visual signals such as lip rounding or spreading, which are lost in the purely auditory record. Even if the interview is well and carefully recorded with good high-fidelity field equipment, the fieldworker will still have to make phonetic notes from time to time, even if he does not transcribe everything on the spot. Gilliéron's fieldworker, Edmont, though originally a grocer by trade and lacking general linguistic training, had an excellent ear and was a rapid and accurate transcriber.

At the opposite pole from Gilliéron, dialectologists such as W. G. Moulton argue for well-trained linguists as fieldworkers, prepared to make structural analyses and judgements in the field. They view the fieldworker's task as more than simply to bring home a collection of disparate facts – pronunciations, lexical items, grammatical constructions. Instead they feel that he should use the opportunity of direct contact with the informant over a period of several days to make conjectures and hypotheses about the structure of the dialect, especially its phonology. The danger here, of course, is that in so doing he may compromise the data. Doubtless the fieldworker should be more than a mere recording machine, but he should first be that, even though he may carry an electronic one with him. However, as Gino Bottiglioni points out, the fieldworker is normally too busy with the primary task to indulge in much theorizing or slanting of the data:

... the autosuggestion and the prejudice feared by Gilliéron cannot influence the man who, linguist or not, is devoted with all his mind to
the difficult task of selecting an informant, establishing a rapport, and
transcribing so smoothly and so quickly as not to interrupt the contact
which has been forming and binds the questioner to the questioned.
The field worker, even if he is a specialist in linguistics, is so absorbed
wiith this exhausting work that he could not, though he would, think
of rules, phonetic laws, linguistic schemes. (Bottiglioni 1954, *p* 383)

One form of training for fieldworkers can all too easily be
overlooked – some knowledge and preferably firsthand experience with the culture and day-to-day ways of life of the informants he is going to interview. The questionnaires of most of the
traditional surveys, for example, deal, often in rather fine detail,
with the work of the farm in all its diversity, much of which
would be foreign to the experience of a city-bred fieldworker.
Certainly he should study the questionnaire closely before going
into the field and make sure that he knows exactly what each
question refers to and how it fits into the daily and seasonal patterns of life in his region. If he knows enough to make comparisons between one kind of plow or haystack or fish-net and
another, he will both insure the accuracy of his questions and
command the respect of his informants. Anthropological and
ethnographic training should be part of every fieldworker's equipment, whether he is going to work with rural informants, as in the
traditional survey, or with a wide range of urban types in a
sociolinguistic investigation. Much of his knowledge in these
areas will come from experience, the wider the better. Perhaps
we should paraphrase Gilliéron's observation about the questionnaire and say that the fieldworker is only properly prepared to
undertake a survey after he has completed it.

Above all, the fieldworker should have the qualities of personality that will allow him to enlist the enthusiastic cooperation of
his informants, indeed of all the inhabitants of the localities
where he works. Patience is perhaps the foremost requirement.
Although he works constantly under the pressure of time, he cannot afford to push the informant too insistently to get on with the
interview. No matter how persistently obtuse the informant may
seem to be about answering the questions, the fieldworker cannot
reveal his irritation, but must continue patiently to try new lines
of questioning to keep the information flowing. He should have a
great deal of natural curiosity not only about the informant's dialect, but about his way of life, his daily routine, and his life history. As Professor Orton often observed, he must put himself

into the position of pupil, who has much to learn from his instructor, the informant. He must have a broad acceptance and understanding of all sorts and conditions of people, and the ability to establish a ready rapport with them. Especially if the questionnaire is a long one, necessitating many hours of interviewing, he must convince the informant of the value and interest of what is going on. The best interviews arise out of a mutual understanding, respect, and ultimately affection, which can be long-lasting. Fieldworkers often establish lasting friendships with their best informants, visiting or corresponding with them for years after the survey is completed. Such friendships are one of the unexpected rewards of the arduous work of collecting dialect data.

Throughout the above discussion I have referred to the fieldworker as *he/him*. This is merely the result of an accident of English grammar; it is not meant to imply that fieldworkers must be men. It is true that in the early days of dialectology in the nineteenth and early twentieth centuries virtually all of them were, but this merely reflects the fact that philologians and linguists were almost exclusively men. More recently, as more women have gone into linguistic study, some of them have undertaken dialect work and have been successful fieldworkers. Two of the ten fieldworkers for LANE and one of the nine for SED were women. For the French regional survey of the Lyonnais, four out of six fieldworkers were women. The director of the survey says of them:

The four female fieldworkers of our team had in general as good results as those of M. Girodet and myself. Those who interviewed in areas where they were known, among informants who claimed common friends, often received a particularly sympathetic welcome. (Gardette 1968, *p* 44)

In fact, the directors of at least six of the French regional atlases now wholly or in part completed are women. I might add that one of my own woman students while still an undergraduate was a very successful fieldworker for DARE; at the time she was only nineteen years old.

It has been pointed out that women do have one disadvantage: the kind of old-fashioned rustic who constituted the usual informant in traditional surveys is likely to be squeamish about discussing some topics and using some lexical items considered to be improper in the presence of women. This is true, but such items constitute a very small part of most questionnaires. On the other side it may be said that a woman fieldworker may have much better success than a man in eliciting some of the special vocabulary of women from female informants.

Selection of informants

Except in the more rigorously sociological surveys, where informants are determined by impersonal and objective methods, the
decision as to what informants to use is almost always left to the
fieldworker. In the more narrowly focused traditional surveys,
where the qualifications for informants greatly limited the possible candidates, the task has often been as much to find suitable
informants as to choose them, as was discussed in the last chapter. In any case, the fieldworker has to be sufficiently familiar
with the social organization and daily life of the community to be
able to find informants as rapidly as possible. Whether the
tavern, the post office, the village shop, the town clerk's office, or
the church is the best place to begin depends on the role these
gathering places play in the social life of the community. The
fieldworker must know the degree to which he can be explicit
about his goal – whether it is safe to admit bluntly that he is collecting dialect, or whether it would be more prudent to talk
vaguely about being interested in 'the old ways of doing things'.
First meeting with a suggested informant is a critical time. On the
one hand, the fieldworker must find out as unobtrusively as possible
if the candidate meets the requirements of birthplace, residence,
occupation, and the rest; otherwise he may waste precious time
interviewing an informant who later turns out to be unqualified.
On the other hand, he must reveal enough of his own background
and mission to win the informant's confidence and cooperation.
In most cultures the countryman is suspicious of the stranger,
especially if he smacks of the city or the gentry. The slightest hint
of exploitation is likely to put him off, and even if he agrees to be
questioned, a successful interview cannot be conducted in an
atmosphere of suspicion. But once he has got past his original
caution and become convinced that the fieldworker is both legit-
imate and genuinely interested in what he has to say, the countryman – like most people anywhere – will accept the situation and
enjoy the opportunity to talk to a sympathetic listener. When this
point is reached, it usually becomes the fieldworker's problem
not to get the interview going but to control it and steer it into
the channels required by the questionnaire.

The question as to how many informants can be used to complete the questionnaire in a given locality is again a matter which
varies from survey to survey. On the one hand, some surveys follow Gilliéron in requiring that the whole questionnaire should be
answered by a single informant. Only in that way, it is felt, can a
consistent idiolect be presented and variables between individuals
be kept out. On the other hand, those surveys whose aim is to record 'the local dialect' or basilect common to the locality may feel

free to use several informants for different parts of the questionnaire, on the ground that not every speaker is equally competent
in all parts of the subject matter covered. It is especially common
for the interviewer to shift to a woman – often the wife of a principal male informant – for those parts of the questionnaire which
deal with the house, the kitchen, the children, and other areas
commonly considered to be women's province. Some investigators, notably Gardette, favor the group interview, where several
informants – a family group or a gathering at the local tavern –
supply the information jointly. Working with a patois rapidly becoming extinct, Gardette claims that no single speaker could
supply all the needed answers:

> There were of necessity gaps in their answers, words which they did
> not remember, but which another informant could recall. That is why
> it was necessary to complete an interview begun with one informant by
> an interview with another and, when possible, to conduct the interview
> with several informants together. This established a conversational
> atmosphere propitious for bringing back the best *patois*, giving mem-
> ory to the tongue. Also it is well known that the vocabulary of women
> does not completely coincide with that of men and vice versa: men
> may not know the old name for the swaddling clothes or wrapper for
> the baby, while women don't know the names of all parts of a cart. It
> is clear that we needed several informants so that the record would not
> be too incomplete. (Gardette 1968, *pp* 56–7)

He goes on to point out that having more than one informant in a
locality can expedite the work; when one informant tires or has to
go to his work, the fieldworker can turn to another. This is true
provided the fieldworker has inexhaustible energy, but I am sure
that most fieldworkers have found the work of interviewing at
least as fatiguing for themselves as for the informants. The
fieldworker also needs time between interviews for reviewing his
record, sorting out his notes made rapidly in the course of the interview, listening to the tape-recording to make sure that it is
technically adequate, noting gaps to be filled in, and planning his
strategy for the next interviewing session.

Eliciting the responses
The heart of the interview and the ultimate test of the fieldworker's skill is his success in eliciting the desired responses indicated by the questionnaire accurately and with a minimum of lost
time. As in many other phases of the collection process, there is
difference of opinion as to the best method for doing this. The
greatest opposition is that between what the Italian dialectologist

Bottiglioni calls the 'rigorists' and the 'free collectors'. This was discussed from the point of view of the questionnaire in Chapter 3. The rigorists maintain that the only way in which accuracy and comparability of responses from one locality to another can be assured is by furnishing the fieldworker with a set of prefabricated questions which are to be put to the informant verbatim, the field-worker being allowed to use his own ingenuity only if the pre-formed question fails to elicit the response desired. The questions are formulated to present the desired notion or referent without using a word, standard or dialect, which refers directly to it. Thus the question for the SED which was originally 'What do you call the place where you keep pigs?' (I.1.5) was changed to 'What do you call the place where you keep the animals that go ——?', at which point the interviewer was supposed to grunt like a pig. Underlying this position are several assumptions: that all infor-mants will be sufficiently familiar with the standard language to understand the question as originally formulated; that the area is culturally and geographically homogeneous enough so that the same question will serve equally well in all localities; and, perhaps, that the fieldworker is not to be trusted to use his own judgement in finding the best way to elicit a response, even from an informant whom he has come to know, in an environment which both share and which may be rather different from that en-visaged by the formulator of the question. One question in the SED questionnaire which always drew a blank with my own Nor-folk informants referred to certain berries which grow 'on the moors' (IV.11.3). There are heaths in Norfolk, but no moors and no bilberries.

Another rigorist position is that the first response of the infor-mant is always to be taken as the correct one. This doctrine, which goes back to Gilliéron, is based on the reasonable assump-tion that the first response to a stimulus is most likely to be the most instinctive and deep-seated one, and that second or later answers are likely to be conscious corrections motivated by the informant's wish to use more 'proper' language or to impress the interviewer with his knowledge of the standard vocabulary. But the reverse may also be true; the informant, influenced by his awareness of the standard speaker who is questioning him, may first come out with the 'proper' form of pronunciation and then, remembering that the purpose of the interview is to get at the authentic local speech, correct himself and give the dialect form, with or without comment. Incidental material and free discourse collected during or after the interview frequently reveal discre-pancies of this sort. The English informant who gives 'isn't', 'wasn't', 'backwards' and 'forehead' [fɔəhèd] in response to questions will often be found to use 'ain't', 'wasn't', [bǽkədz] or [fɔɹəd] in his more informal speech. Dialect speakers, like everyone else, have more than one register.

The 'free collector' school, as the name suggests, places much confidence in the fieldworker's ability to elicit the desired material in the method best adapted to the informant and the situation of the moment. He tries as much as possible to catch words and phrases called for by the questionnaire in the context of conversation, without direct stimulus. Or, at least, he adapts the questions to the individual informant, to his own style, and to the immediate situation. The danger is, of course, that he may misunderstand a usage by the informant and report an erroneous item as a response. For this reason the fieldworker must have sufficient familiarity with the dialect of the region to follow free discourse with ease. Above all, he should be so familiar with the questionnaire that he can catch the items he wants on the wing, as it were, without having to interrupt the informant to repeat a term or make sure of its correct meaning.

The most effective form of free collecting, especially if the interview is being tape-recorded (as all interviews should be today), is what the French dialectologists call the 'directed conversation' (*la conversation dirigée*). Gardette describes this technique as follows:

> It will be seen that our questionnaire is divided into chapters of about
> 50 questions, and that each forms a conversational topic [see Table 3.1
> above]. For example, the first chapter entitled 'Meadow, hay, rake,
> fork . . .' covers the history of the grass from the moment when a field
> is turned over to meadow until that when the hay is gathered and
> brought in. At first it deals with different techniques of grass culture,
> the irrigation of dry meadows, the drainage of wet ones; then the
> growth of the grass, then the kinds of hay, the mowing, the operations
> of drying the hay and putting it into heaps against the rain, then
> the return of the hay to the hayloft, and finally the regrowth of the
> grass. It is easy with a good informant to explain that you expect him
> to describe to you in this way and in *patois* the story of his meadows
> and of the hay, and to let him go his own way, interrupting him as lit-
> tle as possible, but getting him going again when he stops and taking
> him back when he has forgotten something important. At the end, you
> can ask him the questions which have not been answered. The order of
> words and phrases in the record of the interview will be a bit upset; to
> recover it it is enough in the evening to indicate alongside each re-
> sponse the number of the question. (Gardette 1968, *p* 49)

This method obviously produces the most natural language, especially if the informant gets carried away by his topic and expatiates on it. It also will produce the richest body of incidental material – dialect items of interest not specifically asked for by the questionnaire. But it puts a heavier responsibility on the field-worker to make sure that the wanted items actually appear and that they are correctly identified.

There are informants as well as types of subject matter which do not lend themselves readily to the directed conversation technique. For these, the free collector has other resources: the objects themselves, pictures, whether brought along in advance or sketched on the spot, gestures, paraphrases, completion questions, and the rest. Only under special circumstances of understood and accepted bilingualism (including bidialectalism) does he resort to translation of standard words and expressions into dialect. The usual response to a question like 'What do you call a pet lamb in your dialect?' is all too likely to be, 'Why, we call it a *pet lamb*', when some such term as *cade* may be the indigenous word. In his survey of Welsh, however, Thomas sometimes asked the informants to translate an English word into Welsh, with success.

Sociolinguistic surveys may require a variety of modes of elicitation, calculated to bring out various styles or registers of discourse. In his New York survey, for example, Labov was interested in studying a limited number of phonological features such as presence or absence of postvocalic /r/ and substitution of /t/ and /d/ for /θ/ and /ð/ as they appeared in various styles of speech by informants of different social classes. This required him to use various techniques of elicitation, including reading connected passages, reading word-lists, rather formal description of a topic ('common sense'), and narratives designed to get the informant so involved in the story that he lapsed into his everyday casual speech. A topic used successfully for this was: 'Have you ever been in a situation where you thought you were in serious danger of being killed...?' (Labov 1966, *pp* 90–112, 136–51)

Making the record
No matter how skilful the interviewer may be at eliciting responses, the value of his work is lost if he does not make an accurate record. In earlier surveys this inevitably meant either writing down the responses or checking them off on a check sheet. For purely lexical material, the written record could be in standard orthography, which could be more or less successfully improvised for those dialect words lacking a written form, with diacritics to indicate the position of stress or other details of pronunciation to be preserved. But for phonological surveys, including general sur-

veys any of whose responses might be used for phonological purposes, standard writing systems used by most languages are ambiguous and imprecise; some sort of phonetic writing system is needed. At first, investigators commonly devised their own systems or adopted those already being used by philologists in dealing with historical records. The system adopted by Gilliéron and Edmont for the ALF was originally devised by Jean-Pierre Rousselot (1846–1924), a pioneer dialectologist. It is based on the italic form of the Latin alphabet, with accents, diacritics, and miniature superposed letters to increase the number of available symbols. It has continued to be used by French dialectologists, including the editors of the regional atlases of France, with occasional modifications to deal with sounds not recognized by

NOTATION PHONÉTIQUE

L'alphabet phonétique utilisé dans cet ouvrage est celui auquel l'abbé P. Rousselot a donné son nom et qui a servi notamment à l'Atlas Linguistique de la France de J. Gilliéron et E. Edmont. En voici le détail :

Voyelles

à = a de *patte*
á = a de *pâte*
ȧ = a entre *à et è*
ä = a entre *à et o*
a = a moyen, entre *à et á*
ạ = a entre *a et è*

œ́ = eu de *feu*
œ̀ = eu de *bœuf*
œ = eu moyen, entre *œ̀ et œ́*

ò = o de *botte*
ó = o de *peau*
ọ́ ou ọ̈ = o plus fermé, entre *u et ó*
ọ̀ et ọ̈ = o entre *ó, ò et œ́, œ̀*
o = o moyen, entre *ó et ò*

è = è de *paix*
é = é de *fée*
ẹ́ = é très fermé, proche de i
e = e moyen, entre *é et è*
ę = e dit muet de *Grenoble*

i = i de *fils*
í = i plus fermé
ì = i plus ouvert

u = u de *mur*
ú = u plus fermé
ù = u plus ouvert
ü = u entre *u et œ̀*
ʊ = ou de *lourd*

Les voyelles, moins nettement prononcées (ce qui arrive lorsqu'elles sont à la fin d'un mot ou dans une diphtongue) sont écrites au-dessous de la ligne. Ex : Feᵢ ra , trèbl₀

Lorsque les deux éléments d'une diphtongue sont d'égale importance, ils ont la même grosseur et on inscrit au-dessus le signe ⌢ pour indiquer qu'il s'agit d'une diphtongue et non d'un hiatus. Ex : fáèra .

y, w, ẅ sont les semi-voyelles de pied, moins, puis.

i, y, ẅ sont les phonèmes ambigus dont on ne sait s'ils sont les voyelles i, u, ẅ ou les consonnes y, ẅ, w .

, souscrit indique la voyelle qui porte l'accent d'intensité. Nous avons fait l'économie de ce signe toutes les fois que l'accent tombe, comme en français, sur la dernière syllabe du mot.

~ suscrit indique que la voyelle est nasalisée. Ex : mē = fr. main .

˜ indique une nasalisation incomplète .

Les voyelles accentuées sont normalement longues, les voyelles atones sont normalement brèves. La longueur et la brièveté ne sont indiquées que lorsqu'elles sont très apparentes ou lorsqu'elles jouent un rôle morphologique. On les indique par les signes usuels ⁻ ᵕ suscrits .

Consonnes

p, t, k, b, g, d, f, v, l, m, n, s, z, j ont la même valeur qu'en français.

e est le son écrit ch dans chat ; ç̌ est le son écrit ch dans all. ich .

ˌ souscrit indique que la consonne est palatalisée : t, k, d, g .

ṇ est l'n palatalisé de agneau .

k̑, g̑ sont les médiopalatales articulées entre k, g et t, d .

, souscrit indique un point d'articulation interdental : s est le th dur de l'anglais , z le th doux .

r = r usuel dans tout le domaine. Cet r a été apical et devient partout grasseyé-uvulaire; il suit l'évolution de l'r français. Dans le Nord (Saône-et-Loire) il est encore souvent apical et très roulé. Dans le Rhône et la Loire il est de plus en plus grasseyé-uvulaire : les vieillards ont encore souvent un r apical peu roulé, les jeunes ont de plus en plus l'r grasseyé-uvulaire . Il n'a pas été possible de distinguer les générations. Nous avons écrit toujours r cet r en voie d'évolution .

ᵣ = r vocalique .

ᵣ̥ = r dévibré, plus ou moins interdental . Il arrive parfois à être ẓ .

ᶠ = r longuement vibré .

FIG. 5.1. Phonetic alphabet from ALLy (Gardette 1968).

Edmont. The version used by Gardette in the ALLy appears in Fig. 5.1. Based on standard French orthography, without extra characters from other alphabets, it has the advantage, according to Gardette, of 'not upsetting the untrained reader, since it uses virtually only the letters of the Latin alphabet' and yet it 'allows many nuances by means of accents, diacritical signs, and superscript vowels' (Gardette 1968, p 59). It thus resembles the respelling systems used by American dictionaries to indicate pronunciation.

For Italian, Jaberg and Jud used in AIS a system devised by A. Ascoli, considerably modified to accommodate newly recognized sounds (Jaberg and Jud 1928, pp 24–9). It makes use of Greek letters such as θ, χ, and γ for some consonants having no usual equivalent in the standard alphabet. In this regard it is similar to the IPA, the alphabet of the International Phonetic Association, which is favored by English and American dialectologists, (Orton 1962, pp 18–19; Kurath et al. 1939, pp 122–42). This alphabet, developed at the end of the nineteenth century primarily for language teaching purposes, has been modified over the succeeding years to include new symbols and diacritics, and is the form preferred in those areas where an older traditional system, like those of France and Italy, has not become the standard.

German dialectologists have developed their own phonetic alphabet, which is used for such major undertakings as the *Deutscher Sprachatlas* (DSA) and the Swiss *Sprachatlas der deutschen Schweiz* (SDS). This system was originally proposed in 1924 by H. Teuchert as the standard for the journal *Teuthonista*, which later became the *Zeitschrift für Mundartforschung* and still later the *Zeitschrift für Dialektologie und Linguistik*, the most important German journal for dialect research. Forty years later, the original system having proven inadequate for modern phonetic transcription, a revised and expanded system was developed by a committee of the Research Institute for German Language, under the chairmanship of its director, Ludwig Erich Schmitt (Schmitt and Wiesinger 1964). In devising the new system, the committee was guided by five considerations:

1. The traditions of the existing system should be preserved, so that previous dialect studies might remain readily accessible.
2. The system should enable the transcription of all the sounds occurring in German. . . . It should be simple enough for phonological purposes, yet be able to be refined for exact phonetic notation.
3. Experience has shown that this is only possible with a diacritical system. As it must be readily legible and easily handled the basic symbols are to be taken from the Latin (and where necessary from the Greek) alphabet.

4. Methodologically the whole system must be as homogeneous and consistent as possible. . . .

5. In choosing and arranging the symbols the technical limitations of the printer should be borne in mind. (Schmitt and Wiesinger 1964, p 61)

The authors claim that their system meets all these requirements. In the use of Greek letters ɸ, χ, ɣ for fricative consonants this system also resembles the IPA. But its vowel system, using standard roman and italic characters with numerous superscripts, subscripts, and following diacritics, is independent of the IPA. It also has provision for indicating pitch and tone as well as stress.

It may at first seem unfortunate that no universal standard system of phonetic transcription has been adopted by dialectologists. Certainly for those interested in comparing the art and techniques of dialect research in various languages, this is a disadvantage. But in practice most dialectologists work within one language or language family. For them it is convenient to have a system developed specifically for that language, and used more or less consistently in all dialect studies dealing with it. If the modern regional atlases of France, for example, had adopted the IPA, this would have imposed upon those working in French the necessity of constantly shifting from one system to another as they compared the older records of the ALF with the newer regional studies.

A more important question than what system to use is how detailed and refined the phonetic transcriptions should be. This is related to other questions about the role of the fieldworker, such as Gilliéron's view that he should not be a linguist at all, and the rigorist position which very much constrains his freedom in asking questions. All of these matters concern the degree to which the fieldworker is to be allowed to exercise his own judgement in making his collections. With regard to the phonetic transcription, the more rigorist position regards the fieldworker primarily as a 'recording machine' (Moulton 1970a, 1980). This is the usual position of traditional surveys. Jaberg announced it unequivocally in his lectures at the Collège de France in 1933, later published in expanded form as *Aspects géographiques du langage* (Jaberg 1936):

We call *unregularized phonetic transcription* or *impressionistic transcription* that which takes account only of the instantaneous acoustic impression which the answers of the subject interviewed (or in a general sense, everything spoken) make on the interviewer, and to this we contrast normalizing transcription, which attempts to give the normal or average pronunciation of a speech-variety. . . . Combining the direct interview with normalized transcription – which is equivalent, at least in part, to the study of the phonological systems of the speech-varieties under study – is a method of research which will yield valuable results in controlled studies made by experts in the course of living in the same region for a long time; but I am deeply convinced that this method cannot be applied to those surveys which cover a wide area, since such investigations are not sufficient to distinguish accurately in a given speech-variety what is accidental from what is essential for its system.... When it is a matter of rapid surveys of the kind which practical necessity imposes on the authors of national atlases, one must be satisfied with reporting the phonetic facts – or what, trusting one's own ear, one believes them to be ... (pp 17–18).

The same position was taken by Orton and Dieth for the SED. As Orton states it:

> The phonetic recording was carried out impressionistically. The merits and demerits of the impressionistic method need not be re-stated here. Our fieldworkers, all of whom were trained to the same pattern, tried hard to write down as accurately as possible what they heard. They were briefed to regard each response as an individual phonetic problem and not to attempt to normalise. (Orton 1962, p 18)

American work on the Linguistic Atlas of the United States and Canada under the direction of Hans Kurath followed the same principle. Great care was taken on LANE to assure that, as 'recording machines', the various fieldworkers performed as nearly identically as possible in their phonetic transcription. Residual differences and idiosyncrasies were observed and carefully recorded in the *Handbook* (Kurath et al. 1939, pp 50–3, 122–42). In a later work Kurath showed himself in agreement with Jaberg as to the impossibility of establishing an accurate phonological system in the course of a brief field visit:

> How can a full record of relevant phonological information be best obtained under the conditions confronting the fieldworker charged with the task of eliciting and recording a large number of lexical, morphological, and phonological responses in a limited time? Could he reliably, or even tentatively, establish the phonemic inventory and the phonic range of the individual phonemes, say, in the first two hours and thereafter record purely phonemically? (Kurath 1972, p 8)

In what follows, Kurath makes clear that in his view these are rhetorical questions. Even if the fieldworker were able to make the suggested phonemic analysis, the process would be so boring to the informant that he would cut off the interview.

The opposite position holds that the fieldworker should use his linguistic knowledge to draw what conclusions he can while in direct face-to-face contact with the informant. He may not be able to make a full phonological analysis, but he can certainly draw some conclusions about the system the informant is using and allow these conclusions to be reflected in his later more 'normalized' transcriptions. Among other things, this practice can expedite the transcription by reducing the number of fine distinctions the transcriber is obliged to indicate. A general statement such as 'All initial voiceless stops are aspirated' or 'Final voiced obstruents are partially devoiced' would save the transcriber from having to mark every occurrence of these phenomena. In fact, even a trained phonetician who is a native speaker of English might occasionally neglect to mark features such as these, which are common to most dialects of English, thus inadvertently giving a misleading record. On the other hand, if he adopts a more general normalized or quasi-phonemic ('broad') transcription, the fieldworker can note any exceptions as they occur. The important thing is for him to make a complete and accurate statement of his practice for the guidance of those who are to use his material in the future.

In spite of these advantages, however, traditional dialect surveys have not adopted the policy of permitting the fieldworker to operate as a linguist as well as a recording machine. One dialectologist who supports this position, however, is W. G. Moulton. As he puts it:

> What really bothers me about the traditional use of fieldworkers is that it is such a tremendous waste of talent. Here are these highly qualified people, usually with Ph.D.'s, and trained in phonetics, phonemic theory, and the history and structure of the language they are investigating. And what are they asked to do? Perform like recording machines, i.e. make use of their phonetic training but of nothing else. They could just as well be grocers, like Edmond Edmont. (Personal letter, June 1979)

Tape-recording

For recent surveys, this question has been rendered largely irrelevant by the availability of high-fidelity portable electronic 'recording machines', which permit the entire interview to be recorded for later transcription and study. Auditory mechanical recording of dialectological field records predates the tape recorder, which has been developed since the Second World War. The most extensive early use was for LANE. In 1933–34, Miles L. Hanley made a total of 657 phonograph recordings throughout New England (Hanley 1933, p 368; Kurath 1934, p 419). Although many of the speakers recorded had earlier been interviewed for the Atlas, no recordings of actual interviews in pro-

gress were made; the equipment was too cumbersome for the
fieldworker to handle along with all the other things he had to do.
The same is true of the tape-recordings of the SED informants.
Beginning in 1953, recordings were made of at least one speaker
in all but 76 of the 314 localities surveyed. Much of the recording
was done by Stanley Ellis, using a tape recorder weighing about
40 pounds and requiring a power take-off from a Land Rover car
in those localities where electricity was not available. Later the
fieldworkers made their own recordings with more portable
equipment. My own recordings in Norfolk were made in 1957
with a Magnemite recorder which weighed 20 pounds and had a
clockwork tape-drive which had to be wound every five minutes.
Batteries supplied the current for the recording. Although to the
modern reader with a transistorized recorder weighing one-tenth
as much such equipment sounds primitive indeed, it still made excellent records. None of the SED recordings, however, were of
actual complete interviews; they were used instead to gather incidental material, primarily connected discourse of the 'directed
conversation' type, and to check the impressionistic recordings of
pronunciation.

> The material so procured was never rehearsed, and, of course, never
> recited. It was spontaneous, and as a rule consisted of personal re-
> miniscences or opinions, or discussed some task connected with the
> speaker's occupation, e.g. ploughing, harvesting, hedging, stacking,
> pig-killing, bread-making. The themes would crop up naturally – so it
> seemed to the informant – in the course of his conversation with the
> fieldworker, who, by further skilful management, would ensure that
> these informal and uninhibited remarks were secured on his tapes for
> permanent record. (Orton 1962, p 19)

Over the last fifteen years or so, tape-recording equipment has
improved greatly in both fidelity and portability. It is now possible for the fieldworker to record an entire interview without
allowing the operation of the machine to be so conspicuous as to
distract the informant. At first this was done concurrently with a
phonetic transcription. But as it became apparent that tape-
recordings were as accurate as could be desired both for later
transcription and for analysis by sound-spectrograph and other
electronic aids to acoustic analysis, some fieldworkers abandoned
the simultaneous phonetic transcription, thus saving a great deal
of interviewing time. One current survey which has taken this
step is the *Linguistic Atlas of the Gulf States* (LAGS) under the
direction of Lee Pederson. In this survey, 'rather than serving as
a supplement to field notes, such a [tape-recorded] text is the
basic document, for which several kinds of interpretations can be

constructed' (Pederson 1974, *p* 11). This text is then later used as
the basis for various working versions which Pederson calls *analogues*. He suggests five of these, only the last of which is imprac-
ticable on the basis of the time it would require:

> (1) the initial written record and guide to the text, transcribed in im-
> pressionistic phonetics and supplemented with marginal commentary
> on the pages of the workbook; (2) an orthographic typescript of the
> complete running text; (3) a broad phonic transcription; (4) a
> phonemic transcription; (5) a narrow phonetic transcription of the
> complete running text. (Pederson 1974, *pp* 11–12)

The first of these, which Pederson calls a *protocol*, is parallel to
the usual field record in form, but it has the advantage of representing 'the best efforts of a phonetician to record the field record
when he listens to it as a transcriber, not as a participant in a conversation' (*pp* 12–13). There are two obvious advantages to this:
since the recording can be played over and over, the transcription
can be more accurate, and since the fieldworker is freed from
preoccupation with phonetic transcription while making the interview, he can devote all his attention to the informant himself and
to the process of eliciting the material called for by the questionnaire.

It should be pointed out, however, that the tape recorder does
not do away with the phonetic transcription altogether; it will still
be needed for editing and publishing the results. What it does do
is to transfer the difficult task of making the phonetic transcription from the busy fieldworker in the field to the phonetician in
the laboratory – who may or may not be the same person. The
situation has been well summed up by Raven McDavid:

> The tape recorder does not materially shorten the time of interviewing.
> It provides a permanent record and catches more conversational re-
> sponses than even the best fieldworker can note and write down. On
> the other hand, it cannot ask the question or probe for additional or
> alternative responses or think of future questions. What time is gained
> by not writing down the responses as they are given is far less than the
> time required to listen to a tape, transcribe, note conversational re-
> sponses, and enter them in their proper places – perhaps four times
> the length of the interview itself. (McDavid 1974, *p* 56, n. 31)

In connection with McDavid's last statement, however, it should
be pointed out that the time saved by the tape recorder is the
most precious sort, informant time. The dialectologist is willing to
spend whatever time is necessary, but the informant may become
tired or bored at any time and cut short the interview. So anything that makes the best use of the time he is willing and able to
give is of great value.

The format of the field record

Especially in those surveys making use of more than one fieldworker, it is important that a standardized form be established and insisted upon for the field records, whether they are actually made in the field or transcribed from tape later. The handling of a large mass of material can easily become chaotic if provisions are not made in advance to facilitate filing, processing,

72   SURVEY OF ENGLISH DIALECTS: INTRODUCTION

BOOK V   THE HOUSE AND HOUSEKEEPING

5   8   And when the milk does that, what do you call the stuff you get? **Curds*, whey*.**

      9   In hot weather, fresh milk will soon . . . . **curdle.**

     10   . . . the first milk of a newly-calved cow? **Beestings.**

6   BAKING

     1   What do you make your white bread out of? **Flour*.**
       And your brown bread? **Meal*.**
       State what difference there is between them.

     2   Now to make bread, you put flour and water into a dish, and what else, to make it rise? **Yeast.**

     3   . . . all that stuff together, when you've mixed it up? **Dough*.**

     4   What do you do to the dough before you roll it? **To knead*.**

     5   . . . that flat wooden thing you knead the dough on? **Paste-board.**

     6   Where do you bake the bread? **In the† oven*.**

     7   When your bread or cakes come out all black, then you say they are . . . . **burnt.**
       If *burnt* doesn't emerge, suggest *burn* to get *burnt†*.

     8   And why have they been burnt? Because the oven has been . . . . **too hot*.**

     9   Rev. What do you mean by **loaf***?
       Ascertain the pronunciation of *loaf* and **bread***, and contrast their meanings.

    10   . . . the thin piece you cut off from the loaf with the bread-knife? **Slice.**

    11   What might a child ask for when it's hungry, e.g. on coming home from school? **Piece of bread and butter.**
       And if there's something on it? . . . . **and jam/sugar.**

    12   When your bread or pastry has not risen, you say it is . . . . **sad.**

7   COOKING

     1   For breakfast, some people eat oatmeal boiled in water or milk. What do you call that when it's thick? **Porridge*.**

     2   And when it's very thin? **Gruel*.**

     3   You can burn your mouth in eating porridge, if . . . . **it is‡** too hot.

     4   . . . that thing with bars you use in cooking a fish over the fire? **Grid-iron.**
       And that iron plate that cakes were baked on over the fire? **Girdle.**

FIG. 5.2.   Page from SED Questionnaire (Orton 1962).

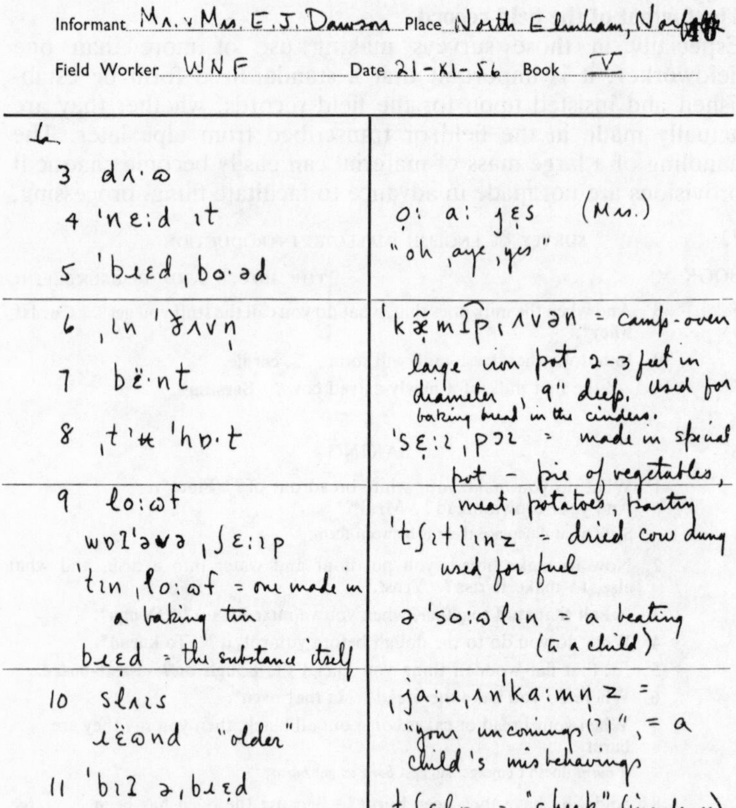

Informant _Mʌ. v Mᴿˢ. E. J. Dawson_ Place _North Elmham, Norfolk_

Field Worker __W.N.F_____ Date _21 - XI - 56_ Book __V__

6.	
3 dʌ·ɵ	
4 'neːd ɪt	ọ: aː jɛs (Mᴿˢ.)
5 'bɹɛd ˌboˑəd	"oh ˌaye ˌyes"
6 ˌɪn 'ʒʌvn̩	'kæ̃mĩp̂ ˌʌvən = camp-oven
7 bë·nt	large iron pot 2-3 feet in diameter, 9" deep. used for baking bread in the cinders.
8 ˌt'ʜ 'hʊ·t	'sɛ̣ːʲ ˌpɔɹ = made in special pot - pie of vegetables, meat, potatoes, pastry
9 ɭoːʊf	
wɒʔ'əvə ˌʃɛːʲp	'tʃɪtlɪnz = dried cow dung used for fuel
'tɪn ˌɭoːʊf = one made in a baking tin	
bɹɛd = the substance itself	ə 'soːɒlɪn = a beating (to a child)
10 slʌɪs	
ɹɛ̈ənd "older"	ˌjaː.ɪ ˌʌnˈkaːmn̩z = "your uncomings (?)", = a child's misbehavings
11 'bɪʒ əˌbɹɛ̣d	
'ɹɛ̈ənd əˌbɹɛ̣d n̩ 'bʌʒ	tʃɛlp = "cheek", (insolence)
or 'dɹɪpɪnz	
or 'dʒæ·m	
12 'hɛvɪ	ˌbɔːə ˌʒæs 'hɛvɪ ɪf ˌʒæ? ˌdonʒ 'ɹʌɪz
	"bor that's heavy if that don't rise"

FIG. 5.3. Page from SED Field Record from North Elmham, Norfolk.

and cross-reference. It is a common practice to use a divided page, with the responses to the specific questionnaire items on the left hand side and incidental material taken from conversation on the right. Figure 5.2 illustrates a page from the SED questionnaire and Fig. 5.3 gives the corresponding page from one of my Norfolk field records. The same format was used for the American atlas surveys, with the added specification that each response should appear in the same position on the same numbered page in every field record. Since the records were made in duplicate, this permitted one file of complete records and another file of the same single pages from all localities. Unfortunately SED did not follow this simple procedure, and therefore the editing process required that each item from each questionnaire be copied off by hand onto lists, which was both time-consuming and a potential source of error. With the development of cheap facsimile copying equipment, it is no longer necessary for the fieldworker to be encumbered with carbon paper and duplicate pages in the field; a Xerox copy of the whole field record can be made when it is returned to the survey center.

The indirect method

The indirect or postal questionnaire type of survey was described above in Chapter 3. Primarily used for collecting lexical material, either for the lexical component of a general survey, as in the *Linguistic Atlas of Scotland* (LAS), or for a survey limited to word geography, as in LGW, collecting by this method differs from the direct method in three important respects:

1. The professional fieldworker is replaced by a willing and interested but virtually always amateur INTERMEDIARY, who undertakes the responsibility for selecting the informants and instructing them in filling out the questionnaire, or else eliciting the responses and recording them himself.
2. The elicitation is carried on primarily by translation: the informant is given a word or phrase – sometimes a whole sentence – in the standard language, either in writing or orally by the intermediary, and is asked to write out or speak a version in his own dialect.
3. The responses are recorded in the standard orthography, leaving it to the informant or intermediary to improvise a representation of those words which do not have a standard spelling.

The intermediary

As the fieldworker is the key figure in a direct survey, so is the intermediary in a postal survey. Ideally he should be a native or at least long-time resident of the area, with at least an amateur's interest in language and dialect, sufficiently well educated to handle the problems of transcription, yet with a broad acquaintance and acceptance among the members of the community designated

as suitable informants. This combination is most commonly found –
in European countries, at least – in the two professionals whose
duties involve them daily with all members of the community on
a basis of confidence: the schoolmaster and the clergyman. Since
the director of the survey is seldom able to select the intermediaries personally (unless they are his own students), he must rely
on his knowledge of the culture to guide him to the class of persons most likely to meet the requirements described above. In
Western countries, at least, the one most usually chosen is the
schoolmaster, and the success of the German, Scottish, and
Welsh postal surveys corroborates this choice. But it is obvious
that in other countries lacking a well-organized and broad-based
educational system, some other class of persons would be chosen.
In any case, the director should ask for biographical information
about the intermediary as well as the informants, in order to alert
him to any bias the intermediary might, consciously or unconsciously, give to the material.

Elicitation by translation

All methods of collecting dialect material assume to some degree
or other that the informants are at least receptively bidialectal,
that is that they can understand questions put to them in the standard dialect, though they may not be productively competent in
that dialect. Very seldom is the interviewer able to question the
informant in his own dialect; indeed, to do so might be counter-
productive, since the informant would be likely to see no point in
answering a number of questions about the dialect words for
things, put to him by a person fluent in the dialect himself, who
thus ought to know the answers to his own questions. But, as we
have seen, the direct method of interviewing commonly uses an
indirect method of questioning, in which even the standard words
for the notions involved are avoided lest they be too suggestive.
But this indirection cannot be used in the postal questionnaire.
As the editor of LGW puts it:

> For a postal inquiry, much of this [indirect] technique is inappropriate:
> circumlocution and paraphrase, when the investigator is not at hand
> to control them, may give rise to ambiguity. (Thomas 1973, p 7)

Instead, the postal questionnaire simply calls for a translation of
the keyword or phrase into the dialect, either by the informant
himself, as in the Scottish and Welsh surveys, or by the intermediary, as in Wenker's German survey. This introduces a factor of unreliability undoubtedly larger than that of the direct
interview, and requires the editor or director of the survey to
appraise the reliability of individual responses or entire question-

naires and reject those he considers unsatisfactory. Commonly this rejection has been done largely on subjective grounds. On the basis of his wide and deep knowledge of dialect, the editor simply finds something about a response or a questionnaire that leads him to doubt its authenticity, and since he is not usually in a position to make a further investigation, he takes the safe course of rejecting the suspect item. Thomas has attempted to rationalize this subjective basis for rejecting responses by studying the overall pattern of responses for the area:

> A potential problem in an investigation of this kind [*ie* by postal questionnaire] is the difficulty of ensuring the validity of the responses, in the absence of personal supervision of the informant by a trained fieldworker. However, a reliable measure of the validity of results is contained in the response-pattern obtained. Where a particular response-pattern is consistent and relatively uniform through the main areas of distribution of specific words, it is evident that a high percentage of informants have interpreted the relevant question in the same way. For

001662 NAME (Mr, Mrs, Miss) ADDRESS How long have you lived in the above place ? Born : Place Year Father's Birthplace Mother's Birthplace	001662 2. BOY (aged about 12) USUAL LOCAL WORD(S) LESS COMMON LOCAL WORD(S) BY WHOM USED COMMENTS (Have you different words for a boy according to his age ?)
001662 GRID (nothing to be written here) NAME ADDRESS COUNTY	001662 3. GIRL (aged about 12) USUAL LOCAL WORD(S) LESS COMMON LOCAL WORD(S) BY WHOM USED COMMENTS (Have you different words for a girl according to her age ?)
001662 1. CHILD Line 1 USUAL LOCAL WORD(S) Line 2 LESS COMMON LOCAL WORD(S) Line 3 BY WHOM USED Line 4 COMMENTS Line 5	001662 4. YOUNG MAN (around 20) USUAL LOCAL WORD(S) LESS COMMON LOCAL WORD(S) BY WHOM USED COMMENTS

We reproduce as a sample of the first page of the questionnaire (Fig. 1). Every book has a number which appears in the top right-hand corner of each slip and facilitates its identification. The first two slips on the left-hand side, the 'name-slip' and the 'grid-slip' respectively, contain the *personalia* of the informant and overlap partially, but are essential for cross-indexing. The national grid (see p. 15) was entered on both these slips on the return of the books to the Survey.

FIG. 5.4. Page 1, Postal Questionnaire 1, LAS (from Mather and Speitel 1975, *p* 11).

that particular response a valid speech-area is defined. A multiplicity
of responses in an area which is typically uniform – or an incidence of
thinly scattered and disparate responses – indicates ambiguity in the
questionnaire. (Thomas 1973, *p* 5)

He goes on to show how analysis can distinguish between invalid
and ambiguous responses.

A further danger of the translation method is the one which
the indirect questioning methods of oral interviewing are designed to avoid – the parroting of the keyword by the informant,
especially if it exists as a loan-word in the dialect. For this reason,
postal questionnaires frequently ask for other commonly used
words in addition to the first response. This can be seen in
Fig. 5.4, which presents the first page of Postal Questionnaire I of
the Scottish survey. The methods suggested by Thomas can be
used to check the validity of the first response if it is the same as
the keyword. If so, the more authentic regional word may turn up
in the 'Less Common Local Word(s)' section of the response.

Transcription

The chances of the intermediary being adept in the use of a
phonetic transcription system are remote, and of the informant
having such a skill virtually nil. An early attempt to get around
this difficulty was that of Alexander Ellis, in a postal survey
which he conducted as part of his extensive collection of material
for his book *The Existing Phonology of English Dialects* (1889).
Along with his word-list of 971 items, which he sent to 1,700 intermediaries 'chiefly... clergy', Ellis sent 'a list of the principal
sounds to be observed, with their glossic representation and a
number attached' ('Glossic' was a phonetic alphabet of his own
devising). The results were disappointing. Ellis reports that only
500 of the lists were returned, 'with some though often very little
information' (Ellis 1889, *pp* 2–3). Apparently the English clergy,
university graduates all, had their limitations when it came to
learning phonetics by correspondence.

More commonly, the instructions simply ask the informant or
intermediary to spell the words as best he can in the standard
alphabet. Since precise phonological information is not being
sought, this will usually suffice to identify the lexical items and
their approximate pronunciation. In the Welsh survey,

> ... no phonetic or phonological information was required in the
> majority of responses, although informants were encouraged to simu-
> late regional pronunciation by manipulation of standard Welsh
> orthography. Where phonological features were explicitly investi-

gated, informants were asked to select, from a set of variant orthographic forms, that form which most closely reflected their local pronunciation. (Thomas 1973, *p* 5)

The editors of the LAS in their introduction discuss at some length the questions and problems raised by the informants' spellings (Mather and Speitel 1975, *pp* 16–20). The situation in Scotland is especially complicated in that there are two orthographies involved: standard English and the standard system for Lowland Scots. Mather and Speitel find that, as in English generally, the greatest variation in pronunciation is in vowels, and therefore 'in a given response, the skeletal framework of written consonants (graphs or digraphs) is of more general utility in the display of lexical distinctions than written vowels' (*p* 17). It is thus usually possible to know how many different lexical forms appear as responses to a given question, but precise phonetic differences are not recoverable.

Format of the postal response
In general, the postal responses can be in the same format as the field records of a direct survey. But the experience of those who have used the postal method shows that, as with all types of postal questionnaire, the easier it is made for the informant or intermediary to report the responses, the more likely it is that the questionnaire will be returned. What seems like an excellent method is that devised for the Scottish survey and followed by Thomas in Wales. The questions are printed in a book made of stiff sheets which can be cut up later into cards for filing (see Fig. 5.4). If it is desired to keep one copy of the complete record in addition to filing the separate responses, the response book can be copied before it is cut up into separate cards. In this way the convenience of both the informant and the editor can be served.

The postal response, like the worksheets from the direct interview, must contain the essential biographical information about the informants: date and place of birth, birthplace of parents and, if possible, grandparents, amount of schooling, occupation(s), amount of time spent away from the locality, birthplace of spouse. Similar information about the intermediary should also be included.

Chapter 6

Publishing the findings

The ultimate aim of a dialect study, whether it be a monograph dealing with a single locality or a survey of a region, is, of course, publication of the results for the use of linguists or, in some cases, the general reader. For a survey of any size, the task of preparing the data and the actual cost of publication are so great that there is often considerable delay between collection and publication, and in some cases the data never reach the public. On the other hand, when adequate staff and funds are available, the result may be a large and impressive DIALECT ATLAS, furnishing the reader or scholar with material for further study and interpretation of the materials collected.

Much study, experimentation, and theorizing have gone into the preparation of dialect atlases. Two basic questions face the editor:

1. What format is to be adopted for presenting the material?
2. To what degree and in what ways is the material to be processed, *ie* edited, summarized, formalized, etc., by the editor?

The primary choice of format is between tabulated lists on the one hand and maps on the other, or perhaps a combination of the two. The primary choice with regard to processing is between presenting the field data unaltered, or at least in recoverable form, and editing it to display conclusions and interpretations at the cost of obscuring or losing much of its detail. Decisions on these questions must be made at an early stage of the editing process.

Facsimile reproduction

The simplest mode of presenting the data is to reproduce the field

notes of the investigators and the transcriptions of the tape-
recordings exactly. This has the obvious advantage of putting the
user in possession of all the information gathered by the fieldworkers, to use as he sees fit. In effect, it makes the scholarly
user a part of the enterprise. Before he can proceed to interpretation, however, he will have to read the records and establish his
own methods for sorting and displaying the information they contain. The scholarly user may find this an advantage; at least he will
be left with no questions or doubts about how the material has been
handled. But even the scholarly user may find this more of a task
than he wishes to undertake, especially if he is simply making
quick reference to the material, rather than studying it in depth.
Let us say he is interested in what the local words are in England
for a small stream, and how they are distributed. In order to prepare a map like our Map 2.1 (p 21), he would have to go to the
record for each of the 314 localities surveyed by the SED, find
the appropriate response or responses, and list them. Only then
could he decide how he wanted them represented on a map and
proceed to enter them. Even to produce a rough map in this way
would be a matter of several hours' work. And certainly the
general reader who might have an interest in dialect distribution
would be completely excluded. Even if he could interpret the
transcription correctly – which is quite unlikely – he would find
the hastily written field notes difficult and the whole procedure
much too forbidding.

A final objection to reproducing field notes in facsimile is the
sheer bulk of the result. The field records of SED average about
100 pages apiece, so that the complete records for that survey
would fill over 30,000 pages. The only feasible means of publishing such a bulky document would be microfilm or microfiche,
which greatly reduce the bulk but increase the cost and introduce
the necessity of a machine to read them. Nonetheless some records, notably those of the *Linguistic Atlas of the North Central
States* (LANCS), have been reproduced in micro-form (McDavid
and Payne 1976). Their cost is such, however, that individual researchers would ordinarily find it impossible to acquire them. The
aim of this publication was primarily to give scholars access to the
material for study at their own institutions without having to
travel to Chicago, where the records are now located. Eventually
they will be edited and published in atlas form.

List or tabular publication

A method of publication which overcomes the major disadvantages of facsimile reproduction, though at the same time introducing some of its own, is in the form of lists. Here all the responses to a given item in the questionnaire are brought together and listed, each one being identified by the number of the locality from which it comes. To save space, a number of such lists can be placed in parallel columns, forming a tabular matrix with item numbers across the top and locality identifiers down the side. The user interested in the variation and distribution of a given item need only find the correct column of the matrix and run down it, referring to the side column for geographical locations as needed. If he wishes to prepare a rough map, he can do so quickly and with a minimum of error, since all the necessary data are together. Conversely, if he is interested in the incidence of a particular phenomenon – say glottal stop as an allophone of intervocalic /t/ – at a given locality, he can run across the appropriate row of the matrix, stopping at each item which he expects to contain an intervocalic /t/ (because of lexical variants, of course, some of these may not be represented). Table 2.1 above (*p* 24), giving the SED responses to five questions at seventeen localities, is a miniature illustration of a matrix list.

The most obvious disadvantage of this method of publication is again size. A moderate-sized survey like SED, with over 1,300 items at 314 localities, has more than 400,000 individual items, each of which would have to have its own cell in the matrix. Allowing 30 localities (rows) and 10 items (columns) to the page, the master matrix would have to be subdivided into over 1,300 submatrices, each filling a page. The user wishing to trace the distribution of a single item would now have to look on eleven different pages, not necessarily in consecutive order (depending on whether the pages were grouped by vertical or horizontal slices). This is a great improvement over the 314 separate look-ups required by the facsimile method, but still cumbersome. And to trace the complete record of a single locality would take him to 130 separate pages, in contrast to the 100 of the facsimile method.

A further disadvantage of this tabular matrix approach is the fact that unless there is to be a considerable waste of space, each cell of the matrix must be limited in size, thus preventing the recording of longer phrases or of several variants of a given item at a single locality. Considerable ingenuity in coding and abbreviation would be required to overcome this difficulty without rendering the records hopelessly complicated to read.

More commonly, instead of the matrix permitting immediate comparison of at least a few items with other items at the same

WVA

36a mæsətʃʉˑˑzəts

b mæsətʃuˑˑɾəs

37a mæsətʉˑsəts

b mæsətʃʉˑsəts

38a mæsətuˑˑsəts

b mæsəstʃʉˑˑɾəs (✓)

39a mæsətʃʉˑsəs

b mæsətʃʉˑˑsəts

c mæsətʃʉˑsəts

40a mæsətʃʉˑˑsəs

b mæsətʃʉˑɾəs

41a mæsətʃʉˑˑzəts

b mæsətⁱʉʃəz

42ab mæsətʃʉˑˑɾəs

43a mæsətuˑˑʃəs

b mæsətʃʉˑɾəs

44a mæsətuˑˑsəs

b mæsətʃʉˑˑɾəs

45a mæˑsətʃʉˑˑɾəs

b mæstʃʉˑˑsəs

46a mæstʃʉˑsəs

b mæsətʃʉˑɾəs

WVA

52c mæsətʃʉˑˑsəts

53a mæsəstʃuˑˑɾəs

b ---

c mæsətʃʉˑˑsəts

54a mæsətʃʉˑsəts

b mæsətʃʉˑɾəs

OHIO

1a mæsətʃɫuˑsɫts

b mæsətʃɫuˢɫˑts

c mæsətʃuˑˑsɫˢts

2a mæsətʃʉˑˑɾəs

b mæsətʃuˑˑsəs

3a mæsətʃuˑˑsəts

b mæsətʃʉˑˑsəts

4a mæsətʃusəts (✓)

b mæsətʃuˑˑsəts

5a ---

bc mæsətʃʉˑˑsəts

6a mæsətuˑˑsəs

b mæsətʃʉˑsəts

7a mæsətʃuˢɾəts

b mæˑsətʃʉˑˑɾəs

FIG. 6.1. Part of page from LAMSAS (McDavid and O'Cain 1980, p 86).

locality or with the same item at other localities, the lists simply give all responses to each item in turn, as in Fig. 6.1 from the *Linguistic Atlas of the Middle and South Atlantic States* (LAMSAS; McDavid and O'Cain 1980, p 86). This is about one-third of a complete page, and reports the pronunciation of the state name *Massachusetts* from 14 of the 54 localities surveyed in West Virginia, as well as 7 from Ohio. In this survey, at least two informants were usually recorded from each locality, one of 'Type I' (a minimum of education and travel) and one of 'Type II' (some years of high school education). In 112 of the 518 localities, a 'Type III' or cultured informant was included. The responses are listed in this order at each locality, and the designator of a cultured informant is underlined. Thus at locality 1 in Ohio, one of each type was interviewed; their pronunciations of *Massachusetts* were identical except that the cultured informant used a simple vowel rather than a diphthong in the third syllable. As is usual in lists of this sort, where consecutive responses are identical, space is saved by combining them, as at locality 42 in West Virginia and locality 5 in Ohio. Each volume of the atlas contains a map of the region with the localities indicated, which the user is permitted to photocopy so that he can make his own maps to suit his needs and interests.

Bulk becomes a problem with lists of this sort to only a slightly less degree than with facsimiles of field records. To report the approximately 1 million items of LAMSAS (787 items from 1,216 informants, plus extras) will require some 7,000 pages. The addition of indexes and a 500-page handbook (Kurath et al. 1979, *p* 37) will bring the whole work to 8,500 pages – a truly massive document.

Considerable space can be saved, at the cost of some loss of ease of reference, by printing the lists in running form, rather than in columns. Figure 6.2 shows the responses to question V.6.10 of SED from fourteen East Midland and East Anglian counties of England, as reported in part 2 of volume 3 of the published records (Orton and Tilling 1969, *pp* 637–8). The exact form of the question is given first, followed by the five different responses in standard orthography. Then follow the lists, by counties, numbered according to a system that permits identification of each locality by a four-digit number. Thus 2105 identifies North Elmham in Norfolk, a page of whose field record was given above (Fig. 5.3, *p* 98). It will be seen that in addition to the primary response at this locality, a second response with the informant's comment ('older') has been given. Where the same word was found elsewhere in the field record in the 'incidental material', it is preceded by a small raised circle, as at 1401. A raised numeral indicates the number of the informant reported. Space is saved in two ways: by collapsing successive identical entries, as at localities 4 and 5 in county 10 (Lincolnshire), or by us-

V.6.10 SLICE

Q. What do you call the thin piece you cut off from the loaf with the bread knife?

Rr. ‡BIT, ROUND, ROUNDEL, SLICE, STULL

Note—For additional exs. of SLICE, see V.6.11.

9 Nt 1 slaɪs 2 ᵈslaɪsəz 3 slaɪs 4 slaɪs

10 L 1–2 sla·ɪs 3 ᵈsla·ɪsɪz 4–5 slaɪs 6 slaɪs, ɹaɵnd 7 sla·ɪs 8–9 sla·ɪs 10 ᵈɹæɵndz 11–12 sla·ɪs 13 sla·ɪs 14 slöɪs 15 ᵈslãɪ̈sɪz

13 Lei 1 ‡bɪt 2–3 sla·ɪs 4–6 sla̱·ɪs 7–8 sla·ɪs 9 sla̱·ɪs, ᵒ~² 10 ‡bɪt

14 R 1 sla·ɪs, ᵒslaɪs² 2 ‡bɪt

18 Nth 1–3 slaɪs 4 slaɪs, ᵒᵒslaɪsɪz¹ 5 slöɪs

19 Hu 1–2 slaɪs

20 C 1 ᵈɹɛ̨ɵndz 2 slaɪs

21 Nf 1 sloɪs 2 slʌis 3 slʌis 4 ɹɛund 5 slʌɪs, ɹɛ̃ɵnd [“older”] 6 slʌis, ɹəund 7 slʌis 8 n.r. 9–10 slʌis 11 slʌɪs, ɹɛɵnd [“older”] 12 slʌɪs 13 ɹɛund

22 Sf 1 ᵈstʌłz, stʌł, ᵒᵒstʌłz¹ 2 sloɪs 3 slʌĩs 4 sloɪs 5 ɹɛɵndł

26 Bk 1 ᵈsloɪsɪz 2 sloɪs 3 slʌɪs 4 slä̈ɪs 5 ᵈslo̱ɪsɪz 6 n.a.

27 Bd 1–3 slaɪs

28 Hrt 1–2 slaɪs 3 slöɪs

29 Ess 1 slo̱ɪs 2–4 sloɪs 5 sloɪs, ᵒᵒsloɪsəs 6–7 slöɪs 8–10 sloɪs 11 ʂlaɪsɪz 12 slöɪs 13–14 sloɪs 15 slä̈ɪs

30 MxL 1–2 ᵈslaɪsɪz

FIG. 6.2. Data on ‘slice’ from eastern England (SED, vol. III, *pp* 637–8).

ing a wavy line for a succeeding identical response from the same locality, as at 1309, where the symbols⁰~² indicate that in the incidental material the second informant at this locality was reported as using the form [sla̱·ɪs], identical with the official response given by the first informant.

By this careful use of symbols and condensation, much additional information beyond the basic first responses has been included in the SED lists, while space is saved by using the run-on rather than tabular format. But SED is still a bulky document. Twelve volumes totaling about 4,400 pages are needed to report the approximately half a million items of data. Furthermore, the division of the whole country into four regional sections means that the user wishing to see all responses to a given question is required to look in four different places, rather than a single table, as in LAMSAS. Once again a blank map with the numbers of the localities is furnished, which the user can copy and use for making his own maps.

The list mode of publication thus has certain clear advantages. By bringing together all responses to a given question in a single list, it facilitates comparison of responses across the area covered, which is certainly the primary interest of geographical linguistics. In this respect it is vastly superior to the reproduction, by facsimile or otherwise, of complete field records. Furthermore, it is easier and cheaper than the preparation of maps, and hence more likely to make the data of a survey available for use within a reasonable time after the completion of the fieldwork. Its major disadvantage, in comparison with maps, is that it does not immediately reveal geographical relationships, which is certainly one of the major interests of traditional dialectology. Unless the user carries in his mind a clear vision of the territory covered, including the relative positions of all localities surveyed, he cannot visualize the position of isoglosses and dialect areas simply by scanning a list. He must stop and take the time – perhaps an hour or two – to make a map of the feature or features he is concerned with. He has been supplied with the data, to be sure, but to make use of it he must himself undertake some of the work that might well have been done by the editors of the atlas.

Publication in map form

Ever since the two pioneer national linguistic surveys – Wenker's *Deutscher Sprachatlas* and Gilliéron's *Atlas linguistique de la France* – the favored mode of publishing the data has been in the form of a collection of maps, as indeed the word *atlas* in the titles of these two works indicates. Since the major, virtually exclusive, interest of traditional surveys has been in the 'horizontal' geographical dimension of linguistic variation rather than in the 'vertical' social dimension, the most logical and effective mode of displaying the distribution has been in maps. This continues to be the case, even though financial exigency may dictate list or tabular form. The lists, after all, are directly related to the geography, and the user is given all he needs to create his own maps. Actually, in spite of costs, true atlases continue to be produced, ranging in size and expense from the lavish volumes of the regional French atlases to more modest volumes like those of the Scottish LAS and the English *Word Geography of England* (WGE).

Maps, then, remain the favored mode of publication. But the maps used vary widely: in the amount and type of data included,

in the mode of display, and in the amount of synthesis, generalization, simplification, and other editorial intervention between
the field data and the visual presentation. It is not possible here
to deal with all the details of variation in mapping procedure,
which are as many as there are atlases. Instead we will select
typical examples for discussion and illustration.

Raw data maps

By far the most common type of map is the raw data map, in
which the actual field responses from a survey are lettered or
printed on a background map of the area covered. This was the
method of the ALF, which established a tradition that has been
followed by Jaberg and Jud's AIS, by most of the regional atlases
of France, by Kurath's LANE, and by many other national and
regional atlases. This type of presentation differs from the list
method only in the fact that the transcriptions of responses, instead of being arranged in lists or tables, are spread about on a
map, each response being lettered in as near as possible to the
locality where it was collected. Maps of this sort have the obvious
advantage over lists of displaying the geographical distribution of
the data directly and visually. But they have certain disadvantages as well. For one thing, they require the user who is looking
for the distribution of a given form to search carefully over a two-
dimensional area, rather than simply running his finger down a
list. For another, if the area covered is relatively large and the
network of localities dense, either the maps become so crowded
as to be difficult to read, or the scale must be so large that the
maps themselves are very large. Unless they are folded, as in the
Dutch–Flemish Netherlands atlases (RNDA) and the recent
volumes of the DSA, they must be published in large unwieldy
volumes or portfolios, which are expensive to produce and awkward to handle.

Maps 6.1 and 6.2 illustrate this type of mapping applied to the
data from eastern England shown in list form in Fig. 6.1 above.
Map 6.1, giving only the responses from the county of Norfolk
and a few localities in the neighboring counties of Lincolnshire,
Cambridgeshire, and Suffolk, is quite easy to read, since the
large scale, small area, and rather sparse network allow plenty of
room. The three lexical forms *slice, round*, and *stull* are easily
seen. Phonologically, two types of the /ay/ diphthong are striking,
one with a rounded syllabic, [ɒ] or [ɔ], and the other with unrounded [ʌ], with an isogloss obviously running south through
west central Norfolk and trending eastward between Suffolk
localities 2 and 3. It is a clear and unconfusing map.

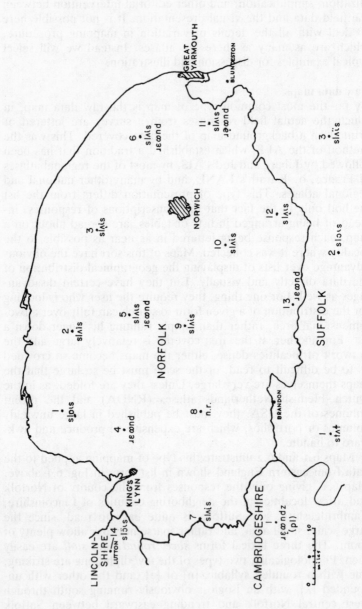

MAP 6.1. Raw data map of 'slice' in Norfolk (data from SED, V.6.10).

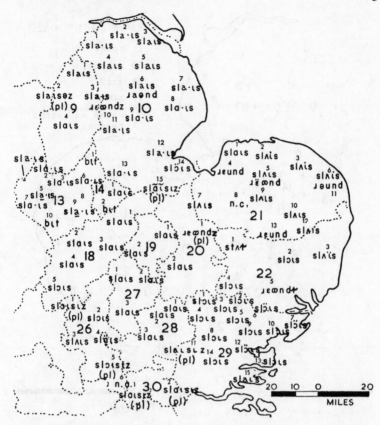

MAP 6.2. Raw data map of 'slice' in eastern England (data from SED, V.6.10).

If we reduce the scale to one-third that of Map 6.1 in order to include the whole eastern area, as in Map 6.2, it is a different story. In order to fit in all the responses and place them as near as possible to the localities they represent, it has been necessary to reduce the size of the lettering and in some places, as in the county of Leicestershire (13), which has a closer network than the rest of the area, to crowd the map too greatly for easy reading. The user interested in either of the matters mentioned above – the lexical items for 'slice' or the phonetic realizations of the /ay/ diphthong – will do better to trace off the map and include just the items he wants, leaving out confusing details. Map 6.3 shows how this could be done for the lexical information, disregarding the phonetics.

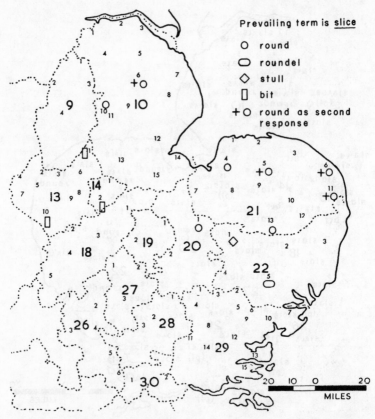

MAP 6.3.   Symbol map of unusual words for 'slice' in eastern England
(data from SED, V.6.10).

If the area becomes very large, the scale small, and the network dense, it can become impossible to place all the actual responses in their phonetic transcriptions directly on the map. One
solution for this is to replace the lettered forms by symbols, which
can be made small enough to fit the space and yet remain distinctive enough to be read. Map 6.4 illustrates an extreme form of
this method, that used by the DSA. This is a part – less than half –
of Map 11, volume 20 of the *Deutscher Wortatlas* (DWA),
which is the word-geography component of the DSA. It maps the
local variants of the word for 'mouth' occurring in eastern
Austria – Vienna is in the rectangle whose coordinates are s' and 65.
Each small rectangle covers an area approximately 12.5 by
9.5 km (7.5 × 5.8 miles). The terms are derived from translation

into local dialect of the sentence 'Junge, halt den Mund!' ('Young man, be quiet/hold your tongue'). Reference to the legend indicates that there is a large number of lexical terms, some of which, such as *Maul* and *Schnauze*, have many phonological variants, each given a separate symbol. The symbols attempt to indicate graphically which word-group a phonetic variant belongs to: thus vertical lines with short offshoots at right angles denote variants of *Mund*; horizontal lines with offshoots at right angles, variants of *Maul*; diagonals inclined to the left, variants of *Schnauze*, and so on. As the note in the upper right hand corner of the legend states, numbers refer to a list of rare forms and multiple equivalents.

Since the maps in this atlas cover the whole German-speaking area of Europe, the scale is quite small (it is somewhat reduced in our reproduction) and the symbols difficult to distinguish, especially when they are closely crowded together, as they are in heavily populated areas of Germany proper; in fact, the full map shows all of the nearly 50,000 localities of the original Wenker survey. A magnified version of four rectangles will show more clearly how the information is recorded: Map 6.5 shows the four rectangles at the intersection of coordinates h', i' and 65, 66, magnified about four times. Within this area, measuring approximately 25 by 19 km, seventeen localities are reported. The curving line down the middle is part of an isogloss that separates a predominantly *Mal* area to the west from a *Maul* area to the east. The local word is *Gosch(e)n* in five localities, *Mund* in two, *Maul* in two, *Papp(e)n* in two, and *Maui* (a variant of *Maul*) in one. Two localities are marked only by small dots, indicating that the response was the predominant one for the particular area in which they fall, in this case *Maul*. Three localities are represented by numbers, referring to the supplementary list, a portion of which is reproduced in Fig. 6.3. This shows that at the point marked 1 in the h' – 66 rectangle the term is *Gouschen*, with the alternative expression *Mach's Maul auf* for the whole phrase, and that both *Gouschen* and *Maul* are used at the point marked 2, while point 1 in i'–66 has both *Maul* and *Kuschen* (an obvious phonetic variant of *Goschen*, but too infrequent to be given its own symbol).

Some of the worst crowding on this map is avoided by printing the predominant term in an area in large type on the map. This allows it to be assumed that localities marked only by a location dot have that term, and that only the exceptions are given symbols. Hence the more homogeneous the responses, the less crowded the map. Thus in the central part of the area shown, the

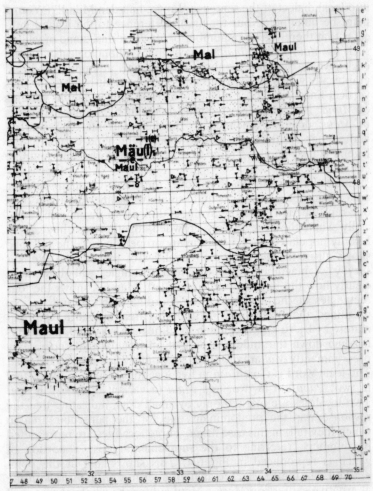

MAP 6.4.   Section of map for 'Mund' in Austria (from DWA, vol. 20,
          Map 11).

predominant forms are indicated as *Mäule, Mäu,* and *Maul,* so
the corresponding symbols ⌣ , ⌞⌣ , and ⸺ do not appear in
that area. Instead, the localities having these forms are indicated
by a dot. The information of the records is thus all there, but it
may legitimately be questioned whether the geographical display
is not so complicated that a simple table would be better, allowing the user to select the items he wishes and make his own map.
But, as the editor points out, even a simple list of the nearly 50,000

Mund (Junge, halt den Mund!)

I Mund	✓ Fresse	↓ Schnabel	⌒ Babbel	Zahlen *verweisen auf die Zusatzliste*
⌈ Mond ₋ₜ	✗ Freß ₋ₐ₋	↕ Snabel	∪ Sabbel	*der Seitenheiten und Mehr-*
⌋ Mound ₋ₜ	⋋ Fressen	↑ Schnaw(w)el	∨ Hals	*fachmeldungen*
⊦ Monk ₋g ₋gk	✗ Frasse	∫ Schnobel	+ Keek	, *vor einem Zeichen = auch*
⊢ Munk ₋g ₋gk	✗ Fraß	⅃ Snobel	∆ Mu(u)lwerk ₋a₋	*die Leitform wurde gemeldet*
	⟨ Fret(t)		⌐ Muppe	
— Maul	/ Frät	⊤ Gusche	⩊ Schlabber(n)	
⊢ Mao(u)l ₋oau₋	⌃ Freit	↓ Kusche	⩘ Schlopp	
⊣ Ma(a)l	⸌ Friet	⊥ Gusch	⊢⊰ Schluck	
⊢⊣ Mail ₋ei₋		⊥ Gusch(e)n	> Schnuffel	
⊢⊣ Moal	⟍ Schnauze	⊤ Gosche	∧ Swiegstill	
⊢⊓ Mo(o)l	⟍ Schnauz	⊤ Gosch	⟍ Schlädde(n) ₋ett₋	
⊓ Moul	✗ Schnoute(n)	⊥ Gosch(e)n		
⊔ Mäul ₋ey₋ ₋io₋ ₋ou₋	× Snaute	⟋ Beck ₋a₋	⊠ Flappe	
	⤬ Schnute ₋d₋	⟨ Ba(c)k	□ Flo(a)ppe	
⊩ Mau	⟍ Schnut			
⊢⊣ Maj ₋ei	⟨ Snute	→ Fo(t)z(e)n	D Schnutz *und* Frät ₋a₋	
⊔ Mäu ₋ey₋ ₋oi₋	⟨ Snu(u)t	⤙ Pfou(t)z(e)n	▽ Fresse " Maul	
⊢⊣ Mäui	⟍ Schnuten	↦ Foz(z)a	⅁ Maul " Schnauze	
⊔ Maui	✗ Snuten		♀ Fresse " Schnauze	
⊢⊣ Ma(u)ö ₋aü₋	⟍ Schniute(n)	⟻ Papp(e)n	ⅅ Gosch(n) " Papp(n) ₋b₋m	
⊤ Mu(u)l	⟨ Sniuten	⟝ Pappe	D‑ Gosch " Maul	
⊔ Muel ₋o₋	⟜ Schnuß		ⅅ Gusche " Schnauze	
⊣ Mu(u)le	⟋ Schnuß(e)n ₋s₋	⟍ Bart	⊸ Gusche " Frasse	
⊤ Mull	⟿ Schnüß	⟍ Bo(a)rt	⊶ Gusche " Fresse	
⊢ Mua	⟋ Schniß		ⅇ Gusche " Klappe	
⊔ Muil	∿ Schneß	J Lappe ₋bb₋	⌒ Fresse " Klappe	
⊓ Miul ₋ju₋ ₋üu₋	✗ Schnutte ₋dd₋	∟ Lawwe	☼ Freß " Maul	
	⟨ Schnutt	⅃ Lapp	♀ Freß " Schnauz	
⊢ Miule	⟋ Schnütt		◁ Klappe " Schnauze	
⟂ Mül	⟋ Schnu(t)z	⅄ Klappe	Œ Klappe " Rand	
⟂ Müll	⟍ Schnu(t)ze	Υ Rand	☐ Klappe " Schnabel	
⟂ Müol ₋e₋	⟋ Schnurre ₋a₋	↑ Rachen	☿ Schnabel " Maul	
	⟋ Schnorre ₋a₋	⊂ Spei	♦ Schnauze " Fresse *und* Gusche	
	⟍ Schnörre	⤛⊣ Müs(s)		

Legend for MAP 6.4.

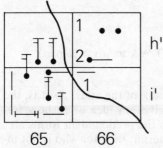

MAP 6.5. Enlarged section of Map 6.4.

e'	4, 1	Monn
	7, 1	Schniß, Gosch, Freß, Maul
	8, 1	Maul, Schniß, Schnawwel, Gosch
	8, 2	Schniß, Mul, Freß
	8, 3	Maul, Schnabbel, Gosch, Schniß
	9, 1	Glabb, Freß
	9, 2	Maul, Schniß, Freß
	9, 3	Maul, Gosch, Schniß, Freß, Klapp
	9, 4	Schniß, Maul, Freß, Klapp, Schnauz, Schnabel
	31, 1	Maul, Schlappm, Gosche
	32, 1	Schlappm
	33, 1	Maul (auch: Schlabbm) Schlabbern
	34, 1	Schleppern
	35, 1	Maul, Rand, Gosche, Schnute
	44, 1	Goschn, Fotzn
	60, 1	Maul, Goschn, Freß
g'	43, 1	Mal, Fotzn, Goschn, Schnobl
	43, 2	Mai(l), Goschn, Fotzn, Terutschn, Waffl, Lebron, Plebron
h'	33, 1	Schlappn
	40, 1	Mal, Fotzn, Läsch'n
	42, 1	Meil, Goscha
	49, 1	Mau, Goschn
	66, 1	Gouschen (halt de Gouschen; dagegen: Mach's Maul auf)
	66, 2	Gouschen, Maul
i'	13, 1	Müahl
	20, 1	Lappel, Gosch
	30, 1	Maul, Lad, Gosch
	32, 1	Schlappm
	34, 1	Mal, Goschn, Fotzn, Schnäbben
	36, 1	Pfotzn, Mail
	36, 2	Mal, Fotzn
	40, 1	Meil, Fozn, Schnawl
	66, 1	Maul, Kuschen
k'	30, 1	Schlapp
	38, 1. 2	Meol
l'	10, 1	Müal
	11, 1	Mül, Schnuffel, Gosch
	13, 1	Schnuffel, Schnurr, Schnutz, Gosch
	14, 1	Schnurr, Mül, Gosch
	28, 1	Sau-Gosch
	35, 1	Fotzn, Gwaf
	37, 1	Mai, Maul (auch: Fotza)

FIG. 6.3.   List data on 'Mund' in DWA (DWA 20, *p* 121, in part).

responses would vastly increase the bulk of the atlas. As it is, the degree of diversity of the symbols gives an idea as to how frequent or infrequent the exceptions to the predominant forms are, and the carefully contrived symbols permit the user who is not in-

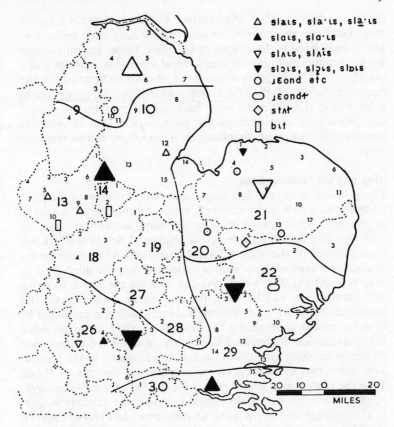

MAP 6.6. Isogloss map, words for 'slice' in eastern England (data from
          SED, V.6.10).

terested in precise phonetic detail to get an idea as to what the
exceptions are from a fairly rapid glance. Thus in the southern
Maul area of Map 6.4 it can be seen that the exceptions are
Mund, Pappen, Goschen, and various phonetic variants of *Maul*.

The DWA maps thus avoid impossibly dense crowding of symbols by omitting the predominant form in an area, which is over-
printed in large type. The areas are then separated by isoglosses
showing their extent, and rare or unusual forms are indicated by
numbers referring to the supplementary list. This kind of simplification can be carried further at the cost of some loss of
phonetic information by lumping together phonetically similar
but not necessarily identical forms under a single symbol. Return-

ing to our data on 'slice' from eastern England, Map 6.6 is such a map. Here eleven phonetic versions of *slice* have been reduced to four, symbolized by four types of triangles. Other lexical variants are represented by other shapes: *round* by circles, *stull* by a diamond, etc. The large symbols serve the same function as the large-type words on the DWA map – to indicate the predominant form within the bounded area. Such a map presents the lexical data accurately and perhaps the phonological, but it sacrifices phonetic detail to gain simplicity. It is no longer a true raw data map.

Map and list combinations

The problem with raw data maps, especially for surveys covering a large area with a dense network, is how to indicate all the detail of the field data without making the maps either too large for easy handling or too crowded to be legible. A solution which has been adopted by the atlas of Swiss German (SDS) is to combine a generalized symbol map with a tabulated list, as illustrated in Map 6.7 and Fig. 6.4, which give the data for the words meaning 'the mumps'. As can be seen, the map (here both reduced and somewhat cut down from the original size) has been simplified by to some extent generalizing the symbols, leaving lesser phonetic detail to the list. Fourteen different lexical items are represented by the contrasting symbols in the left hand column of the legend. The other two columns give major phonetic variants of these. Thus the larger open triangles indicate the base form *Ooremügge-li*, or with various minor alterations in shape, the variants *Müggeli, Ooremünggeli, Ooremüggel, Ooremügerli*, and *Ooremügge(e)-ler*. This is the prevalent form in the western canton of Bern, and the exact phonetic forms of the responses from the 112 localities surveyed in Berne can be seen in the list in Fig. 6.4, which shows only a part of one page from the atlas. This is an elaborate and expensive way to present the data, but it has the advantage of allowing the user to choose how much detail he wishes to use. If his interest is primarily lexical, the map gives him all the detail he needs. But if he wants detailed phonetic information, he can derive it from the list.

The *Linguistic Atlas of Scotland* (LAS) has also combined simplified maps with a full listing of forms, but using a different kind of map from those in SDS. As Map 6.8 shows, various kinds of hatching are used to indicate the principal variant forms. This has the advantage of allowing localities where more than one response was recorded to be indicated simply by overlapping two or

FIG. 6.4. List data on 'der Mumps' in Switzerland (part of p 56, vol. IV, SDS).

der Mumps

(Entrundung der Ohrspeicheldrüse)

Frage 118.5

Zeichenerklärung

Zusätzliche Orte

BA 13a	⧫	ZH 5a	—
SO 2a	⧫	ZH 42a	—
AG 3 F	◉	GR 12	♥
AG 18 J	⚲		

Hinweise der Gewährsleute

SO 11: „Müggeli" im Kt. Bern.
BE 47: ᵂ. In der Ostschweiz sagt man 'Mum.
WS 76: „ In Saas (WS 81) 'Mops'."

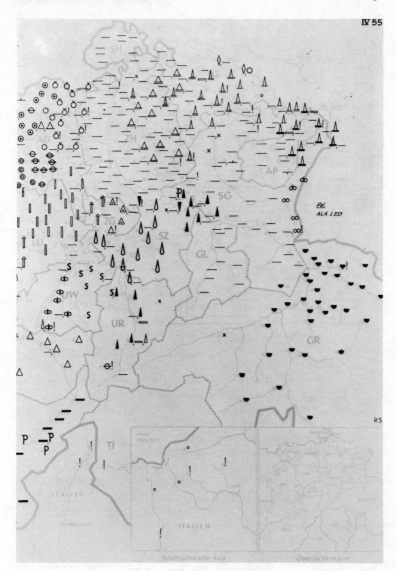

MAP 6.7. Words for 'der Mumps' in Switzerland (from SDS, vol. 4, Map 55).

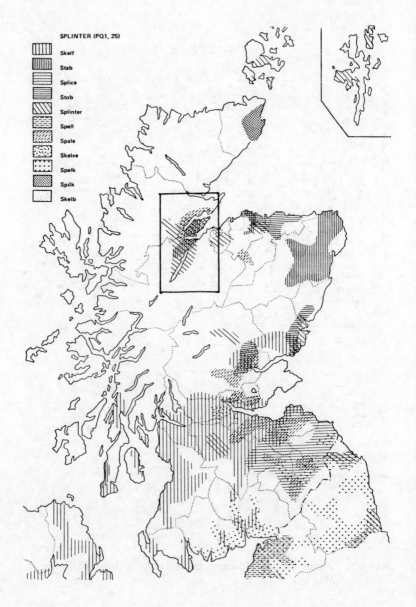

MAP 6.8. Words for 'splinter' in Scotland (from LAS, vol. 1, Map 4).

4 SPLINTER (tiny fragment of wood driven into finger etc.) (PQ1, 25)

For the recurrence of stab, stob, see 5 to prick, 13 three legged stool, 26 bradawl and 42 fence posts.

Shetland
Bit o' wid — 20
Fliss — 2, 21b, 30
Peerie bit o' wid — 30
Peerie fliss — 30
Skelfen — 14
Skilf — 22
Something — 33
Spale — 11, 26
Speeger — 5
Speelick — 25
Spell — 17, 24
Spellick — 17, 24
Spjolk — 19
Spleet — 2, 6
Splint — 15
Splinter — 1-2, 4, 7-8, 10, 15, 17, 21a, 22-23, 27
Spoilk — 3
Spolk — 12
Nil — 9, 13, 16, 18, 28-29, 31-32

Orkney
Bit of wid — 6
Bit of wood — 9
Jag — 5
Skliver — 15
Sliver — 7, 13a
Slivver — 17
Speel — 7-8
Spell — 16
Splint — 13b
Splinter — 2-5, 8, 11, 13ab, 15, 17-21
Sprack — 2, 4, 15
Nil — 1, 10, 12, 14

Caithness
Bit — 4
Pirk — 12b
Purr — 11, 13
Skelf — 2a, 12c, 15
Skelp — 16a
Spale — 1, 11, 13-14, 16b
Speeling — 12c
Spilk — 2b, 5-6, 8-9, 12abc, 14-15, 16b, 17
Splinter — 8, 16b
Nil — 3, 7, 10

Sutherland
Jag — 3
Skelf — 10
Spale — 8, 11, 14
Speal — 13
Spike — 8, 15
Splinter — 3, 5-8, 9a, 13, 16
Stab — 1-4, 6, 9b, 10, 15-17
Nil — 12

Ross & Cromarty
Bit wood — 9
Skelding — 31
Skelf — 5-6, 25a, 26-27, 38-39
Skelve — 23
Slipe — 25a
Sliver — 20
Spale — 9, 13-14, 18, 20-21, 25a 28, 32b, 33, 35-36
Spaleack — 20
Speel — 11, 25b, 34
Spellack — 29
Splinter — 1, 5-6, 8-9, 16-17, 20, 23-24, 26-27, 29-30, 32a, 36, 39
Stab — 3-4, 11-12, 15-17, 19, 22, 31, 32c, 34
Stick — 36
Stob — 22, 27, 31, 37ab
Thorn — 22
158

Whittle — 13
Nil — 2, 7, 20

Inverness
Chop — 1
Fire — 13a
Jag — 30
Skelf — 12, 13b, 19, 22, 24, 27, 35-38, 40
Sleeshack — 13d
Sliver — 13a
Spailach — 14, 20
Spale — 9, 13e, 26, 33
Spealg — 26
Spell — 31
Spellack — 24
Spirack — 18
Splinter — 1-8, 10, 13ce, 18-20, 21b, 23, 29, 33, 35
Split — 1
Stab — 6, 8-9, 11, 13abc, 16-17, 21ab, 22, 25, 27-28, 32, 34, 36, 38-40
Stob — 29, 33
Thorn — 6
Nil — 15

Nairn
Spalach — 4
Spale — 1b, 2-3
Splinter — 5-6
Stab — 1ac, 2

Moray
Bit stick — 7
Scob — 17
Skelb — 1, 2a, 6a, 8b, 10, 12-13, 16, 22
Skelf — 3, 13
Skelp — 5, 8bf
Spale — 2b, 9b, 18, 21-22
Spalin — 9a
Splinter — 6b, 8d, 9a, 11, 14
Stab — 3-4, 7, 8bc, 13, 15, 21-23
Steug — 9a
Stob — 5, 6a, 8ae, 9a, 19-20, 23
Stobe — 8d

Banff
Skelb — 4-5, 8, 15, 18bcd, 23, 26, 29, 31
Skelf — 2c, 6b, 18c, 28, 30, 32
Skilf — 20
Sliver — 34
Spale — 32-34
Speel — 22
Splinter — 15, 21, 34
Stab — 5, 9, 16, 25
Stick — 13, 19
Stob — 1, 2ac, 3, 5, 6ab, 7, 9-11, 13-14, 17, 18bd
Stowb — 2b, 3
Nil — 12, 18a, 20, 24, 27

Aberdeen
Bit (of) stick — 32, 44, 62, 86, 108
Bittie (of) stick — 10, 35
Brob — 16
Brod — 5c, 14
Jag — 39
Job — 1, 9, 40, 63, 74, 105
Jobbie — 9
Piece of stick — 70
Skelb — 3b, 5bd, 11-12, 20-21, 23, 26-27, 28abc, 42, 47a, 50-51, 53, 65, 77, 80-81, 88, 97-98, 103-104
Skelbie — 35
Skelf — 2, 14, 19, 28a, 51, 80, 96

Skelfin — 19
Skellie — 9
Skelp — 27
Skelve — 51
Skiff — 30
Skilf — 60
Slether — 71a
Sliver — 5b
Speel — 23
Spell — 69, 79
Spilk — 14
Splint — 59
Splinter — 6, 8, 22, 45-46, 72, 75, 83, 90, 94
Stab — 48, 74
Stick — 29, 47f, 79
Stob — 1, 3a, 4, 5ab, 7, 9, 14, 17, 19, 24-25, 28b, 31, 34, 36, 40-41, 47abcde, 48-49, 51-52, 54, 56, 60, 63-64, 66-67, 70, 71abc, 73-74, 76, 78, 82-84, 92-93, 95-97, 99-102, 104, 106-109
Stowb — 7, 47d
Nil — 13, 15, 18, 33, 37-38, 43, 55, 57-58, 61, 68, 85, 87, 89, 91

Kincardine
Bit stick — 11, 19, 26
Chip — 3, 8
Skelb — 14, 17a, 18, 21, 23, 28
Skelf — 7, 23, 25
Skelve — 1
Slither — 27
Sliver — 7, 22
Speil — 1
Spell — 2, 16
Splice — 17b
Splinter — 5-6, 8, 10, 17c, 21, 27
Stob — 4, 12, 15, 17abcd, 20, 22, 24
Stobe — 18
Nil — 9, 13

Kinross
Skelb — 1-5, 7
Skelf — 1, 6
Spale — 3, 7
Splinter — 1

Angus
Bit stick — 15
Bittie stick — 33b
Crum — 33b
Jobie — 5a, 8
Prickle — 33b
Scliff — 14a
Scroag — 10
Skelb — 4, 5c, 6, 8-10, 14abcd, 15, 19, 22, 32, 35-36
Skelf — 9, 12, 14b, 17a, 19, 23, 25-26, 29a, 30, 33a, 37
Skelb — 14d
Skelve — 14a, 28
Skiff — 34
Sliver — 27
Spale — 7, 13, 32, 34, 37
Speel — 5b, 31
Spelk — 29b
Splice — 17b
Splinter — 1, 3, 17b, 18, 20, 24-25, 29b, 34, 36
Stick — 2
Stob — 2, 5b, 14c, 21, 24, 35, 37
Stobbie — 24
Stobie — 5a
Stog — 21
Thorn — 33b
Nil — 11, 16

Perth
Drob — 41a
Jag — 26
Jobe — 20
Jug — 69
Scare — 47
Skale — 25
Skelb — 11, 15, 20-21, 23, 27-28,

more types of hatching. (We used this technique for Map 2.5 (*p* 37) to show overlapping areas of the forms for *saw*.) Maps of this sort are suggestive only; they omit such details as the number and actual location of the localities covered by each patch of shading and the frequency of each variant. For example, within the rectangular area outlined on Map 6.8, which covers the north central part of the county of Inverness and the southeastern part of Ross and Cromarty, the shading shows three overlapping forms for 'splinter': *stab, splinter*, and *spale*. Reference to the list associated with this map, part of which is reproduced in Fig. 6.5, reveals that these are indeed the two most frequent forms in these three counties, but that a fourth, *skelf*, occurs in quite a few localities but has not been indicated, presumably because to add a fourth type of hatching would have made the map difficult if not impossible to read. As the editors explain, 'there was a technical limit to the number of overlapping areas which could be depicted by our means of representation' (Mather and Speitel 1975, *p* 21). This same consideration led them in many cases to omit a response of especially high frequency and wide distribution, thus leaving blank areas. But in order to determine whether a blank area results from this kind of omission or from the absence of postal returns from that area (the network for this atlas, it will be remembered, was determined by the usable questionnaires returned), the user must consult both the list and the key map of localities, which is included in each volume of LAS. It can be said, then, that this type of mapping, even more than that of the SDS, is an illustration or comment upon the lists, which themselves constitute the primary presentation of the data.

The use of maps and lists together is thus an attempt to present the data in generalized form on maps which are not too complicated to be read even by amateurs, while insuring that all information about the responses is still available in accompanying lists for the use of the specialist. In such combinations the range is from the method of the DSA, where the map contains all the data and the list is merely a device for giving special information about a relatively small number of localities, to that of the *Linguistic Atlas of the Upper Midwest* (LAUMW, Allen 1973–78), where the list is the principal mode of presentation, with the insertion of small maps for occasional comment or clarification. The systems of the Swiss German and Scottish atlases, with rather detailed maps complemented by full lists, lie between these extremes.

Edited maps

All the maps we have so far considered have the aim of displaying either on the map alone or with the help of an accompanying list the responses of informants in full detail, item by item, one item to a map. The justification for such maps is that they allow the user full access to the data of a survey without any intervention of an editor or interpreter. In one sense this shows admirable restraint; the compiler of the material passes on to the user the results of his labors and those of his assistants without intruding any of his conclusions or interpretations as to their significance.

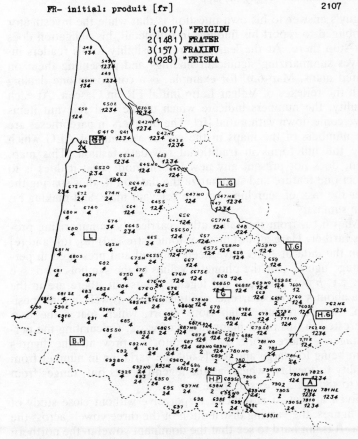

MAP 6.9.   Distribution of initial [fr] in four words in Gascony (from ALG, vol. VI, Map 2107).

But from another point of view, it can be considered a shirking of responsibility. After all, the director of a survey has usually spent literally years of his time over this material; is it not part of his function to share with his readers his estimation of the meaning of what he has collected? As Jean Séguy, director of the *Atlas linguistique de la Gascogne* (ALG), puts it:

> At the first glance over a linguistic atlas in the tradition of Gilliéron, one is struck by the abundance of phonetic distinctions. One admires the honesty and scrupulousness of the investigators. But in the course of association with the atlas, one question arises: what is the import of these minutiae? (Séguy 1973a, *p* 3)

Séguy's answer to his own question is that while the investigator is obliged to report his findings in full detail, his obligation does not stop there. At the least, his responsibility to his readers involves summarizing significant findings and presenting them on edited maps. Map 6.9, for example, is a composite one dealing with the reflexes of Vulgar Latin initial FR- in Gascon. At each locality, the numbers indicate which of the four relevant items have come down with initial [fr]. The numbers in parentheses are the numbers of the maps in the earlier volumes of ALG which give the full forms in traditional raw-data fashion. This map, then, does not present any new information; what it does is to select one feature and summarize the data on it, thus sparing the user the task of searching out the relevant maps and making his own summary.

Map 6.10, from the same atlas, carries the summarizing process further. Here all instances of tonic (stressed) [é], [e], and [è] from the data of ALG have been counted and presented in percentage figures (for the phonetic values of the symbols used, see Fig. 5.1, *p* 90). Since, as the legend points out, there are in the data about 57,000 occurrences of these three vowels in tonic position, this represents a laborious effort, which spares the user interested in this point many hours of work. Calculating the percentages – more work by the editor! – prevents the figures from being too large and levels out the variation in number from locality to locality, which, as the legend points out, ranges from 110 to 589 occurrences of these vowels.

Even at that, it is difficult to perceive without close study of the figures, the varying distribution of the three vowels across the area. It is not hard to see that the dominant vowel in the northern part of the area is [è] (IPA [ɛ]) and in the southern part [é] (IPA [e]), but further details are hard to work out from the figures. Accordingly, the editor has obligingly converted the figures to [é] [e] [è] toniques : statistique synchronique en pourcentages, toutes occurrences additionnées sans égard à l'état primitif.

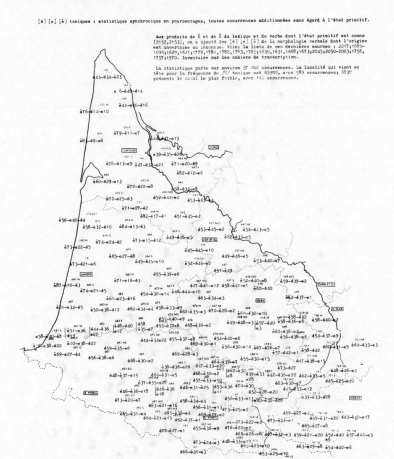

Aux produits de é et de è du lexique et du verbe dont l'état primitif est connu (2152,2153), on a ajouté les [é] [e] [è] de la morphologie verbale dont l'origine est incertaine ou inconnue. Voici la liste de ces dernières sources : 2017;1685-1696;1629,1621;1779,1781,1782,1783,1785;1630,1631,1668;1673;2045;2050-206);1756, 1757;1970. Inventaire sur les cahiers de transcription.

La statistique porte sur environ 57 000 occurrences. La localité qui vient en tête pour la fréquence de /é/ tonique est 693NO, avec 589 occurrences; 683M présente le total le plus faible, avec 110 occurrences.

MAP 6.10. Frequencies of [é], [e] and [è] in Gascony (from ALG, vol. VI, Map 2150).

graphs, as shown in Map 6.11. In this map, while the precise percentages are lost, the distributional facts are displayed with admirable clarity.

Since these maps are presented in addition to raw data maps of the Gilliéron type, Séguy maintains that they do not interpret the material, but merely summarize it. Nothing is lost. Nor does he draw linguistic conclusions from the distributional facts. He does not, for example, come to any conclusion from the data presented in Maps 6.10 and 6.11 as to the number of phonemes – 1,

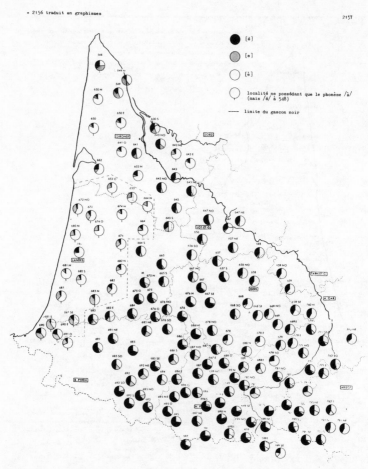

MAP 6.11.   Graphic representation of data from Map 6.10 (from ALG, vol. VI, Map 2151).

2, or 3 – in the mid-front unround sector of the Gascon vowel system. This is for the linguist using the material to judge. As he puts it:

> ...the principal task which we gave ourselves...was to bring together in synthetic maps the facts of diachronic phonetics and of phonology which are carried by the words in volumes I–V – facts which the reader would have been able to grasp and collect only at the cost of discouraging labor, while the author of the atlas seems naturally designated to undertake that enterprise....

The synthetic descriptions which we give are no more and no less objective and impersonal than the contents of analytical maps since we never formulate an explanation – a conclusion in terms of finality or causality. We have confined ourselves to using only those methods, mathematical in the broad sense, in which subjectivity has no part. Interpretation properly so called is left to the free choice of the reader. (Séguy 1973a, *pp* 1–2)

Summarizing maps of this sort are particularly helpful for presenting phonological data. The phonetic transcription of an individual word, as in raw data maps in the Gilliéron tradition, serves only to indicate the pronunciation of that particular word in each of the various localities surveyed. It gives no indication as to what type of variation is being displayed (neither, of course, does a facsimile or list presentation). The variation may be incidental, affecting only that word, as in the [təméto, təmɑto, təmǽto] variation in American English. Or it may be allophonic, affecting certain sounds only in the particular environments present in the particular word shown. Finally, it may be systematic, illustrating one part of the phonological systems at the various localities. Thus a map like our Map 6.2, while presenting clearly the pronunciations of *slice* in eastern England, says nothing about the structural position of the diphthongs [ɔi], [ɑi], [ai], and [ʌi] in this area, nor about their allophonic constituency. Is there a common /ay/ diphthong in the area, of which these are simply localized allophonic realizations? Or are they distinctive phonemes, distributed differently in different parts of the area? Do the particular phones here represented occur in all word positions, or only before voiceless obstruents/fricatives/sibilants? If the latter, what allophones do occur in other environments?

In short, a single phonetic transcription says nothing about the phonological system at the locality where it appears, or how that system compares with those of neighboring localities. To come to any significant conclusion on these points, the linguist must compare the whole body of data before him. It is the feeling of dialectologists like Séguy that this process can be aided by the presentation of summary maps such as Maps 6.10 and 6.11, but that conclusions going beyond such summaries must be left to the user of the material. They draw a sharp distinction between the function of the dialectologist as investigator, whose role is to assemble the data and make it available in the most convenient form he can think of, and the function of the dialectologist as linguist, whose role is to draw conclusions from the data concerning the dialectal structure of the language area concerned and the nature and significance of its regional variation. These two may be the same person, as in the case of Gilliéron, who, after completing the ALF, went on to write a series of articles and monographs based on the material it reported. But since the type of training of the theorist is quite different from that of the collector-investigator, they are often different persons, leaving the collector with only the responsibility of furnishing the theorist with the amount and kinds of data he requires. This is, of course, easier if the investigator has some understanding of linguistic theory and is capable of carrying on theoretical work himself.

Interpretative maps

Maps which go beyond simply presenting the field data in the direction of organizing it so as to direct the reader toward specific conclusions are INTERPRETATIVE. Most commonly these are secondary; that is, they handle data which has already been made available in its original form, so that the mapper is relieved of the responsibility of making the primary report. This is the case with the maps in volume VI of ALG (from which we drew our Maps 6.9, 6.10, and 6.11), which are based on the material reported in volumes I–V of that atlas, or with those in Orton and Wright's *Word Geography of England* (WGE), which are based on the data listed in SED. Kurath's *A Word Geography of the Eastern United States* (WGEUS), from which we derived Map 1.1, is a special case, since it is based in part on the field records of the Middle and South Atlantic States, which had not yet been published. It was understood, however, that they eventually would be, and this expectation is now being fulfilled in the publication of LAMSAS. It is still generally accepted that one part, at least, of the primary publication resulting from a survey should make the original data recoverable by the user interested in doing his own analysis and interpretation. Some recent surveys (for example LAGS) are making available not only the transcriptions of field interviews but copies of the tape-recordings on which they are based. The user can thus verify the accuracy of the transcriptions if he wishes. In very few fields of study is primary data made so readily accessible.

Isogloss maps

The most common type of lexical map is concerned with showing the different words or word-variants used in different localities to represent the same referent or concept. Such a map is based on the type of question which in Chapter 3 we call ONOMASIOLOGI-CAL. There are several assumptions behind such a map: (1) that the referent is well known to the informants over the whole area mapped; (2) that the question is put so clearly that the informant always understands just what is wanted; (3) that if an informant knows several words – synonyms – to describe the referent, he responds first with the one that he and presumably the other inhabitants of the locality he represents use regularly and naturally. It is, of course, the duty of the interviewer to make sure of these conditions. The mapper, unless he is also the fieldworker, can only map what he finds in the field records. Even so, he must be constantly aware of the possibilities of error, ambiguity, or misleading emphasis.

A common type of lexical map is the isogloss map. We have already seen some examples of these (Maps 1.1 and 2.1, *p* 3 and *p* 21), where the isoglosses are lines separating large areas characterized by contrasting words for the same referent: *pail* and *bucket* in the first case; *burn, beck, brook*, and *stream* in the other. Since, as we noted in Chapter 1, there is more commonly a transition area in which both contrasting terms may be used interchangeably or with slight differences in meaning, isoglosses of this sort represent rather strong simplification of the data. They also reflect the evaluation or interpretation placed upon the data by the dialectologist, consciously or unconsciously. Minor phonetic detail, for example, is commonly omitted, on the assumption that it is irrelevant from the point of view of lexicon, where the interest focuses on contrasting words rather than pronunciation. But the decision as to what is a different word rather than a mere variant pronunciation is not always easy to make. Lexicographers commonly make this decision on the basis of etymology. If two forms closely resembling each other phonologically can be shown to have different etymologies, they are held to be different words, no matter how much alike they may be semantically as well as phonologically. The etymologically unrelated words *isle* from Old French, ultimately Latin *insula*, and *island*, from Old English *ig* 'island' and *lond* 'land', are an example. Conversely, *riband*, an old-fashioned form of *ribbon*, is considered the same word, while the homophonous *riband*, a term from shipbuilding, is considered a different word because of its different etymology.

But even this fairly objective distinction often does not work. In the first place, the dialectologist is often at least as much concerned with the informant's own notions about his words as with precise etymological fact. Certainly most native speakers will consider *isle* and *island* to be related words – perhaps that the former is a clipped form of the latter – on the grounds of their phonological, semantic, and even graphic similarity, while the semantic

distance between the adjectives *rear* and *rare* (as of meat) will prevent them from associating these words, though the etymologist
claims that they are historically the same word. Related to this
situation is the fact that FOLK ETYMOLOGY – 'the transformation of
words so as to give them an apparent relationship to other better-
known or better-understood words' (Webster III) – is a common
cause of dialectal variation. Take, for example, the two forms
swingle-tree and *single-tree* used to designate the wooden crossbar
to which a horse's traces are fastened. The older of these, and
apparently the only one used in England, is *swingle-tree*, the first
element of which is related to the verb *swing*, and the second is a
common term in dialect for a piece of wood. When two horses
are hitched together side by side, their swingle-trees are fastened
to a larger crossbar often called a *double-tree*. Apparently this led
to the alteration of *swingle-tree* to *single-tree*, and the two are
separately listed with different etymologies in Webster III. The
Oxford English Dictionary (*OED*), however, treats them as
variants of the same word, commenting: 'An altered form, SINGLE-
TREE, due to association with *double-tree* (= the crosspiece to
which the swingle-tree is attached) is common in U.S.' We must
then conclude that these are different words in the US but the
same word in the UK.

Map 6.12 is an example of an isogloss map representing a simplification and interpretation of the SED data by the editors of
WGE. Their concern was to illustrate the contrasting distributions of two synonymous local terms for a newly born female
lamb, *ewe-lamb* and *gimmer-lamb*. The editors describe their
mapping procedure as follows:

> Our [maps show] areas of lexical distribution, i.e. regions character-
> ized by the employment of an individual word. They do so by means
> of isoglosses, which enclose areas throughout which a particular ex-
> pression is found. Thus the isogloss is a boundary line marking off
> clearly on the map one distributional area from an adjoining area in
> which the expression under consideration is either not recorded or else
> occurs only exceptionally. When two adjacent localities use different
> words, the isogloss in question is drawn approximately midway between
> them. Thus isoglosses do not in fact mark off separate divisions pre-
> cisely, but are only rough boundaries between one feature and
> another.
> The chief novelty in our mapping procedures concerns the method
> of indicating in the labelled areas of distribution the occurrence of
> words listed in the map legend. The practice in this case differs from
> that followed in non-labelled areas, where distributions are not under
> consideration. In these labelled areas, the locality dot has been given
> the additional function of representing an occurrence of the labelled

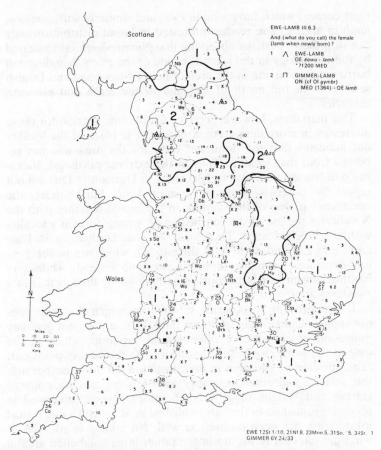

MAP 6.12. Words for 'ewe-lamb' in England (from WGE, Map 44).

form, but not so in non-labelled areas, where it always retains its primary function of representing one locality in the network of places investigated. (Orton and Wright 1974, *p* 3)

Map 6.12, therefore, has three kinds of areas bounded by isoglosses: two contrasting labelled areas, marked 1 and 2, and an unlabelled area in the East Midlands, embracing most of Lincolnshire (10 L) and parts of Northamptonshire (18 Nth), Rutland (14 R), and Huntingdonshire (19 Hu). The labelled area 2 splits the area 1 into two parts, a small one along the Scottish border, and a large southern one covering most of the country. Every numbered locality in area 1 marked only by a dot reported some phonetic variant of *ewe-lamb*, except for six listed in the lower right corner, which have simple *ewe*, and similarly with *gimmer-lamb* in area 2. The reader interested in broad distribution only can stop there, perhaps observing that *gimmer-lamb*, as indicated by the etymology in the legend, is one of the many Scandinavian borrowings occurring in the area of heavy Norwegian and Danish settlement in the north of England in the tenth and eleventh centuries.

This map does, however, convey further information for those interested in more detail. An X occurring in place of the locality dot indicates that the dominant term for the area was not reported from that locality. Thus in the extreme northeast, localities 6 in Northumberland (1 Nb) and 1 in Durham (3 Du) did not report the otherwise prevalent *gimmer-lamb*. Furthermore, the occurrence of one of the symbols in the legend together with the X indicates the use of the contrasting or 'wrong' form at a locality within a labelled area. Thus localities 5 in Durham, 2 in Lancashire (5 La) and 20 in Yorkshire (6 Y), which are in the *gimmer-lamb* area, actually reported *ewe-lamb* instead, while 4 in Nottinghamshire (9 Nt) reported *gimmer-lamb*, though it is in a *ewe-lamb* area.

It is interesting to note the information which this map does *not* supply. Unlike Map 6.4 from the DWA, it does not give any indication of phonetic or phonological variation, which in the case of the word *ewe* is quite extensive. As the editors point out: 'The question of variation in pronunciation did not arise because this atlas is concerned primarily with lexicon, not phonology.' (Orton and Wright 1974, *p* 2) Therefore anyone interested in phonology must go to the lists published in SED. But some lexical information has been omitted as well. No inkling is given as to what the relevant terms are in the rather large unlabelled area in the East Midlands. Likewise the X's within labelled areas are purely negative; they do not indicate what word, if any, is used instead of the dominant terms. Thus for this information as well the user would have to resort to the SED lists.

This map, then, is well designed to fulfil its single function: to illustrate the distribution of a Scandinavian loan-word in contrast to that of the otherwise dominant word of Anglo-Saxon origin. In the chapter on 'Analysis of the maps', the senior editor, Harold Orton, comments:

Some of [the Scandinavian words] are still widely distributed and mark off clearly those parts of England, more particularly in the North and L[incolnshire], which the Vikings colonized after abandoning their piratical activities. ... *Gimmer*(-lamb) (M44) persists vigorously *vis-à-*

vis ewe, except in L, where it was not recorded. (Orton and Wright 1974, *p* 26)

It can be said, however, that the map could have been designed to furnish considerably more lexical information without complicating it unduly or otherwise obscuring its main purpose. The X's in labelled areas, for example, stand for three different things. Ten of them stand for the notation 'n.a.' for 'question not asked'. Three more stand for 'n.k.', meaning that the term, or rather the notion which the term represents, was not known in the area, or at least to the informant questioned, presumably because he was not familiar with the raising of sheep. Four represent the response *lamb*, a general term which may or may not indicate the informant's ignorance, rather than local absence of sheep culture. Eleven indicate that the informant reported a local term different from the two in the legend. This ambiguity could have been avoided by employing different simple symbols, say + and =, for 'n.a.' and 'n.k.', leaving X to stand for 'alternative word given; see legend'.

Furthermore, the map fails to show that three of these alternative terms have local concentrations which might be of some interest to the reader studying lexical distribution. One of these, *chilver(-lamb)*, is represented by eight of the X's in the southwest counties of Gloucestershire, Somerset, Wiltshire, and Dorset. This is a native English word, from OE *cilfer*, having a stem ultimately related to *calf*.

The other two, *she-lamb* and *sheeder(-lamb)*, which are etymologically related (*Sheeder*, according to the *OED*, is from the pronoun *she* plus *deer* in the general sense of 'animal'), are reported each from nine localities in the unlabelled East Midland area of Lincolnshire and bordering counties. Since this area is within the Scandinavian settlement region, and since the editor, as quoted above, comments on the absence of the expected Scandinavian term in this area, the map might well have indicated just what terms actually were reported from there.

Map 6.13 is our own attempt to show how this extra information could have been included without unduly cluttering the map or detracting from its primary purpose.

One criticism of the isogloss map is that, in a sampling survey with a rather open-meshed network, it appears to give more information than the data warrant. If single informants in two villages 15 or 20 miles apart give different responses to a question, to place a boundary at some arbitrary point – say halfway – between them seems to indicate that the survey shows just where

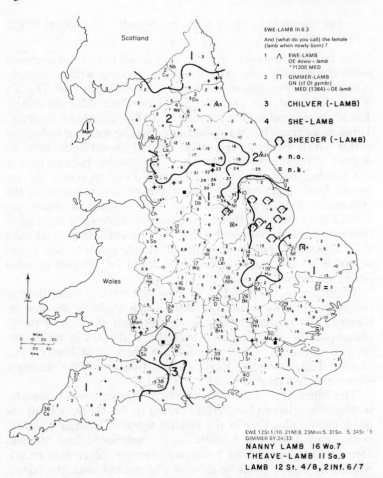

EWE-LAMB III.6.3

And (what do you call) the female
(lamb when newly born)?

1 ∧ EWE-LAMB
       OE *ēowu + lamb*
       *?1200 MED

2 ∏ GIMMER-LAMB
       ON (cf OI *gymbr*)
       MED (1364) + OE *lamb*

3   CHILVER (-LAMB)

4   SHE-LAMB

∩   SHEEDER (-LAMB)

+   n.a.

=   n.k.

EWE 12St.1/10, 21Nf.8, 23Mon.5, 31So. 5, 34Sr. 1
GIMMER 6Y.24/33
NANNY LAMB 16 Wo.7
THEAVE-LAMB 11 Sa.9
LAMB 12 St. 4/8, 2 Inf. 6/7

MAP 6.13. Modified form of Map 6.12 (additional data from SED,
III.6.3).

the lexical shift occurs. But a finer-meshed survey might reveal
more precisely the location of the shift, or, what is more likely,
the changing proportions of the numbers of speakers using the
two forms. As the geographer Hägerstrand has remarked in
another connection: 'When studying changes we cannot draw
boundary lines and observe their displacements. Instead, we must
ascertain *the spatial diffusion of ratios*.' (Hägerstrand 1952,
quoted in Trudgill, n.d.) To do this, of course, requires abandoning the survey based on single informants considered representa-

tive of their localities in favor of a statistically valid sample of the whole population, as described above in Chapter 4. The traditional dialectologist who uses the isogloss technique is, of course, usually aware of the possible overinterpretation of his presentation, and may enter a cautionary comment about it, such as that by the editors of WGE in the quotation from their introduction above: '...isoglosses do not in fact mark off separate divisions precisely, but are only rough boundaries between one feature and another' (Orton and Wright 1974, *p* 3), or the comment by Séguy on his use of straight lines instead of the usual smooth curves, because 'curving lines suggest to the reader an illusory precision' (Séguy 1973a, *p* 4). Isogloss maps, in short, though easier to read and more graphic than symbol maps, are more capable of misinterpretation. A map such as Map 6.4 above, though heavily cluttered and difficult to read, tells us only that certain responses have come from certain precise localities, without suggesting anything about the responses from intervening unsampled localities. It thus more accurately reports the degree of precision of the survey data.

A type of isogloss map designed to indicate the degree of difference between the speech of contiguous localities is illustrated by Map 6.14, representing phonological contrasts in French-speaking Belgium (Atwood 1955). Unlike the usual isogloss map such as Map 6.12, which plots a single feature, or a multiple isogloss map like Map 1.1 (*p* 3), which shows a bundle of 4 isoglosses running rather close together, this map is based on a number of features – 150 in all. The lines separate individual localities surveyed by the *Atlas linguistique de la Wallonie* (ALW), and their thickness indicates the number of contrasting items at each intermediate point. Since the ability of the eye to distinguish small differences in size is limited, the composite lines have been reduced to 6, representing contrasts in 10 or more features out of a possible 150. The broadest lines, then, approximate to what might be called dialect boundaries, while the narrower ones represent degrees of variation within the larger dialect areas. Such a map, therefore, while less precise than a collection of single isogloss maps, gives more of an idea of the changing degrees of differentiation across a linguistic area.

It is of interest to compare this map with Map 6.15 from the same source, which shows three bundles of four isoglosses each in the traditional manner. Note that when the position of the heavy lines has been established as in Map 6.14, certain isoglosses can be selected which follow the heavy lines and can thus be considered representative of a dialect boundary. Thus No. 2 of the

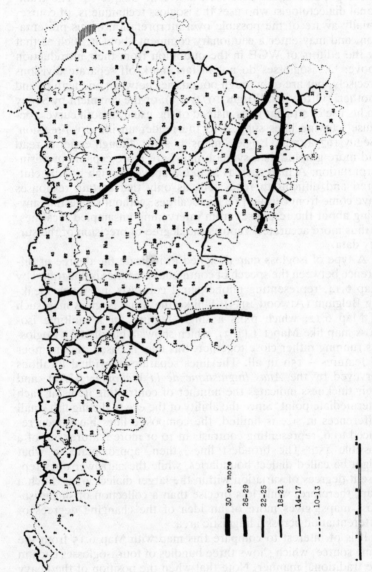

MAP 6.14.   Bundles of isoglosses in Walloon area of Belgium (from Atwood 1955, Map 1).

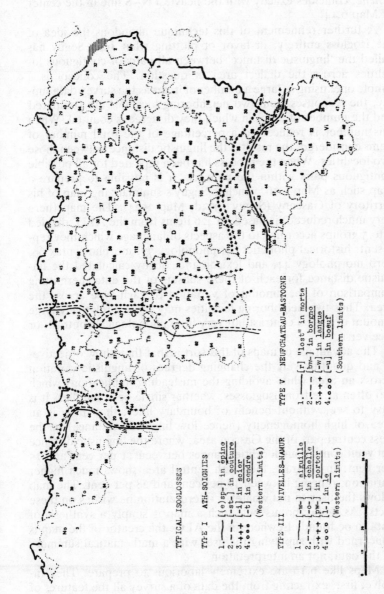

TYPICAL ISOGLOSSES

TYPE I ATH-SOIGNIES

1. ——— [(e)sp-] in épine
2. – – – [-st-] in couture
3. +++ [-i] in soier
4. ∘∘∘ [-b] in condre
          (Western limits)

TYPE III NIVELLES-NAMUR

1. ——— [-w-] in aiguille
2. – – – [-o-] in échelle
3. +++ [pw-] in porter
4. ∘∘∘ [l-] in le
          (Western limits)

TYPE V NEUFCHATEAU-BASTOGNE

1. ——— [r] "lost" in morte
2. – – – [bw-] in borgno
3. +++ [-w] in longue
4. ∘∘∘ [-u] in boeuf
          (Southern limits)

MAP 6.15. Isoglosses in Walloon area of Belgium (from Atwood 1955, Map 2).

second set (Type III), representing the western limit of [o] in *échelle*, coincides exactly with the heaviest N–S line in the center of Map 6.14.

A further refinement of this technique abandons the idea of the isogloss entirely, in favor of plotting what Jean Séguy has called the 'linguistic distance' between all pairs of contiguous localities across the dialect area in question. The concept is a simple one: using as large a number of items as the survey data supply, the responses from two neighboring localities are compared and the number of items in which they disagree is counted. When this number is reduced to a percentage of the total number of items considered, the result is the linguistic distance between those two localities. When the process has been repeated for all possible contiguous pairs within the network, it is possible to prepare a map such as Map 6.16, which is Séguy's summarizing map of his territory of Gascony (Séguy 1973d, Map 2524). The map (here very much reduced) is based on 426 items from the ALG, divided into 5 groups according to the aspects of language which they represent: historical phonetics 67, phonology 77, morpho-syntax 68, verb morphology 44, and lexicon 170. Séguy calculated the linguistic distance for each of these subsets of the data, permitting comparison of the amount of variation of each type across the area. Thus two neighboring localities may show a relatively large amount of lexical contrast but very little phonological contrast, or vice versa.

The advantage of maps of this sort is that they show objectively and quantitatively the changing degrees of linguistic variation across an area while avoiding the misleading implications which too often arise from isoglosses, whether single or in bundles. It is easy to see, without benefit of boundary lines, that there is an area of high homogeneity (hence low linguistic distance) in the west central part of the Gascon area, where the linguistic distance between contiguous localities ranges between 11 per cent and 15 per cent. In contrast, the south central area shows much higher variation, ranging between 18 per cent and 28 per cent. The map allows the user to put whatever interpretation he wishes on these facts. As Séguy points out, such a map is simply a synthesis of data to be found elsewhere in the ALG: the creator of the map is concerned with supplying the user with a mathematical summary of the data, not an interpretation.

Maps like 6.16 are extremely laborious to prepare. They involve, first, extracting from the data of a survey all the features of linguistic significance that can be recognized. A single response, for example, may supply data from various fields: lexicon, pho-

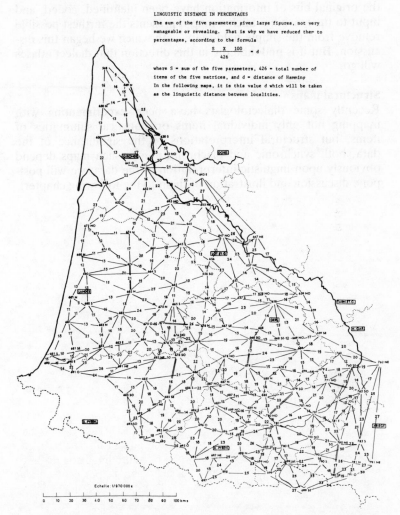

LINGUISTIC DISTANCE IN PERCENTAGES
The sum of the five parameters gives large figures, not very
manageable or revealing. That is why we have reduced them to
percentages, according to the formula

$$\frac{S \times 100}{426} = d$$

where S = sum of the five parameters, 426 = total number of
items of the five matrices, and d = distance of Hamming
In the following maps, it is this value d which will be taken
as the linguistic distance between localities.

MAP 6.16. Linguistic distances in percentages, Gascony (from ALG,
vol. VI, Map 2524).

nology, morphology, and even syntax. All of this must be tabulated for each locality. Then the data from each locality must be
compared with that from three to six contiguous localities, and
the differences recorded. Séguy estimated that the preparation of
Map 6.16 involved 2,660 individual matchings. The actual comparison can, of course, now be done by computer, but only after

the original bits of information have been identified, coded, and input to the machine. Such a map represents the furthest possible remove from the simple field-maps with which we began this discussion. But it is undoubtedly in this direction that dialect atlases will go.

Structural maps

Recently some dialectologists have been experimenting with mapping not only individual items or statistical summaries of items, but structural interpretations of the significance of the data, both synchronic and diachronic. Since such maps depend obviously upon linguistic interpretation of the data, we will postpone discussion and illustration of them to the following chapter.

Chapter 7

Dialectology and linguistic theory:
I Traditional, structural, generative

As we have seen throughout the preceding chapters, the main concern of dialectology – in fact, its whole subject matter – is variation in language, in all the forms and aspects described and illustrated in Chapter 2. Primarily it has occupied itself simply with collecting and displaying this variation in as much detail as possible, and it has developed elaborate and effective means of doing so. To some dialectologists, the responsibility of the discipline goes no further than this collection and display. Others, however, have felt that dialectology is not just a museum of linguistic oddities but a branch of the field of general linguistics, and hence responsible for developing theories of language variation and distribution which are compatible with or contributory to a general theory of language. On the whole, dialectologists have not been noteworthy linguistic theorists (with some notable exceptions). But by insistently confronting the theorists with carefully collected and presented facts about language as it is found in the field, they have been able to demonstrate the errors and inadequacies of overly abstract theories and suggest, if not force, amplification and amendment.

Faced with a body of facts which his theory fails to accommodate, the theorist must do one of three things (if he is to continue theorizing): he may (1) prove that the facts are wrong, or at least questionable to the point of requiring further verification, (2) demonstrate that the facts are either irrelevant to the theory or provided for within it, or (3) modify the theory to accommodate the facts. Linguistic theory has not always responded in one of these ways to the presentations of dialectology; it has sometimes taken a fourth course, simply to ignore them. On the other side, dialectologists have often gone their own way without attending to current theory. Fortunately we are now in a period when both sides are working toward a desirable synthesis of their interests and conclusions.

The Neogrammarian Hypothesis

It is the nature of scientific theory to attempt the explanation of some aspect of the universe in as general terms as the facts will permit, expressing its conclusions in rational terms which will strongly suggest, if not demand, their acceptance by rational men, and which will indicate lines of future study and thought. A notable example in linguistic history is the so-called Neogrammarian Hypothesis, the claim that 'Every sound change, inasmuch as it occurs mechanically, takes place according to laws that admit no exceptions.' (Osthoff and Brugmann 1878, *p* xiii) This theory was not the product of sudden inspiration or brilliant intuition; it was reached after a long and intensive period of comparative study. It was put forward as an explanation not of why phonological changes take place but of how they do. It is a claim of great generality, and rests on equally general assumptions: first, that sound changes, or at least some of them, take place 'mechanically', which means without the conscious will or even the awareness of the members of the speech community involved, and second, that all speakers of all languages are subject to this limitation. A further assumption, characteristic of much nineteenth-century thought, was that a 'mechanical' process allows no room for variation and uncertainty; given a certain set of conditions as input, the result of the process will be completely predictable, in the form of exceptionless 'laws'.

To realize how momentous a contribution to linguistic theory this hypothesis was, it is only necessary to remember that only a century or so earlier some wag (reputedly Voltaire) is said to have remarked that in etymology consonants count for very little and vowels for nothing at all; that is, that sound changes must occur capriciously and randomly if the claims of etymologists are true. A century of close study of the Indo-European languages demonstrated that both vowels and consonants change according to orderly and definitely formulable 'laws'. The elaborate and detailed demonstration of how these laws had brought about the greatly diversified phonologies of the members of the Indo-European family established etymology on a scientific basis which is one of the triumphs of nineteenth-century thought. But the theory was so sweeping that it challenged verification or disproof.

The two great pioneering efforts in dialectology – Wenker's

Deutscher Sprachatlas and Gilliéron's *Atlas linguistique de la France* – were undertaken in the climate of the Neogrammarian Hypothesis and in part at least with a view to supplying the verification or disproof which it demanded. The theory had been built by philologists, working with those fragments of older languages which history and chance had preserved in written texts. They perforce viewed their linguistic material through the clouded and distorted window of writing systems; before they could deal precisely with phonological problems, they had to understand and allow for the habits, traditions, and vagaries of scribes. Since writing systems almost universally have dealt with a standardized form of language, the texts always incline to the normative; they present a more or less idealized form of the language. Thus the material with which the philologists worked was at two removes from the actual language of the ordinary speaker: it lacked the spontaneity and irregularity of ordinary talk, and it avoided the wealth of variation which we have seen to be characteristic of language in use by a community of native speakers. In Saussurean terms, it was a reflection of *langue* rather than *parole*.

What the pioneer dialectologists succeeded in doing was to collect rather large bodies of data drawn more or less successfully from the actual language being used by contemporary speakers. Gilliéron particularly, with his insistence on direct face-to-face contact between fieldworker and informant, sought to correct the philologists' preoccupation with written texts. By requiring the responses to be recorded phonetically, he hoped to eliminate the problem of the phonological interpretation of writing systems. By deriving his data from ordinary people in towns and villages throughout the country, he sought to avoid the limitation of the philologist to more or less standardized forms of language. Though the ALF survey was conducted on a synchronic descriptive basis, it was clearly intended to make possible a more profound and more accurate understanding of the ways in which language changes through time. This is apparent from the use which Gilliéron himself made of the ALF data: he produced a series of brilliant, lively, often aggressively argumentative papers and monographs, demonstrating in rich detail that many other factors beside unconscious mechanical change are involved in both phonological and lexical history.

This was, in effect, the first major confrontation of a sort which the Swedish dialectologist Dahlstedt has described in these terms:

Since modern dialectology was born, at the end of the nineteenth century, it has fulfilled and is still fulfilling the role of confronting scrupulously collected empirical data, from sociolinguistic microstructures as well as from whole domains of languages, with the visions and models of dominating linguistic schools. (Dahlstedt. 1970, *p* 158)

It can be summed up in the two succinct statements which we have previously quoted: on the one side, 'Sound laws are without exception', and on the other, 'Each word has its own history.' Reconciliation of these apparently completely contrary summations became the preoccupation of a generation of linguists, and is still going on. The French linguist Dauzat saw the conflict at least partially in nationalistic terms, as an opposition between Teutonic scientific rationalism and Gallic humanism:

> This young science [linguistic geography], essentially French, while sending out some roots into neighboring countries, marks a reaction against the doctrines of the German school of Neo-grammarians, who had triumphed during the last third of the nineteenth century and who had had their *raison d'être* in that period, but who, too dogmatic and too absolute, threatened to weaken linguistics by imprisoning it in rigid formulas and by causing it to lose contact bit by bit with the infinitely delicate and changeable realities of life. Once again the spirit of *finesse* has got its own back against the geometric spirit. (Dauzat 1922, *pp* 5–6)

This view, while understandable coming from a Frenchman writing not long after the First World War, is rather overstated. The real opposition is one common to science generally, between the intellectual need to produce clear, easily formulable, predictively powerful theories on the one hand, and on the other the stubborn variety and intractableness of the facts with which the scientist must deal. It is out of this conflict that new and more successful syntheses arise.

As we saw in Chapter 2, dialect variation is evinced in all parts of language: in phonology, morphology, syntax, semantics, and lexicon. No part of language is proof against change, and differential diachronic change is the source of synchronic variation. This was well known to nineteenth-century linguists, whose major focus was on change. It was succinctly put by Saussure, whom many consider the founder of modern linguistics. Time '. . . is actually the cause of linguistic differentiation. Geographical diversity should be called temporal diversity.' (Saussure 1959, *p* 198) The two parts of language on which traditional dialectology has focused are phonology and lexicon. These two were seen to be closely related, in that on the one hand individual words are the clearest and most obvious manifestation of the sounds of language; and on the other, the most obvious way in which words vary is in their phonological constituency. This relationship suggested the traditional method of collection – eliciting from the informant by one means or another individual words from his lexicon. After all, one cannot ask an informant to produce phonemes; he never heard of them, and if he had, it is hardly possible to produce them in a vacuum. As we saw in Chapter 3, the common feeling, as expressed by Gardette, was that a sufficiently large collection of words, phonetically transcribed, would supply the material needed to 'do' the phonetics. Gilliéron found that the 1,900-odd forms of the ALF, though selected as lexical items, supplied ample material for his studies in diachronic phonology. But as we shall see, such collections are too incomplete and haphazard to satisfy modern phonology.

Phonology and lexicon, then, are the two areas of language where dialect studies have had most to offer and hence the areas where dialectology and linguistic theory confront one another (only recently has syntax come into the picture). Of these two, phonology has been by far the more important. The great size of the lexicon and its relatively unsystematic organization have defied reduction to structured theory, and those who have attempted to deal with it in systematic fashion – the lexicographers and compilers of thesauri – have found that their most useful contribution has been to compile masses of facts about words and their meanings in convenient and useful compendia for the use of readers and writers. There have, of course, been areas where theories about the lexicon have been developed, as in the study of word formation (*eg* Marchand 1969) or semantic fields (Trier 1973; Stern 1931). But in general the area where lexical dialectology has been most fruitful is the anthropological and ethnographic, as in the work of the *Wörter und Sachen* school.

Phonology, on the other hand, with its rather small body of highly systematic data, has been the principal field of operation of linguistic theory, at least until the syntactic explosion of the last quarter century. So it is to phonology that we must look for the most interesting relationships between dialectology and linguistic theory. These may be grouped into four schools of dialectal phonology: the traditional, the structural, the generative, and the sociolinguistic. These four approaches to phonological theory appeared in that order chronologically, and all are still more or less current. The traditional approach is diachronic and item-centered; the structural approach is synchronic and system-centered; the generative approach is panchronic (*ie* both synchronic and diachronic) and rule-centered; the sociolinguistic approach is panchronic and speaker-centered.

Traditional dialectology

Traditional dialectology, as we have seen, grew out of the nineteenth-century interest in historical and comparative linguistics. It saw the development of dialectal variation within a language area as a microcosm of the processes which on a larger scale produce language variation; in fact, dialectal variation was seen as the first stage through which the diverging varieties of a proto-language must pass on the way to the development of independent languages. Its theoretical base was, therefore, the same as that on which historical and comparative linguistics rested. This involved several important assumptions and hypotheses:

1. A set of related languages (dialects) derives from an earlier homogeneous language (proto-language) (Pulgram 1964a, *pp* 376–7).
2. Phonological variation is produced by mechanical, systematic sound changes, affecting the original sounds of the language (proto-language).
3. These sound changes, though operating systematically (*ie* affecting all instances of a given sound in a specific environment or set of environments), affect the language of different sectors of the speech community in different ways, thus producing variation where once was homogeneity.
4. Although various forces such as analogy, inter-language or inter-dialect borrowing, and conservative pressure may counteract the mechanical force of sound change, it is powerful enough to assure that, over a sufficient span of time, every homogeneous language will develop dialects, and every proto-language, daughter languages. The only limitation on this endless proliferation of variant modes of speech is that, due to various non-linguistic forces such as wars, invasions, and political domination, many dialects and languages cease to be used and eventually die.

In describing traditional dialectology as 'item-centered', or, as another dialectologist has put it, 'atomistic' (Fourquet 1956, *p* 196), we mean that the interest is focused on individual facts of the variable distribution of a single sound (or other linguistic feature) without attempting to relate them to the overall structure of the dialects involved. The maps and tables discussed in the last chapter, all drawn from traditional dialectology, are sufficient illustration of this. Map 6.9, (*p* 127), for example, merely summarizes the localities in Gascony where one or more of four colloquial Latin words have kept the initial /fr/ cluster in Gascon dialects. There is no attempt to relate this distribution to the phonemic inventory or phonotactics of the individual dialects. In fact, Séguy would have considered any such attempt to be 'interpretation' and hence beyond the function of the dialectologist. 'Interpretation properly so called is left to the free choice of the reader.' (Séguy 1973a, *p* 2) Even a map as complex as Map 6.16 (*p* 143), charting the 'linguistic distance' between contiguous localities across a dialect area, is only a summation of a large number of individual facts. The 426 possible oppositions on which the linguistic distances are based are discrete items, all given equal value, and each one counted without consideration of its relationship to any of the others or to the overall phonological, morphological, and lexical structure of the dialects.

All the great dialect atlases of the twentieth century, from Gilliéron's ALF, which was completed in 1908, to the regional atlases of Germany and France, some of which are still in progress, are in the item-centered traditional mode. Not all are as averse to interpretation as Séguy, but when they do engage in interpretation, it is diachronic and etymological. A characteristic example is the *Phonological Atlas of the Northern Region* (1966), produced by Eduard Kolb from the field records of the SED. The atlas, like the Survey, assumes a homogeneous Middle English sound system, and presents a series of maps showing the modern reflexes of the individual Middle English sounds in the north of England. The maps follow the Swiss tradition, as developed by Hotzenköcherle in the Swiss German atlas (see Map 6.7 above, *p* 122–3), and present the data clearly and elegantly. But no conclusions are drawn about the number and nature of different phonological systems in the region, or their relation to one another or to the hypothetical Middle English proto-dialect.

There is, however, one area in which traditional dialectologists have engaged in considerable theorizing. That is the problem with which we began this book: how is dialect to be defined? what distinguishes one dialect from another? are there boundaries between dialects, and if so, how are they to be identified? Discussion of these points has continued throughout the twentieth century, and has been passed on from the traditional school to its successors and/or rivals, the structural and generative schools. In one sense these are insoluble problems, while from another point of view they are pseudo-problems which give rise to a good deal of scholastic argument which would be better abandoned in favor of getting on with the task of observing and studying dialects.

The naïve view, held by the ordinary person who is aware of dialectal variation but has not observed or studied it, is that there are indeed dialects, that they are indeed distinguished from one another by different words and pronunciations, and that there are fairly sharp boundaries between them. He can tell you that in Scotland they roll their r's, or that south of the Mason-Dixon line people say *you all* and pronounce *fine* like *fan*. He would, in short, expect to encounter a large number of miscellaneous linguistic differences or even absurdities upon crossing such political boundaries as the line between England and Scotland or between Pennsylvania and Maryland.

At the other extreme is the view expressed by Gaston Paris in the passage quoted at the beginning of Chapter 1: 'there really are no dialects' and hence no dialect boundaries; instead there is a gradual but continuous and cumulative change across the countryside. There is no break in the chain of intercommunication from one neighborhood to the next, but nonetheless an accumulation of differences which ultimately results in incomprehensibility between the two ends of the chain. The paradox is that there clearly are dialect differences at the extremes, but between them only a continuous transition area without boundaries or 'local dialects' of its own.

In an important article published in 1903, when the work of the ALF was just beginning to appear, the Swiss dialectologist Gauchat faced the question which he used as his title: 'Gibt es Mundartgrenzen?' – Are there dialect boundaries? He quotes the famous passage from Paris, whose student he had been, only to claim that Paris was intentionally exaggerating in order to clear away a number of false notions or myths about dialect. Chief of these was the prevailing a priori definition, which set up three requirements:

1. A dialect includes certain characteristic features which occur nowhere else.
2. A dialect is separated from neighboring dialects by a bundle of at least two coinciding isoglosses.
3. Within a dialect, an unvarying phonological unity prevails.

Underlying these provisions, which he disposes of one after the other, Gauchat finds two fallacies, that of 'first setting up a definition and only afterward inquiring whether such a thing exists', and that of treating a dialect as if it were a distinct organism, 'a living being, which begins to live on a certain day, ends its existence on an equally certain day, that is physically bounded on every side, that can be transported whole, etc.' Instead, he points out, linguists have long been agreed:

> that language is not an organism but an inter-individual function, which at least at any given moment supposes two persons, whereof the listener is as important as the speaker. In actuality, not two but many or very many persons, whose number can range from two to ten

thousand and more, use the same dialect. And all these persons carry in themselves their changing apprehensions of things, their different temperaments; they vary the dialect according to the variations in their cultural positions. Yet all users of a dialect have something in common, so that it can be seen that when they encounter one another in a foreign land, a joyful feeling of home is awakened in them. (Gauchat 1903, p 396)

A dialect, then, for Gauchat is a psychological reality, a unique combination of features, many below the level of awareness, which allows one speaker to recognize another. Its boundaries are not sharp lines, but gradual transitions, as Schuchardt had earlier pointed out, like the colors of the rainbow, where palpable red yields to palpable yellow, though no sharp line divides them.

A similar view, though more sophisticated in expression, is held by another traditional dialectologist, writing seventy years after Gauchat. Gaston Tuaillon, editor of one of the regional atlases of France, addressing the question of 'frontière linguistique et cohésion de l'aire dialectale', finds the fallacy of precise dialect boundaries a result of confusing 'dialectal geometry' and 'administrative geometry' because both may be placed on the same type of maps. As he puts it, 'the confrontation of dialects and politico-administrative maps has been the source of several false problems for which even more erroneous solutions have been found' (Tuaillon 1973, p 195). He concludes his discussion as follows:

The precise boundary of a dialect is, most often, an ungraspable chimera. I believe that there is an incompatibility between the business of the dialectologist and that of the real-estate geometrician. For, while between two neighboring properties the owners frequently are accustomed to raise a barrier or a wall, dialects, on the other hand, erect a complex array of gangways as soon as there is a risk of too great a rift becoming established between them. And yet the dialectal field exists; one can, if not delimit it, at least define it thanks to several particular characteristics. One may even seize upon certain behavior patterns of the whole; or rather, one may see that features which appear elsewhere in gallo-roman as tendencies are the habitual rule of the particular dialectal region. It is then that our mind, too Cartesian to take in a space as complicated as dialectal space, is faced with the problem of the correct use of specific terms: 'do they apply to all of the thing defined? to that thing alone?' There are no answers, at least not the precise answers which our minds, distorted by the simplicity of ordinary geography, wish for. For linguistic geography, with its coherent space with points interconnected in very complex fashion, there would be needed either meticulous observation of an infinitude of facts, to which nobody could ever attain, or a method written by an anti-

Descartes whose first principle would be that one can accept something as true without knowing plainly that it is so, since not all science is necessarily certain and evident, and he who is in doubt about many things is no less knowing than he who has never reflected on them. (Tuaillon 1973, *pp* 205–6)

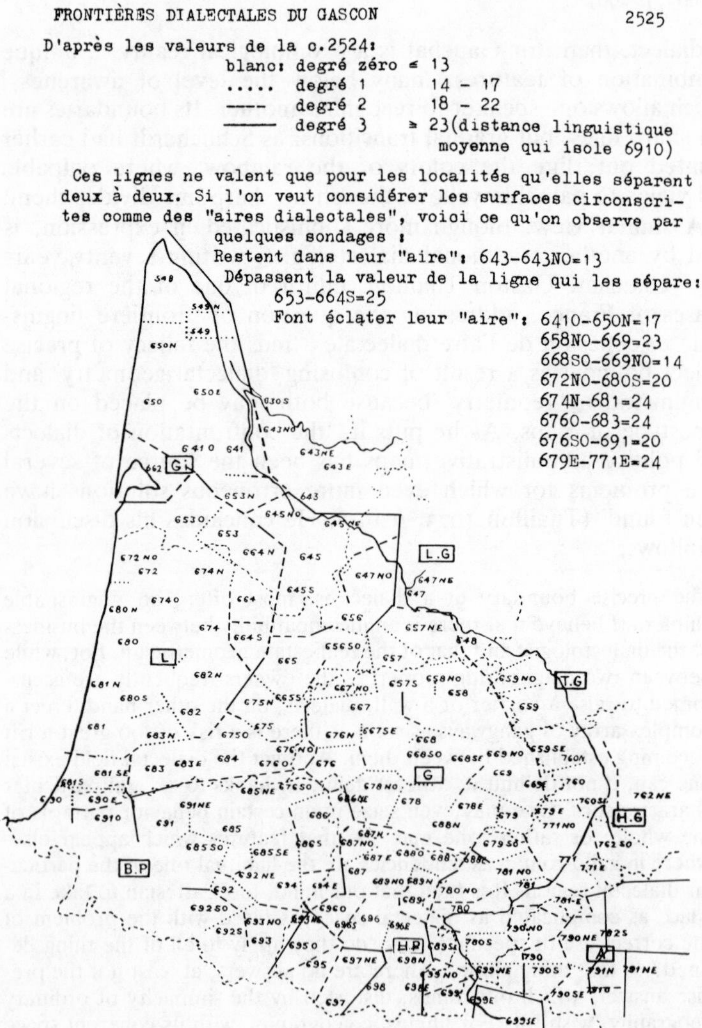

MAP 7.1.   Dialectal boundaries in Gascony (from ALG, vol. VI, Map 2525).

An ambitious attempt to delimit dialect boundaries by statistical means was carried out by J. Séguy in the final volume of ALG (Séguy 1973d). As we saw at the end of the last chapter, he calculated the linguistic distance between contiguous points in Gascony as represented by the percentage of oppositions among 426 features drawn from various aspects of language (Map 6.16 above, p 143). In Map 7.1, he arbitrarily set four degrees of contrast, running from Ø at 13 per cent or lower to 3 at 23 per cent or greater (see legend to Map 7.1). By connecting the interpoints falling into the last three of these degrees by different kinds of lines, he derived a network of dialectal boundaries. Map 7.2 represents a rationalization of these lines by combining those of degrees 2 and 3, that is, lines connecting interpoints of 18 per cent contrast or higher. In the profile charts presented in Fig. 7.1, he shows the exact percentage for each interpoint along the lines, as derived from Map 6.16 (p 143). He explains these charts in the legend of Map 7.2, which may be translated:

> The charts have been obtained by projecting the values on a vertical plane, so that the 'boundaries' resemble a mountain range seen from a distance, since the curves have been flattened out; the boundaries of the regions have similarly been straightened out.
>
> In abscissae: distances in kilometers (1 mm = 1 km)
>
> In ordinates: values of interpoints (1 mm = 1 unit of linguistic distance)
>
> The data of these graphs are more precise than those of Map 2525 [our Map 7.1], where each of the four degrees corresponds to a branch.
>
> The figures are the numbers corresponding to the encircled figures on the graphs.

To see how the charts work, let us trace part of line 2, which begins at point 690 on the west coast and trends eastward across the area. The first interpoint encountered is between points 690 and 691 O, and has the value 24. The next interpoint, between 683 and 691 O, has 25, and so on (these figures can be derived from Map 6.16, p 143). The profile as a whole has a high point of 27 between points 678 NO and 686, and a low point of 16 between 679 SO and 781 NO (the profile actually shows 12, which is an error).

Line 1 is of particular interest, since it sets off the limits of 'gascon noir', as traditionally established by a single isogloss [œ] as the realization of Proto-Romance stressed /e/. In spite of this fact, however, it should be emphasized that the areas enclosed by the lines are not necessarily homogeneous dialect areas. In fact, as Séguy points out in the legend to Map 7.1, within the area

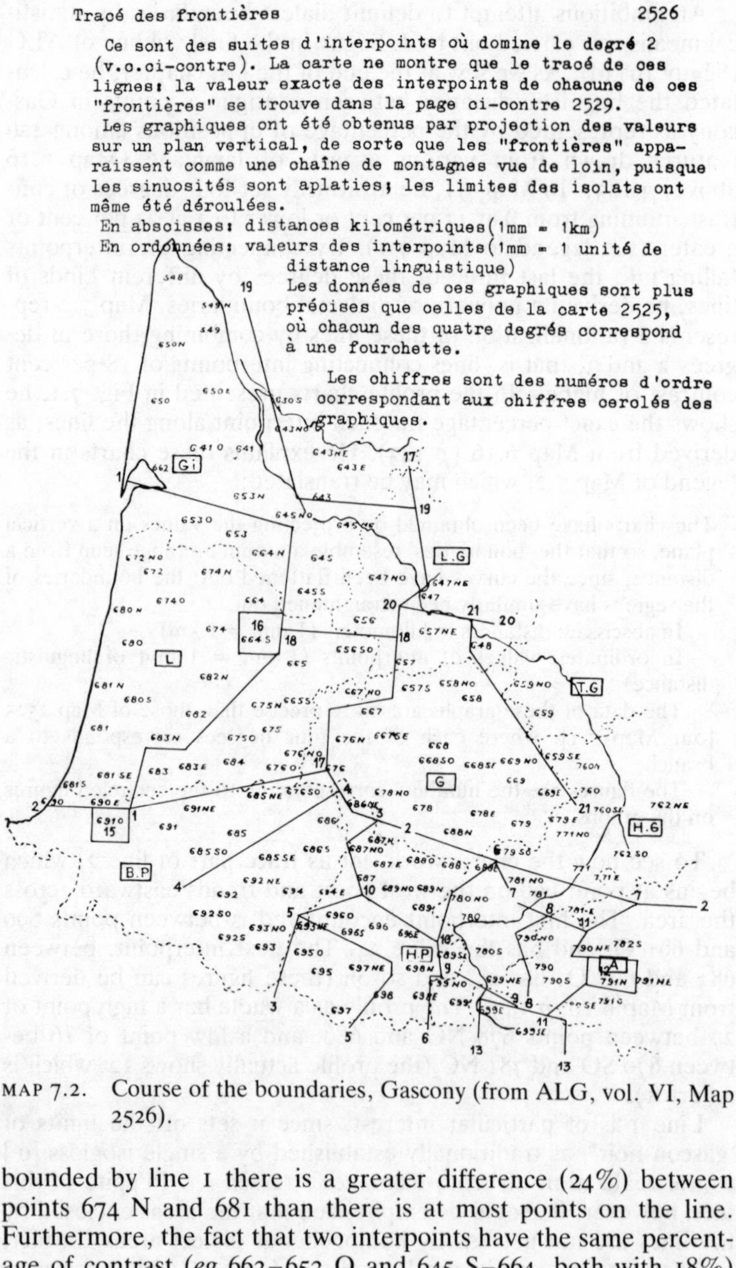

Tracé des frontières   2526

Ce sont des suites d'interpoints où domine le degré 2
(v.o.ci-contre). La carte ne montre que le tracé de ces
lignes: la valeur exacte des interpoints de chacune de ces
"frontières" se trouve dans la page ci-contre 2529.
     Les graphiques ont été obtenus par projection des valeurs
sur un plan vertical, de sorte que les "frontières" appa-
raissent comme une chaîne de montagnes vue de loin, puisque
les sinuosités sont aplaties; les limites des isolats ont
même été déroulées.
     En abscisses: distances kilométriques(1mm = 1km)
     En ordonnées: valeurs des interpoints(1mm = 1 unité de
                        distance linguistique)
          Les données de ces graphiques sont plus
          précises que celles de la carte 2525,
          où chacun des quatre degrés correspond
          à une fourchette.

          Les chiffres sont des numéros d'ordre
          correspondant aux chiffres cerclés des
          graphiques.

MAP 7.2. Course of the boundaries, Gascony (from ALG, vol. VI, Map
          2526).

bounded by line 1 there is a greater difference (24%) between
points 674 N and 681 than there is at most points on the line.
Furthermore, the fact that two interpoints have the same percentage of contrast (*eg* 662–653 O and 645 S–664, both with 18%)

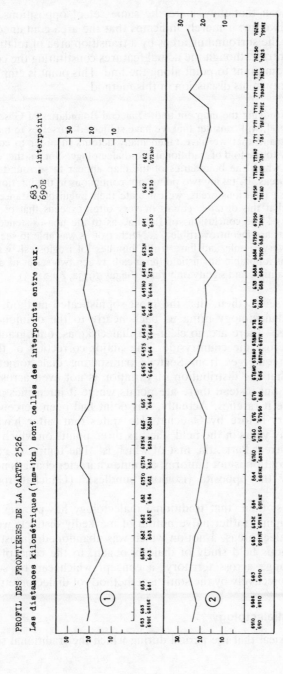

FIG. 7.I. Graphs of Gascon dialect boundaries (part of chart 2529, vol. VI, ALG)

does not mean that they share the same set of oppositions. A 'boundary' like line 1 merely indicates that the area contained is set off from the surrounding areas by a transition area of relatively strong contrast, though the actual features constituting the contrast vary from point to point along the line. This point is emphasized by Séguy in his discussion of this method:

> Some, on studying the map entitled 'Dialectal Boundaries of Gascon' [our Map 7.1], will consider that we have subjected ourselves to many contortions and that we have taken many détours in order to come back finally to the fold of traditional geo-dialectology. Not so: the 'dialect areas' which the boundaries of the map appear to surround are only false areas. If, taking two points not contiguous in the interior of one of these fallacious areas, we calculate their linguistic distance, it turns out that this distance equals or very often exceeds that of the boundary.... The conclusions of Lalanne as to the non-existence of dialect areas are incontrovertible.... Neither of us was able to see [in 1950] the very simple and bare truth: bundles [of isoglosses] signify that there is a notable linguistic difference between two series of contiguous localities, and signify only that. (Séguy 1973a, *pp* 22–3)

It would seem, then, that the most sophisticated methods of traditional dialectology bring us back nearly to the opinion of Gaston Paris – there are no clear-cut dialect areas, only gradual transition across the countryside. The major correction of that view, which emerges from Séguy's painstaking dialectometric studies, is that the distribution of variation is not even across a whole area, but instead there are points where it intensifies and others where it rarefies. Actually, this point had been perceived seventy years before by Gauchat. He states that 'after having worked many years in the field', he has three points on which he wishes to correct Paris, the first of which is: 'The tempo of geographical variation is not uniform; a sound-character changes now slowly, now the opposite (isogloss bundles).' (Gauchat 1903, *p* 399)

It appears, then, that traditional dialectology has progressed from the original rather naïve notion of markedly distinct, well-bounded dialect areas, a notion which was abandoned almost as soon as serious field study of dialects began, to the concept of variable change across territory, a concept which can be substantiated objectively by the statistical methods of dialectometry.

Structural dialectology

It is paradoxical that the period during which the traditional surveys and the resulting atlases were being produced was also the period of the development and flourishing of structuralism in linguistics. Saussure's *Course in General Linguistics*, published posthumously by his students in 1915, is commonly regarded as the starting point of a linguistic revolution, carried on by the Prague School in Europe and the American work of Boas, Sapir, Bloomfield and others in the period between the two World Wars. In brief, and at the risk of oversimplification, it may be said that structuralism shifted the emphasis from the individual linguistic elements to the systems of which they are parts, and from the history of the changes which the individual elements have undergone to the synchronic description of the overall organization of the language or dialect. As a recent writer has put it:

> The essential contribution of structural dialectology has been to stress the importance of comparing corresponding units in structured systems rather than studying the distribution of features whose status within the local system is not taken into account. (G. Sankoff 1973a, *p* 166)

Meanwhile the dialectologists continued their work in the tradition of Gilliéron and Jaberg, taking no account of the new ways of looking at language. The result was a profound split, in which each side virtually ignored the other. Uriel Weinreich, himself both a structuralist and a dialectologist, wrote in 1954:

> In linguistics today the abyss between structural and dialectological studies appears greater than it ever was. The state of disunity is not repaired if 'phoneme' and 'isogloss' occasionally do turn up in the same piece of research. Students continue to be trained in one domain at the expense of the other. Field work is inspired by one, and only rarely by both, interests. The stauncher adherents of each discipline claim priority for their own method and charge the others with 'impressionism' and 'metaphysics', as the case may be; the more pliant are prepared to concede that they are simply studying different aspects of the same reality. (Weinreich 1954, p 388)

In the title of the seminal article of which this is the opening paragraph, Weinreich asks the question: 'Is a structural dialectology possible?' He goes on to answer his own question by proposing some initial steps toward a reconciliation of the two fields which would amount to more than 'a compromise induced by fatigue'. His proposals, the discussion and amplification which they subsequently received from other dialectologist-linguists, as well as their application in subsequent dialect studies, make up the structural school of dialectology, which still is dominant, in spite of newer linguistic and dialectal theories.

At the heart of the opposition described by Weinreich is the structural view that individual linguistic items – particularly but not exclusively sounds – are significant not in themselves but in their position in one of the closed systems of the language. In this view, the set of individual sounds used in a given speech-variety is not a random collection but a system of oppositions; each phoneme is such because it contrasts in certain ways with all other phonemes and thus occupies a unique and indispensable position. In a language with 5 vowels, for example, there are 10 vowel contrasts; in a language with 6, there are 15. The addition of one vowel to a system thus basically changes the ways in which the system may be deployed in the lexicon of the language. Normally the effect of such a change is not simply a 20 per cent increase in the lexicon by the addition of a new set of words containing the new vowel, but a redistribution of the new six-vowel set across the vocabulary formerly fully represented by the five-vowel set. This is diachronically accomplished by phonemic splits and mergers, which produce major readjustments in the phonemic constituency of words. In effect, after a split the functions formerly divided into five sets are now divided into six, which means that there has been a redistribution affecting the original functions of some or all of the original five vowels. If a subsequent merger reduces the number of vowels to five again, depending on where the merger took place, the resulting system may or may not be the same as the original five-vowel system. Looking at the beginning and ending of the double change, it might appear that there had always been a five-vowel system, but that certain words had shifted from one phonemic set to another.

As a hypothetical example, let us assume a language with three front vowels, /i, e, æ/. Suppose a split, by which half the words containing /e/ come to have /ɛ/ instead, resulting in a system of four front vowels. Then suppose a merger, in which the /ɛ/ words come to have /æ/. We will again have a three front-vowel

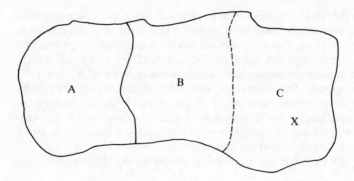

system, but with a different distribution of front vowels across the lexicon. And if the changes took place in only parts of the total territory of the language we might be left with three dialects, two with three front-vowel systems and one with four. In the sketch-map on *p* 160, suppose that both changes originate in the area of the capital city, X, that the first change, the split of /e/, spreads as far as the solid line, and that the second change, the merger of /ɛ/ and /æ/, extends only to the broken line. We will now have three dialects: A and C with three front vowels and B with four. The effect on certain words might be as follows:

Word	A	B	C
pin	/pin/	/pin/	/pin/
pain	/pen/	/pen/	/pen/
pane	/pen/	/pɛn/	/pæn/
pan	/pæn/	/pæn/	/pæn/

The traditional 'atomistic' dialectologist would find that the only 'interesting' word here is *pane*; his map would show it pronounced /pen/ in area A, /pɛn/ in area B, and /pæn/ in area C, while the other words are the same everywhere. The structuralist, on the other hand, would point out that system B is incommensurable with the other two, and that A and C, while superficially similar, are structurally different as a result of the split and merger.

This is a rather simple illustration, but it points up the essential dilemma of the dialectologist who attempts to interpret his material structurally: how can these different systems be compared? This dilemma has been vividly described by Ernst Pulgram:

> In Saussurean linguistics, it does not make much sense to speak of partly similar systems; there is either one system or more than one, and no part of one may be extracted and placed vis-à-vis its alleged counterpart in another, for in a structure where, in Meillet's phrase, *tout se tient*, the removal of a part from its surroundings changes both it and the whole to which it belongs. Accordingly, also the juxtaposition and comparison of several chronological stages of a dialect for the purpose of illuminating its history, even though this procedure eliminates the difficulty of having to deal with a gradually changing system, still contains some theoretical awkwardness, largely inherent in the notion of the history of a dialect (in the singular) as a succession of different structures whose synchronic differentness conflicts with the singularity produced by the diachronic view.... It has in fact been said that 'a strict application of structural principles excludes such classification [*ie* structural classification, or typology embracing different linguistic structures], and indeed any comparison of states of language

whatever. Since each state is a system consisting of members solely defined by their mutual relations, any two non-identical systems must necessarily be incommensurable, for no element in one can be identified with any element in the other.' (Pulgram 1964b, *p* 66; quote from Reid 1960, *p* 12)

The solution proposed for this dilemma by Weinreich is the DIASYSTEM, which he defines as 'a system of a higher level [constructed] out of the discrete and homogeneous systems that are derived from description and that represent each a unique formal organization of the substance of expression and content' (Weinreich 1954, *p* 390). Although he clearly indicates that the diasystem is constructed by the linguist, he claims that it has a certain psychological reality for 'bilingual (including "bidialectal") speakers'. He makes the point that the differences between dialects are of two kinds: 'differences of inventory and differences of distribution'. Clearly the latter has been the active area of traditional dialectology; he claims that the diasystem is the structural key to the former. Using his methodology, we would observe that the diasystem suggested in our example above would have not three but two members, since dialects A and C would share the same inventory, at least with regard to front vowels, which are all that are involved here. He would diagram the relationship between them as follows:

$$
\mathrm{A,B,C} \left/\!\!\left/ \frac{\mathrm{A,C}^{/i \,\sim\, e \,\sim\, æ/}}{\mathrm{B}^{/i \,\sim\, e \,\sim\, ε \,\sim\, æ/}} \right/\!\!\right/
$$

The double slashes here enclose a diasystem; the single slashes (as usual) indicate phonemes, and the wavy line is to be read 'contrasts with'. The whole diagram thus says, in effect: 'Dialects A, B, and C constitute a diasystem in which A and C have three short unround front vowels and B has four.' Weinreich uses this same diagram to show the relation between two dialects of Yiddish. Since nothing is said about phoneme incidence, alternative modes of displaying the same contrast in vowel inventory are possible, such, for instance, as the following:

$$
\mathrm{A,B,C} \left/\!\!\left/ /i/ \approx \frac{\mathrm{B}^{/e \,\sim\, ε/}}{\mathrm{A,C}^{/e/}} \approx /æ/ \right/\!\!\right/
$$

Here it is emphasized that the difference is found in the mid-front area, where B has two vowels and A, C only one. There is no way to decide the merits of these alternatives without consulting the incidence of the vowels in the lexicon, or, what amounts to the same thing, the phonological history of the two vowel systems (Moulton 1960, *p* 175, n.18).

As was very soon pointed out, the inadequacy of the diasystem as used by Weinreich is in its neglect of all phonological aspects except phonemic inventory. There is nothing to show in the diagrams above that A, B, and C are even dialects of the same language; they could be completely different languages. Or they could be dialects, as suggested by our hypothetical splits and mergers, whose history left them with contrasting word forms in spite of similar phoneme inventories. Moulton, in a particularly apposite example, cites two Swiss German dialects which have identical inventories of eleven short vowels, hence, if lexical incidence is disregarded, they not only are diasystemically related but phonemically identical. But when lexical correspondences are taken into account, they have only one 'fully shared diaphoneme' (Moulton 1960, *pp* 176–7). The diagrams are as follows:

1. With lexical correspondences disregarded:

$$\text{Lu, Ap} /\!\!/ \text{i} \approx e \approx \varepsilon \approx \text{æ} \approx a \approx \text{ɔ} \approx o \approx u \approx \text{ü} \approx \text{ö} \approx \text{ɔ́} /\!\!/$$

2. With lexical correspondences included:

$$\text{Lu,Ap} /\!\!/ \frac{\text{Lu}^{/i_0 \sim e_1 \sim \varepsilon_2 \sim æ_{3,4}/}}{\text{Ap}^{/i_{0,1} \sim e_{1,2} \sim \varepsilon_3 \sim æ_4/}} \approx /a_4/ \approx$$

$$\frac{\text{Lu}^{/ɔ_2 \sim o_1 \sim u_0 \sim u_0 \sim ö_1 \sim ɔ_2/}}{\text{Ap}^{/ɔ_2 \sim o_{1,2} \sim u_{0,1} \sim ü_{1,2} \sim ö_{1,2} \sim ɔ_2/}} /\!\!/$$

Here each subscript number indicates a set of lexical items. It is clear, for instance, that the set of words with /e/ in Ap is split between /e/ and /ɛ/ in Lu, and that the words with /æ/ in Lu are split between /ɛ/ and /æ/ in Ap. In a split and merger diagram, the situation with the front vowels is:

For Lu			For Ap		
Proto-vowel		*Lu*	*Proto-vowel*		*Ap*
i	———→	i	i	———→	i
e		e	e		e
ɛ		ɛ	ɛ		ɛ
æ	———→	æ	æ	———→	æ

There have been a split and a merger in each dialect, but in different parts of the system, and a complete lowering of one vowel (e > ɛ) in Lu. As a result, no front vowel in either dialect appears in the same set of words in the other, even though their inventories are the same. The same applies to the front round and back vowels. Only the low central /a/ is the same in both dialects. As Moulton puts it:

If we disregard lexical correspondences, it turns out that LU and AP share not a diasystem but the same identical phonemic system. A Luzerner and an Appenzeller will hardly agree to this. Nor will a dialectologist, since we are treating these two dialects as if they were unrelated. Yet if we treat them as related, and hence take lexical correspondences into consideration, we get a diasystem with just one fully shared diaphoneme: //a₄//. Since we are dealing here with two dialects hardly 50 miles apart, this makes the concept of the diasystem seem of questionable value in dialectology. (Moulton 1960, *p* 177)

This points up the fact that in making a structural comparison of two or more lects considered as dialects of the same language, we must take account of the fact that the relationship between them is a function of two factors, RELATEDNESS and LINGUISTIC DISTANCE. Both of these are variable functions which may range from zero to unity, and to a considerable extent, but not completely, they are complementary. Thus two lects whose relatedness is zero obviously cannot belong to the same language. If they share certain structural features (vowel inventory, for example), this is to be considered either a chance coincidence or the result of language contact and resultant borrowing. There are, for example, many languages, so far as we know totally unrelated, which have five-vowel systems /a e i o u/ like that of classical Latin. This is to be considered as typological similarity rather than dialectal relationship. Similarly, there are languages which share large sections of lexicon, such as the vocabulary of science in Western languages. This, of course, is the result of cultural rather than linguistic relatedness.

At the other extreme, two lects whose relatedness is unity must be considered not simply related but the same dialect. Their linguistic distance will normally turn out to be at or close to zero.

The question arises as to how these two factors are to be measured. As we saw in the last chapter, Séguy and other dialectometrists have devised techniques for measuring linguistic distance in terms of the percentage of items from a fixed set in which two dialects exhibit contrast. This is on the whole a synchronic approach, though Séguy included historical phonology as one of the five aspects of language he measured. It could as well be omitted. But there are two major flaws in the method. One is that, as we saw, it is very cumbersome, at least in its present form. This difficulty can ultimately be overcome by computerization, though, as Séguy has pointed out, the programming would be very complex (Séguy 1973a, *p* 13). Before the method can be used for areas of any size, the data will have to be processed in order to make input to the computer more practicable. Better still, it should be collected and recorded with computerization in mind from the beginning. Meanwhile others are experimenting with related techniques, particularly CLUSTER ANALYSIS, which provides an index of similarity (or, conversely, dissimilarity or distance) and groups related localities accordingly (Pellowe et al. 1972; Pellowe 1976; Shaw 1974, Jones 1979).

The other flaw in the dialectometric method, at least from the structural point of view, is that it is completely item-centered. Each of the 426 items used by Séguy is equal to each of the others in the final tally, so that the method does not directly indicate structural similarity or distance. This could presumably be corrected by weighting the items, but this would be both difficult and arbitrary.

When we turn to the measurement of relatedness, it immediately becomes apparent that the diachronic dimension must be introduced. The essential criterion of relatedness is genetic; two languages or dialects are related if they can be shown to be descended from a common original. Their divergence, *ie* their degree of non-relatedness, is presumably to be measured by the different changes they have undergone since the hypothetically homogeneous language or dialect from which they derive. The danger here is, of course, circularity, since normally the historical linguist makes use of these differences to establish the nature and sequence of the changes which have occurred. The problem is admirably summarized by the Italian dialectologist Giuseppe Francescato:

> If we wish to study linguistic systems according to a *diachronic* point of view, we cannot do other than compare the *monochronic* descriptions of two or more systems. But linguistic systems are not – as a rule – ever isolated; they always can be interpreted as members of a *diasystem*. That is why *diachronic* investigation will have to behave in two ways or by means of two procedures: a) starting from an initial system interpreted on the descriptive (*monochronic*) level, one observes the variations successively encountered in its progressive differentiation into the various member systems of a diasystem (e.g. the Latin system which differentiated into the various systems of the Romance languages); on the other hand, b) by comparing on the *synchronic* level the various member systems of a diasystem, one goes back from their variations to the successive intermediate stages which have differentiated the diasystem into its component systems (that is, from dialect to subdialects) to get back, as far as possible, to the original system. (Francescato 1965b, *p* 1016)

It is clear that, in the view of Francescato, as of others (*eg* Pulgram 1964a, 1964b), the idea of the diasystem has been expanded from the original simple synchronic structural comparison described by Weinreich to a much more complicated notion of relatedness, involving diachronic as well as synchronic information, and ultimately (in the view of some, at least) coming to include the linguistic content of the term *language*, without the social, cultural, political, literary, and other connotations of the term. In Francescato's words:

> Constructing a 'diasystem' means, in fact, not only comparing two or more dialectal structures which apparently reveal a more or less strict parallelism, but also recognizing that this parallelism has validity in terms of paradigmatic as well as in terms of syntagmatic structure: in other words, not only the inventory and distribution of phonemes have to reflect certain types of congruence, but a similar congruence is expected to be manifest also in word structure. . . . In addition, up to this time, there has usually been at least a tendency to leap from the purely synchronic comparison of dialectal data in terms of the diasystem to the diachronic (or 'historical') interpretation of them. In this sense, at least in my opinion, the role of a diasystem consists not only in asserting the validity on a higher level of whatever sort of unity can be found in the dialect structures involved, but at the same time in enhancing and suggesting their derivation from a common ancestral unit, and their development along similar lines. This parallel development is the fundament upon which all explanation of the similar, or identical patterning of a relevant amount of the structural units under consideration is based, independent of the actual divergence of their possible concrete realization. (Francescato 1965a, *p* 485)

It will have been noted that the discussion of the diasystem has dealt with dialects as linguistic systems without relation to their geographical distribution. In Moulton's view, there are three dimensions involved in dialect study: the historical, the geographical, and the structural. Traditional dialectologists were concerned with a two-dimensional, historical–geographical approach. The structuralists concerned themselves with a third dimension, the structural, at first in itself (Weinreich) and then, as we have seen, joined with the historical into another two-dimensional approach, the historical–structural. In Moulton's view, 'the time now seems ripe to combine these two movements and produce a three-dimensional approach to the study of language: historical–geographical–structural' (Moulton 1968b, *p* 574). In a series of articles produced during the 1960s, he used the rich materials of the *Sprachatlas der deutschen Schweiz* (SDS) to attempt this synthesis (Moulton 1960, 1961a, 1961b, 1962, 1963, 1964, 1965, 1968a, 1968b). The material of these articles is too rich and the treatment too detailed for full discussion here; suffice it to say that they represent original and ingenious application of structural models to an area of great dialectal interest. The dominant notions in his work are the pressure of languages and dialects to develop symmetrical phonemic systems, and the

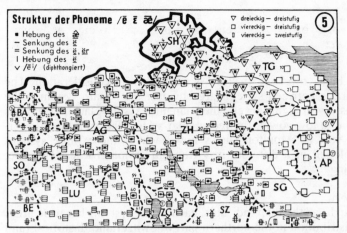

MAP 7.3. Non-high long front unround vowels in northern Switzerland (from Goossens 1969, Map 5, after Moulton 1963, Map 4).

related tendency for phonemes and their allophones to distribute themselves at even intervals across 'phonological space', conceived of in articulatory terms. Moulton attempts to devise maps to illustrate the geographical dimension of these historical—structural notions, so as to bring them into accord with his three-dimensional view of language study.

Map 7.3 represents one of Moulton's most ambitious attempts to display linguistic data of all three sorts: the structural, the historical, and the geographical. It is a very complicated map (capable, as we shall see, of some simplification), but it can be read without great difficulty by the specialist who understands the system on which it is based. For full understanding, one must go to Moulton's own descriptions, which are too long to quote here (Moulton 1963, 1968b). What follows here is simply enough to indicate the kinds of information recorded and the types of symbols used.

Structure

The map deals with the mid and low long vowels of Swiss German and the development of the front unround set of these vowels from Middle High German (MHG). The major structural point is the 'shape' of the long vowel system as a whole. Moulton recognizes three types, the triangular, the 3-level rectangular, and the 2-level rectangular, symbolized respectively by ▽, □, ◻. They consist of the following vowels (the traditional Germanic symbols used by Moulton are here changed to their IPA equivalents):

▽			☐			◻		
eː	øː	oː	eː	øː	oː	eː	øː	oː
ɛː	œː	ɔː	ɛː	œː	ɔː	ɛː	œː	ɔː
	aː			æː	aː		æː	aː

The high vowel set /iː yː uː/ is omitted from consideration. The contrasts between systems are obvious: the square system is the fullest, with eight vowels; the triangular system, lacking /æː/, has only one low vowel; the rectangular system lacks all three lower-mid vowels. Moulton shows how each of these three systems developed in a different way from an asymmetrical MHG one, lacking /ɔː/.

History

Though, as the map indicates, each of the systems has wide areas of distribution in the northern part of Switzerland, historical (and lexical) evidence shows that the local representatives of each differ widely in the sound changes that have produced them and hence in the incidence of phonemes in their lexicons. The following is a somewhat simplified account of these developments and the way they are symbolized on the map.

In the first place, Moulton assumes a homogeneous Alemannic version of Middle High German, with nine short vowels and eight long vowels. Since this map deals only with low and mid front vowels, the proto-vowels concerned are these five:

short	long
e	eː
ɛ	
æ	æː

The developments that have taken place are of four sorts: (1) unchanged transmission, (2) lengthening of short vowels, (3) raising or lowering of vowels, (4) diphthongization. Specifically:

1. MHG /eː/ > /eː/ throughout the region.
2. MHG /æː/ > /eː ~ ɛː ~ æː/ in different regions.
3. Lengthened MHG /e/ > /eː/ everywhere.
4. Lengthened MHG /ɛ/ > /eː ~ ɛː ~ æː/ in different regions, with different distribution before /r/.
5. Lengthened MHG /æ/ > /ɛː ~ æː/ in different regions, with different distribution before /r/.
6. Modern /eː/ from whatever source is in some places diphthongized to /eːⁱ/.

The symbols Moulton uses for these various developments are indicated in the legend in the upper left corner of Map 7.3. The raising of /æː/ is indicated by a small black square; if it is in the center of the figure the result is /ɛː/; if at the top, it is /eː/. Absence of the square indicates that /æː/ remains unchanged. Lowering of lengthened /ɛː/ to /æː/ is indicated by a horizontal line through the symbol, or by a double line if it also occurs before /r/. Raising of lengthened /ɛː/ to /eː/ is indicated by a vertical line through the symbol. Diphthongization of /eː/, which occurs only in the south central part of the area, is indicated by a wedge above the triangle or rectangle.

It is thus possible to derive from each local symbol information about the general shape of the long vowel system, the specific low and mid front long vowels, and their MHG sources. It is hard to imagine much more structural–historical–geographical information crowded into a single map. Yet in a map in a later article (1968b), Moulton does include more information, first by extending the map to cover the whole of Switzerland, and second by including some phonetic detail by means of additional symbols. He admits that this last was in some sense a mistake: 'the map is misleading in all those cases where, along with phonemic structure, I have tried to give some phonetic detail' (p 590). In an earlier article, however, he did use allophonic detail to show that the phonetic realizations of phonemes tend to move towards areas where the neighboring phonemes allow more 'phonological space' (Moulton 1962).

One fault with Map 7.3 has been pointed out by the Belgian dialectologist Jan Goossens. He claims that, though Moulton's map ingeniously includes all the relevant information, it is unclear because the symbols chosen are arbitrary when they could have been iconic. As he puts it:

> Although the *Bezugskarte* [relational map] includes the whole diasystem involved, except for the lengthened æ before r, it seems to me to have one fault: the symbols are not sufficiently clear. The choice of a vertical rectangle to indicate a two-level rectangular system is arbitrary. Although the position in the symbol of the small black square to indicate the open grade in the development of MHG æː is not arbitrary, the choice of this square itself for the development of æː is arbitrary and it is moreover not clear why this square is not placed in the lower part of the symbol to show the realisation /æː/. The choice of vertical lines for raising and horizontal for lowering of lengthened ɛ is likewise purely conventional. The correct interpretation of a square with two horizontal lines demands a bit of deductive skill. The fact that close /eː/ everywhere has MHG /eː/ and lengthened /e/ as sources must be figured out from each symbol. Of course a symbol is by nature a conventional marker, but the bringing together of several arbitrarily

chosen symbols in combined markers ought not to be carried beyond the limits of clarity. It appears to us that Moulton in this respect has gone too far; his map appears too 'abstract'. (Goossens 1969, *pp* 40–1)

Goossens, himself a noteworthy experimenter in structural mapping, proposes a new map for Moulton's data, using 'less arbitrarily chosen markers to build clearer symbols, which are at the same time just as complete in their presentation of the relationship of the dialect systems to an overall relation-system' (*p* 41). He offers Map 7.4, in which he has used the isogloss method to keep the map from becoming overcrowded. His basic symbol is a rectangle, with the present phonemes within solid lines in the center and the MHG sources within dotted lines at the sides, the lengthened short vowels on the left and the long vowels on the right.

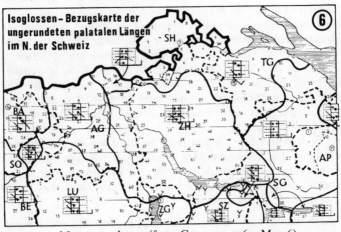

MAP 7.4.   Map 7.3 redrawn (from Goossens 1969, Map 6).

| | Present | |
MHG	dialects	MHG
e	eː	eː
ɛ	ɛː	
æ	æː	æː

Arrows from the sides toward the center indicate the sound changes, and the solid isogloss lines on the map show the range of each distinctive pattern. The heavy line at the bottom of the pattern indicates whether the system is triangular or rectangular. It is not necessary to have separate symbols to distinguish two-level systems from three-level ones, since this is done by the number of squares in the center area. This map does indeed seem easier to read because of the iconic nature of the symbols, and it does indeed include all the information of Moulton's more crowded and 'abstract' one (except for the special development of MHG lengthened /ɛ/ before /r/). But Goossens modestly admits that 'it is obvious that the last word on the cartographic technique of preparing relational maps has not yet been spoken. There must be more extensive experimentation'. (*p* 41)

It is clear that the work of structural dialectologists like Weinreich, Moulton, Goossens, and others has gone a long way toward bringing about the reconciliation described by Dahlstedt:

> I would say that the antagonism between dialectology and structural linguistics has now, at the end of the sixties, been settled to the satisfaction of both parties. Structuralists no longer demand that the whole phonological structure of every dialect be fixed in monographs before any mapping of linguistic expression phenomena is undertaken. They have also learned that the concept of *langue* as a static structure *où tout se tient* is an abstraction, fruitful within certain limits, but all too narrow and dogmatic in a wider sociolinguistic perspective. Dialectologists on their part have accepted phonemic checking in their recording of dialectal materials as routine, even though, to be sure, most of the work of applying the benefits of structuralism not only to phonology but also to other levels of linguistics, e.g. morphology, syntax, and semantics, remains to be done. (Dahlstedt 1970, *pp* 162–3)

Many dialectologists, working on problems in various languages, have taken up the structural model and are continuing to use it. Meanwhile, a new revolution in linguistic theory as fundamental as that of Saussure and the structuralists has opened up new modes of dealing with dialectal variation.

Generative dialectology

The generative school of linguistic theory, which in one form or another dominates the field today, may be said to have begun in the late 1950s as an extension and modification of structuralism, especially in the field of syntax. Chomsky's *Syntactic Structures* (1957) explored various grammatical models and came to the conclusion that a complete grammar – one that can account for all sentences of a language, both actual and potential – has to be both GENERATIVE and TRANSFORMATIONAL. The first of these terms means, essentially, that the grammatical explanation of a linguistic construction should be in terms of an ordered set of processes by which more complex structures can be derived from simpler ones according to established rules, rather than by the arrangement of subassemblies of categorized parts into larger assemblies, which had been the constituent structure approach of structural syntax (as in *eg* Wells 1947; Nida 1960, *pp* xi–lviii). The second term means that some constructions are best explained as remodelings of generated structures according to recognized rules of rearrangement and deletion. There has been much discussion of these two principles, especially the latter, and much alteration of the original theories. Since the impact of syntactic theory on dialectology has been relatively slight, we do not need to trace the history of these complex developments here. What should be emphasized are certain fundamental principles which are openly or tacitly adhered to by all generative schools, however widely they may differ in details.

One of these is the notion of the native speaker's COMPE-TENCE. By this is meant the internalized knowledge about his language which allows the speaker to produce and understand utterances whether or not he has encountered them before. It is often contrasted with PERFORMANCE, the body of actual utterances the speaker produces (Chomsky 1965, *p* 4), which is only an imperfect reflection of competence, since it is subject to all kinds of distractions and interference. Traditional dialectology certainly believed in competence: its whole methodology as we have described it in preceding chapters was based on the conviction that the dialect speaker is an authority about his dialect and the only reliable source of information about it. But the traditional approach did not allow for slippage between competence and performance, as can be seen from Gilliéron's insistence on the first response as the correct one (which Séguy later called 'the Gilliéronian myth of the *"instanté"'* – Séguy 1973b, *p* 34), and his 'iron rule' – 'Le rédacteur ne corrige pas l'enquêteur.'

A second important part of generative theory is the conception of the roles played by the various components of competence: lexicon, syntax, semantics, and phonology. Our concern is particularly with phonology, whose function is to convert the relatively abstract output of syntax and lexicon into 'surface structures' realizable phonetically as speech. The generative approach inherits from the structural the analysis of continuous speech into discrete segments, even though no workable procedure can be found for precisely making such a division (Halle 1964, *pp* 324–5). Unlike the phonemes of structural phonology, which represent contrastive units realized phonetically as allophones, the generative segments, called SYSTEMATIC PHONEMES, are more abstract. They often have to undergo a series of rule-governed changes before they reach phonetic realization. These changes incorporate much of what was called MORPHOPHONEMICS in structural theory.

Thirdly, the whole system of systematic phonemes, phonological rules, and surface phonetics is tied to a system of DISTINCTIVE FEATURES, under which each segment can be represented as composed of positive or negative values (*ie* presence or absence) of various features or characteristics. These features are ultimately phonetic, but there is much disagreement as to how many and what they are, and whether they are based on acoustic analysis of the speech signals, or upon the articulatory maneuvers necessary to produce them. Various sets of features have been suggested, and there is still no consensus on a definitive set. We shall not here enter into this controversial area. In general, in the interests of simplicity, we will avoid the use of features. When it is necessary or convenient to use them, the set given in Appendix A will be employed.

The components of the phonology, then, are the following:
1. A set of UNDERLYING LEXICAL UNITS – morphemes and words – which are composed of strings of systematic phonemes, each of which comprises a set of positive and negative values for the relevant distinctive features.
2. A set of MORPHEME STRUCTURE CONDITIONS (or CONSTRAINTS) which control the ways in which the phonemes may be composed in the lexical items. They play a similar role to phonotactics in structural analysis.
3. A set of PHONOLOGICAL RULES which govern the changes which the underlying forms must undergo to reach the systematic phonetic level.
4. A set of PHONETIC RULES, which specify the nuances of actual pronunciation.

Ideally, all speakers of a language share the same rules and forms on all of these levels. Their lexicons contain the same lexical items, having the same meanings and grammatical privileges and the same systematic phonemic shape, subject to the same morpheme structure conditions. They have the same phonological and phonetic rules, leading to the same surface structures and ultimately the same pronunciations. But of course this is only an ideal; as we have seen throughout this book, variation is everywhere. The problem for the generative approach, as for the others, is how much and what sorts of variation are possible between what can still be recognized as versions of the same language.

Confining ourselves to phonology, it is clear that differences between lects can occur at various levels. They may involve the number and feature consistency of the systematic phonemes – what we have been calling the inventory. As we saw in Chapter 2, Catford found that the number of vowels in Scots ranges from eight to twelve. Although he was dealing with structural (or, in Chomsky's terminology, 'taxonomic') phonemes, it is clear that unless the phonological rules involve complicated splits and mergers, these units will appear in some form or other at the systematic level. Or differences may involve the phonemic constituency of the underlying forms (in Moulton's term, the 'incidence'): those who pronounce *tomato* with [eː] or [ei] in the second syllable have a different underlying vowel from those who pronounce the word with [ɑː] or [æ] in that position. More commonly the differences involve the phonological rules: their presence or absence, their form, and their ordering. A speaker who frequently drops the final [d] from words like *find, hand, ground* has an optional or context-governed deletion rule which is not present in the phonology of a speaker who always retains the final [d]. Or two speakers may have the same rules but in different order. If A pronounces *nothing* as [nʌθɪn] while B says [nʌθɪŋ], both are starting from an underlying form that ends in /ng/, and both have the same two rules, one for assimilating the /n/ to [ŋ] before velar stops, and one for dropping the /g/ from final /ng/ in unstressed syllables. But for A the *g*-dropping rule comes before the assimilating rule, thus rendering that rule inoperative in this case, while B has the rules in opposite order, so that the /n/ gets changed to [ŋ] before the /g/ is dropped. There are also those who lack the *g*-dropping rule altogether and who thus say [nʌθɪŋg], and others who have a rule devoicing the /g/, producing [nʌθɪŋk], or if, like some Cockneys, they also have a rule changing intervocalic /θ/ to [f] they will end up with [nʌfɪŋk]. Finally, there may be more or less subtle nuances in the phonetic realization rules, producing minor differences in pronunciation which may go wholly unobserved except by the phonetician.

In general, the feeling is that the higher up in the phonological process the differences appear, the more serious the variations will be. In fact, some have maintained that if two or more lects are to be considered dialects of the same language, they must start from the same systematic phonemic inventory and the same underlying forms, leaving the differences to be accounted for by variations in rule inventory, rule form, and rule ordering (Agard 1971). As Rudolph Troike puts it:

> [The generative model] has a distinct advantage over static structural comparisons of phonemic and allophonic inventories in that it relates all dialects directly to a single underlying diaphonemic system, on the basis of which they may be compared as to number, scope, order, and form of the rules needed to derive their distinctive phonological characteristics. (Troike 1971, p 342)

The problem with this assumption is that there are no strict limitations on how abstract the underlying forms can be or how complicated and even counter-intuitive the rules. This problem has been much discussed (see especially Kiparsky 1973). Troike himself goes to some length constructing rules to handle an underlying fricative /x/ in English in words like *right* in order to give Scots, the only variety of English which has this sound in its surface phonetics, a position in the 'single underlying diaphonemic system' of English. Subsequently Chomsky and Halle found reason to include /x/ in English underlying forms even without consideration of Scots (Chomsky and Halle 1968, pp 233–4). Certainly the criterion of common underlying forms cannot be used without circularity as a defining test for the distinction between dialect and language if the linguist is free to elaborate the rules to whatever complexity is required to change a single underlying form into quite contrastive forms. Under these conditions, it could be demonstrated that all Romance languages are merely dialects of a common language (as, of course, they were at one stage of history). This seems to some dialectologists to be a *reductio ad absurdum* that breeds skepticism about the whole theory of generative phonology, especially as applied to dialectology. But this need not be so. It can be shown that a reasonably conservative application of generative phonology can clarify and explain dialect phenomena in a more elegant and satisfying way than the traditional or structural approaches. In this sense, Troike's claim is justified:

> Given a generative model, the strategy of dialect comparison can shift from a fixation on superficial phonetic differences to an examination of the underlying, 'deeper' structural unity which ties the dialects together into a single overall phonemic pattern. The nature of dialect differences can also be assessed in a more significant way, e.g. by asking whether certain dialects do indeed possess a different phonological system on a deep level, or whether differences between them are merely in the number, form, or ordering of realization rules. In short, with the use of a generative model for dialect description, a structural dialectology is indeed possible. (Troike 1971, p 330)

As an example of how a generative approach can clarify, if not explain, dialect variation, let us consider the phenomenon of final consonant cluster reduction in English, specifically the dropping of the final consonant in clusters consisting of [s] followed by a voiceless stop, *ie* [-sp, -st, -sk]. This is a frequent phenomenon in rapid speech throughout the English-speaking world, especially before words beginning with a consonant. In careful speech, the [t] or [k] is preserved in phrases like *post box, last chance, desk top*, but in natural speech these will become [pɔ́ːsbɒ̀ks], [làsčáns], [dɛ́strɒ̀p]. The incidence of this phenomenon varies greatly, reaching an extreme in American so-called Black English, where the final stops may appear to be completely lost. Further complications arise with noun genitives and plurals and verb third person singular forms, where there is a sibilant suffix added to the word.

Let us first consider the plural form *desks*. In most varieties of English this will be [dɛsks] in careful speech and either [dɛsː] or [dɛs] in rapid speech. A generative approach would account for these forms as follows:

The underlying form is /desk + z/, where + indicates morpheme boundary and /z/ is the plural morpheme. The following phonological rules apply:

1. Suffix Adjustment. /z/ goes to [-ɪz] after sibilants and to [-s] after other voiceless obstruents. Without going into the technical formalities of writing phonological rules, this may be written:

$$/z/_{\text{suffix}} \longrightarrow \begin{cases} \text{ɪz} & / & [\text{+sibilant}] \underline{\quad} & \text{(a)} \\ \text{s} & / & \begin{bmatrix} \text{+cons} \\ \text{-voice} \end{bmatrix} \underline{\quad} & \text{(b)} \\ \text{z} & & & \text{(c)} \end{cases}$$

The parts of this rule are disjunctive and ordered; that is, only one of them can apply in any given case, and they are applied in top-to-bottom order. Therefore the input to the rule is first examined to see if it has a sibilant before the plural ending. If so, it fits part (a) of the rule, and the suffix is rewritten as [-ɪz] and the derivation moves on to the next rule; if not, the form is examined to see if it complies with the input conditions for part (b) of this rule – a final voiceless consonant other than a sibilant – which would change the suffix to [-s]. If this, too, does not apply, the remainder case applies and the suffix is realized as [-z]. Obviously irregular plurals like *men, teeth, sheep, strata*, etc., have to be excluded from this derivation entirely, since they do not have the /z/-plural suffix.

2. Final Cluster Simplification. Morpheme final /p t k/ are deleted after /s/:

$$\begin{bmatrix} -\text{continuant} \\ -\text{voice} \end{bmatrix} \longrightarrow \emptyset \;/\!/\text{s}/\!\underline{\qquad} +$$

3. Degemination. Long (double) consonants are shortened:

$$\begin{bmatrix} +\text{consonantal} \\ +\text{length} \end{bmatrix} \longrightarrow [-\text{length}]$$

Given these rules and the underlying form /desk + z/, the derivation of the three standard forms of *desks* would be as follows:

Underlying Form	desk + z	desk + z	desk + z
1. Suffix Adjustment	desk + [s]	desk + [s]	desk + [s]
2. Cluster Simplification	---------	des + [s]	des + [s]
3. Degemination	---------	------	des
Surface Form	[dɛsks]	[dɛsː]	[dɛs]

In some varieties of Black English, however, the plural form is [dɛ́sɪz]. There are two ways in which this can be accounted for: RULE REORDERING and RESTRUCTURING OF THE UNDERLYING FORM. By reordering the rules so as to place Cluster Simplification ahead of Suffix Adjustment, we get the following derivation:

Underlying Form	desk + z
2. Cluster Simplification	des + /z/
1. Suffix Adjustment	des + [ɪz]
Surface Form	[dɛ́sɪz]

If, however, the final /k/ never appears at the surface in any mode of speech or any context, we can assume that the underlying form has been restructured by dropping the /k/ completely. The only rule now needed for the plural is Suffix Adjustment:

Underlying Form	des + z
1. Suffix Adjustment	des + [ɪz]
Surface Form	[dɛ́sɪz]

A more complicated situation is presented in British dialects by the word *posts*, which was elicited in the SED in the form *gateposts* in response to question IV.3.2. Parallel to the situation described above in *desks* we would expect the careful form [poːsts] and the optional fast-speech forms [poːsː] and [poːs], and indeed all these appear. But there are also two other forms: [poːstɪz] and [poːsɪz]. The three irregular plural forms have regional distribution, as shown in Map 7.5. In the areas of the map marked off by isoglosses, the form given is the prevalent one, though there may be scattered instances of the others or of other words. In the areas outside the isogloss boundaries, either the dominant form is the standard [poːsts] or another lexical form, such as the northern *stoops, stubs, stumps*, or else some other non-indicative form,

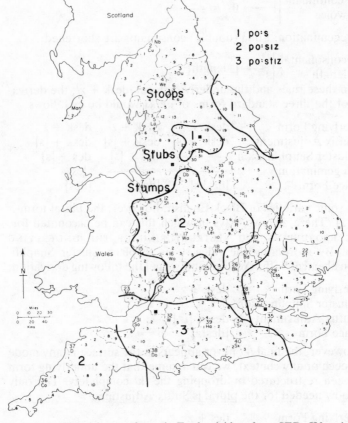

MAP 7.5.   Plural forms of *post* in England (data from SED, IV.3.2).

such as the singular, was given. The most homogeneous areas are
the [poːstɪz] region in the central South and the two [poːsɪz]
areas in the central Midlands and the Southwest. No distinction is
made on the map between [poːsː] and [poːs]. The frequencies of
the irregular plural forms (out of 314 localities surveyed) are:

poːsɪz   60
poːstɪz 46
poːs   34
poːsː   8

The last two figures are suspect, however, since there is reason to
believe that not all fieldworkers distinguished between long and
short final [s] in their transcriptions. Henceforth these two will be

taken together. The realizations of the stem vowel [oː] include a large variety of vowels and diphthongs, and the vowel of the syllabic suffix may be [ə] but these differences, while phonologically interesting, are irrelevant to the morphological point we are considering here.

Fortunately singular forms of the word were elicited from most localities by another question, IV.3.3, which asked the name of the timber to which the gate is attached (most commonly *hanging post*). Since this question immediately follows the *gateposts* one, we are sure of getting the response of the same informant to both. The singulars are all either [poːst] or [poːs], indicating the variable (or optional or stylistic) application of the Cluster Simplification rule. Each singular form is paired with each of the plural forms in rather random fashion, as follows:

Singular	Plural	Frequency
1. poːst	poːsɪz	30
2. poːs	poːsɪz	27
3. poːst	poːstɪz	38
4. poːs	poːstɪz	5
5. poːst	poːs	17
6. poːs	poːs	20

The derivations of some of these forms present some interesting problems. In sets 1 and 5, where the singular is [poːst] with the final [t], the plurals [poːs] and [poːsɪz] can be derived by the same set of rules used above for *desks*, with Suffix Adjustment preceding Cluster Simplification in [poːs] and following it in [poːsɪz]. But where both singular and plural lack the [t], as in sets 2 and 6, the question arises as to whether we are to assume a restructured underlying form without the final consonant, as suggested above for Black English [dɛsɪz]. This is quite feasible for set 2, since the Suffix Adjustment rule would operate normally to produce the 'regular' plural [poːsɪz]. But for set 6, where both singular and plural are [poːs] (the plural perhaps actually [poːsː]), it would require a major change in the Suffix Adjustment rule to produce the suffix [-s] rather than [-iz] after a final underlying /s/. The word would have to be listed among the irregular nouns with no plural suffix, such as *sheep*. Of the three possibilities, the best choice seems to be to postulate underlying /poːst/, even though the final /t/ does not reach the surface in either the singular or the plural. It certainly would not be justified to assume total loss of the final /t/ without further evidence, such as might be provided by words like *postal* and *post office*, where the underlying /t/, if present, would be likely to appear before the following vowel. Unfortunately these words were not elicited in the survey.

The form [poːsti z] is more difficult. It cannot be derived in any way by the rules so far stated. Instead, it seems to indicate a revised version of part (a) of the Suffix Adjustment rule, allowing the influence of the /s/ to extend over the final /t/ to require the [-ɪz] suffix instead of the expected [-s]. The rule can be written:

$$/z/_{\text{suffix}} \rightarrow \begin{cases} \text{ɪz} & / \text{ [+sibilant] (/t/)} \text{——(a)} \\ \text{s} & / \begin{bmatrix} \text{+cons} \\ \text{-voice} \end{bmatrix}\text{——} \quad \text{(b)} \\ \text{z} & \text{(c)} \end{cases}$$

where the parentheses around /t/ indicate that the rule applies whether or not a /t/ comes between the sibilant and the suffix. Since this part of the rule comes before part (b), which assigns [s] after a voiceless non-sibilant consonant, it removes words ending in sibilant + /t/ from the input to that rule. Unfortunately, no nouns ending in /-sk/ or /-sp/ were elicited, so we do not know whether the revised Suffix Adjustment rule is limited to final /t/ or extends to the other voiceless stops after /s/.

For set 3 in the list above, this rule would simply replace the original Suffix Adjustment rule. For set 4, the Cluster Simplification rule would also have to be altered to allow it to apply to the singular but to prevent its application to plural [poːstɪz], perhaps by limiting it to word-final or pre-consonantal positions:

$$\begin{bmatrix} \text{-continuant} \\ \text{-voice} \end{bmatrix} \rightarrow \emptyset \Big/ \text{ s——} \begin{cases} \# \\ \text{(+) [+cons]} \end{cases}$$

This would also produce *postman* [póːsmən] and *postal* [póːstəl]. These are indeed the forms reported by Bertil Widén, who collected material for his monograph on the dialect of Dorset in 1939 and 1946 (Widén 1949). He also reports plural forms of *chest, coast, ghost*, and *nest*, as well as *post*, with a syllabic suffix. In contrast to the data from SED, collected only ten years later (1956), he shows a suffix [-əs], rather than the [-ɪz] reported from Dorset by SED. Widén believes that the syllabic suffix is an innovation in this area, with an epenthetic vowel inserted 'to avoid a cumbersome sequence of consonants' (*p* 72). He further speculates:

[ə] before [s] in the group of nouns ending in -*st* in the singular may be secondary and have developed after the voicing of -*s* in the M[iddle] E[nglish] ending -*es*, and Do. -[əs] was consequently unaffected by this change. All the remaining words with final [-əs, -is] have a medial [z] which may have given rise to a dissimilation resulting in final [s]. (Widén 1949, p 85)

To explain the discrepancy between Widén's data and those of SED we would have to assume a voicing of the final [s] after 1946, perhaps by analogy with the [-ɪz] suffix on other words. His theory of the origin of the disyllabic forms is in line with the distribution patterns of Map 7.5. The strong concentrations of [poːstɪz] and [poːsɪz] in the Midlands and South very much resemble focal areas, which are usually centers of innovation, while the scattered concentrations of [poːs ~ poːsː] look like relic areas, where older forms survive. It is thus unlikely that the forms with [-əs] or [-ɪz] are survivals of the Middle English syllabic suffix.

So far as I have been able to determine, the [poːstɪz] form does not occur in American Black English, which has either the 'standard' [poːs] or the expected [póːsɪz]. The prevalent pronunciation in this dialect of *post office* as [póːsɔ̀fɪs] is presumptive evidence that the /t/ has been completely lost from the underlying form.

This illustration has been discussed in some detail in order to establish several important points about the dialectal application of generative phonology:

1. In order to establish underlying forms and phonological rules unequivocally, it is not sufficient to elicit single words in citation form, after the manner of traditional dialectology. Instead, forms must be elicited in various contexts and probably in various styles, in order to determine the exact-conditions under which rules operate and the degree of variation between various styles of speaking. In short, the confidence of traditional dialectologists that a sufficiently large collection of lexical items chosen primarily for lexical reasons and usually produced in citation form would supply enough information to permit phonological analysis of a dialect certainly does not extend to generative phonology.

2. The 'same form' in different localities or even in different positions in the same idiolect may be the same only on the surface; the derivations may reveal that identical surface forms are arrived at by different processes. The form [poːs] in the singular, for example, derives either from underlying /poːs/ transmitted without change, or from underlying /poːst/ which has undergone Cluster Simplification. The same form in the plural, however, may derive from underlying /post + z/ which has undergone Suffix Adjustment, Cluster Simplification, and Degemination.

3. Many rules do not apply automatically and without exception; speakers often vary the application because of some difference in the situation under which words are produced. For exam-

ple, at many of the localities where the SED formal question elicited the singular [poːst], the incidental material from the same
informant also shows [poːs], and vice versa. Likewise the word
doorposts, which occasionally appeared in response to question
V.I.II, 'What do you call these uprights [*ie* jambs]?' often shows
a different plural form from that appearing in *gateposts*. We can
only conclude that while most phonological performance goes
according to fixed rules, there are areas of variation not only between different speakers of a given dialect, but within the performance of a single speaker. This question will be further dealt
with in our next chapter.

4. It is not necessary that either the phonological rules or their
ordering in synchronic derivations follow precisely the diachronic
changes that may be proved or postulated, though this is very
often – perhaps usually – the case. As we saw above, Widén believed the syllabic plural suffix of *posts* in Dorset to be a recent
development arising from the insertion of a vowel to break up the
awkward cluster [sts]. This may indeed be what happened. But
the simplest way to account for these forms synchronically still
seems to be the modification of part (a) of the Suffix Adjustment
rule. Otherwise the change from Widén's [-əs] to the SED [-ɪz]
will be difficult to account for except perhaps by analogy with
other syllabic plurals.

In contrast, Map 7.6 shows a particularly clear example of a
synchronic situation reflecting a diachronic change. This map,
which is taken from Goossens (1969), covers a small enclave of
Holland, called South Limburg, with neighboring areas of Belgium to the west and south and Germany to the east.

The border between Belgium and Holland begins with the dot-
and-dash line in the north, then follows the Maas River south,
with a loop around Maastricht, to the point marked with a small
4, where it turns east. The German–Dutch border is the dot-and-
dash line in the east. Thus the areas numbered 1, 2, most of 3 and
4, a southern strip of 5, and the southern segment of 6 are in Belgium; the unmarked white area to the east is in Germany, and
the central area, comprising parts of 3 and 4, most of 5, and the
northern 6 area, is in Holland. In spite of the fact that three official languages are spoken in the region – Flemish, Dutch, and
German – there is a dialect continuum from west to east of the
sort described by Gaston Paris in the passage given at the beginning of this book. Goossens illustrates this in terms of the distribution of the phoneme /š/.

Data for relevant items, derived from volume 8 of the *Reeks
Nederlandse Dialektatlassen* (RNDA, Blancquaert et al. 1962),

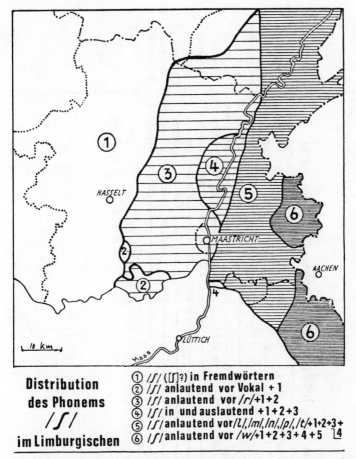

Distribution des Phonems /ʃ/ im Limburgischen

① /ʃ/ ([ʃ]?) in Fremdwörtern
② /ʃ/ anlautend vor Vokal + 1
③ /ʃ/ anlautend vor /r/+1+2
④ /ʃ/ in und auslautend +1+2+3
⑤ /ʃ/ anlautend vor /l/,/m/,/n/,/p/,/t/+1+2+3+
⑥ /ʃ/ anlautend vor /w/+1+2+3+4+5 ⌐4

MAP 7.6.   Distribution of /š/ in Limburgish (from Goossens 1969, Map 9).

are given in Table 7.1. The traditional dialectologist might very well either simply report the individual forms on a raw data map (as is actually done in RNDA) or plot a series of isogloss maps, one for each word, with the isogloss dividing [sχɪp] from [šɪp] following the line between areas (1) and (2), that for [sχreːbə] ≠ [šreːbə] along the line between (2) and (3), and so on. Goossens, the structuralist, sees the situation in terms of the distribution of a phoneme /š/, which exists only in foreign loan words in Dutch and Flemish, but occurs in successively more environments as one goes eastward across this transition area. In his discussion of the map (Goossens 1969, *pp* 51–2), he gives examples and, more im-

TABLE 7.1 Development of /š/ in Limburgish (data from *Reeks Nederlandse Dialektatlas*, vol. 8)

Word	Netherlandic Spelling	Area 1	Area 2	Area 3	Area 4	Area 5	Area 6	Area 7	German Spelling	Proto-form
'ship'	schip	sχγp	šιp					šιf	Schiff	*skip
'write'	schrijven	sχreːbə	šreːbə					šraubən	schreiben	*skriːban
'flesh'	vlees	vleːs			vleːš			flauš	Fleisch	*fleisk
'spin'	spinnen	spιnə				špιnə		špιnən	spinnen	*spinnan
'stone'	steen	steːn				šteːn		štaun	Stein	*stain-
'snow'	sneeuw	sneː				šneː		šneː	Schnee	*snaiw-
'swim'	zwimmen	zwιmə				žwəmə	žwəmə	žwmən	schwimmen	*swimjan
'machine'	machine	mašinə						mašiːnə	Maschine	Fr. *machine*

portantly, etymological information, pointing out that in areas (2), (3), and (4) the /š/ derives from West Germanic *sk*- while in areas (5) and (6) it derives from West Germanic *s*. He points out in an important footnote that although the map is presented as a chart of synchronic distribution, it:

> can also be read, just as well, as a derivational map. This comes naturally from the fact that /š/ in Limburgish is the result of a series of combinatorial sound-changes and not a 'spontaneous' development of a single phoneme or phoneme-sequence of the diasystem in all positions. (*p* 52, n.45)

To the generative dialectologist, the map presents a fascinating example of the gradual generalization and differential spread of phonological rules across a transitional area, with each special rule leaving a record in the form of a line marking its furthest extension, somewhat like wave-lines on a sandy beach on a receding tide. Like Goossens, he can read the map either synchronically or diachronically, and he finds that in this case (as not always in a generative model) the synchronic phonological rules reflect in nature and order the successive sound changes which account for some of the differences between modern German and Netherlandic, both ultimately descending from a common Proto-West Germanic.

Adopting a rather abstract version of generative phonology, we may conclude first that there is no systematic phoneme /š/ in the underlying forms of either Netherlandic or German, but that wherever a surface [š] appears, it derives from either an underlying /s/ or the cluster /sk/. In fact, there are no instances of surface [š] at all in Netherlandic except in foreign words, particularly French, such as *machine*. In German, on the other hand, surface [š] is quite frequent, owing to a series of phonological rules converting underlying /sk/ and /s/ to [š]. These can be lumped together under the general categorization of 'sibilant palatalization rules'. Their effect is to convert all instances of /sk/ and all instances of initial /s/ before consonants to [š]. In both languages there is a general rule which converts all initial /s/ before vowels to [z]. We thus have the following rules for German:

$$\text{G 1} \quad /s/ \rightarrow [z]/ \underline{\quad\quad} V$$
$$\text{G 2} \quad /sk/ \rightarrow [š]$$
$$\text{G 3} \quad /s/ \rightarrow [š]/ \# \underline{\quad\quad} C$$

Netherlandic, on the other hand, has a rule identical with G 1, but instead of G 2 it changes /k/ after /s/ to the fricative [χ]:

$$\text{N 2} \quad /sk/ \rightarrow [sχ]$$

Looking at the Limburgish area on Goossens' map and the words in Table 7.1, we can see that, proceeding from west to east, the sibilant palatalization rules, beginning with very specific environments, become more and more general until they become virtually identical with the quite general German rules G 2 and G 3. Specifically:

In area (2), rule N 2 is followed by

L 1   /sχ/ → [š]/ ____V

This accounts for [šɪp] from underlying /skɪp/.
In area (3), this is extended to include /r/:

L 2   /sχ/ → [š]/ ____r

which accounts for [šreːbə].

In area (4) this rule is further generalized to include /sk/ in medial and final environments. The rule for /sk/ has now extended to the full generality of G 2. Up to this point, all Limburgish [š] derive from underlying /sk/. In area (5), however, we get an important rule which changes initial /s/ before the consonants listed by Goossens – /l m n p t/ – to [š]. Since, with /k/ removed by rules N 1, L 1, and L 2, this list includes all consonants that may occur in initial clusters with /s/ except /w/, which we will come to shortly, the Limburgish rule is now the same as German G 3, with this one exception. What has happened, then, is that starting with two simple Netherlandic rules:

N 1   /s/ → [z] / # ____V
N 2   /sk/ → [sχ]

and passing through more specialized rules, we have again reached a set of simple rules approximating to those of German.

Looking at the situation diachronically, we may conclude that the German development of palatal [š] from West Germanic /s/ occurred in several stages, each of which spread west into the Netherlandic area to a certain limit, where it stopped. Each following stage also spread, but not quite so far as the preceding ones. We therefore have several bands – wave marks on the sand – revealing the extent of each stage of this gradual dissemination. The beginning of sibilant palatalization was the change of /sk/ to [š] before vowels, which went right across Dutch Limburg and into Belgium almost to Hasselt, stopping at the line separating area (1) on Map 7.6 from areas (2) and (3). Over most of this area, the resonant consonant /r/ was included with vowels in the rule, but this stopped short of extending into area (2). Next, the rule palatalizing /sk/ in other than initial environments resulted in a more general rule (G 2), which also spread west, but stopped at the boundary of area (4). Finally, initial /s/ before other consonants was palatalized to [š], and this new rule also spread into Limburg, stopping even shorter, at the line between areas (4) and (5). The map thus gives a perfect picture of the increasingly limited spread of the sibilant palatalization rules westward from Germany into the Low Countries.

One problem with this otherwise clear demonstration is posed by words beginning with underlying /sw/. As the data for 'swim' in Table 7.1 show, this becomes [zw] in Netherlandic and [šv] in German. Furthermore, in area (5), comprising Dutch South Limburg, it becomes [žw], thus seeming to show both the voicing called for before vowels by rule N 1 and the palatalization called for before consonants by rule G 2. In the two areas numbered (6), however, the voicing is not present, and underlying initial /sw/ becomes [šw]. One solution to this problem would be to include /sw/ in the input to rule N 1 but not that of G 1. This would give:

$$\text{N 1a} \qquad \text{/s/} \to \text{[z]} / \ \#\_\_\_\_(\text{/w/})\text{V}$$

where the parentheses around /w/ indicate that the rule applies when there is /w/ between /s/ and a vowel as well as directly before a vowel. If we then generalize the rule for palatalization of /s/ before consonants to include [z] as well, it would change [z] to [ž] before /w/. This would be a Limburgish rule:

$$\text{L 3} \qquad \text{sibilant} \to \text{palatal} / \ \#\_\_\_\_\text{C}$$

We would still have to account for the lack of voicing in areas (6).

A better solution would be to leave our rule N 1 as it is, with /w/ not included, and to add a second voicing rule after the extension of the rule palatalizing /s/ before consonants (G 3) into area (5). This rule would also affect [š] in this environment, and would have the form:

$$\text{N 3} \qquad \text{sibilant} \to \text{[+voice]} / \ \# \_\_\_\_\text{w}$$

Being a Netherlandic rule, its dissemination would be from west to east, stopping just short of the German border to exclude areas (6) from its application. The [žw] area in South Limburg would thus show an overlapping of the palatalization rule, of German origin, coming from the east, and the voicing rule of Netherlandic, coming from the west. This rule is more satisfying, since it accounts not only for the forms with [žw] but also for the forms with [šw] in areas (6). It shows how a transition area may undergo spreading influences from both sides, with the adoption of selected features from each – what in the traditional approach was covered by the rather vague and general term, DIALECT MIXTURE.

The illustrations given above have for the most part dealt with individual items or small sections of the phonology of the respective languages and their dialects, and in the case of Limburgish, at least, with only a small geographical area. It is quite another matter to attempt a generative analysis of the phonology of a whole language, including its dialects. A few such attempts have been made, and though they are on the whole limited to the broader phonological features, with less attention to the details of phonetic realization, they have demonstrated that the generative approach, though technically quite complicated on that scale, is very revealing as to both the synchronic relationship of dialects and their diachronic history. The method gives promise of adding another dimension to dialect study, building upon rather than replacing the results of traditional and structural dialectology.

An early attempt of some significance is that of Vasiliu on the Daco-Romanian dialects, *ie* those dialects of Romanian spoken within Romania proper (Vasiliu 1966). Using the data from Pop (1938) and Petrovici (1956), Vasiliu was able to demonstrate 'that the DRum dialects can be described largely in terms of THE SAME RULES ordered differently' (*p* 83). Specifically he identified eleven phonological rules, not all of which are present in all dialects, and which appear in crucial differences of ordering which account for significant variations. He finds two main classes of dialects, the Muntenian (south) and Moldavian (north), the former with three subvarieties and the latter with two. The presence and ordering of the rules, identified by capital letters, is:

Muntenian A: (A–B–C–D–E–F–H–I–J–K)
           Ba: (A–B–C–D–E–F–J–K–G–A)
           Bb: (A–B–C–D–E–F–H–I–J–K–G–A)

Moldavian A: (A–B–E–F–H–I–J–K)
           B: (A–B–E–F–C–H–I–J–K)

Even without knowing the specific content of the rules (too complex even to summarize here), one can draw several conclusions from this array about the degree of difference between the various dialects. Rules D and G, for example, are totally missing from the Moldavian dialects. The Muntenian B dialects are characterized by the inclusion of rule G after K and the repetition of rule A at the end of the cycle. Moldavian A could be assumed to be the most basic variety, since all the others can be derived from it by the simple addition of one to four rules at various points in the ordering (also the dropping of rules H and I from Muntenian Ba). Vasiliu sums up the advantage of the generative model in these terms:

> The generative approach seems to be more powerful than the purely historical one and more powerful even than the synchronic distributional one.
>
> It is more powerful than the first because it does not limit itself to establishing only WHEN a change occurred in relation to another, but its aim is the inference of all the STRUCTURAL consequences resulting from the different ordering in time of changes X and Y. In such a manner, the generative approach enables us to establish a direct and coherent relationship between historical change and its synchronic implications. Relationships of this kind are not expressed in the traditional historical classification. . . .
>
> We can say, in our case, that the generative approach is more powerful than the purely distributional since: (a) it enables us to establish a hierarchy among various criteria of classification; (b) according to this hierarchy we can put together dialects showing deeper morphophonemic identities (or only similarities) disregarding the more superficial distributional dissimilarities; . . . (c) in terms of a generative model we can detect DIFFERENT RULES BEHIND IDENTICAL DISTRIBUTIONS; *mutatis mutandis*, we can say that it is a specific case of describing (and defining) structural ambiguity by means of a generative model. (Vasiliu 1966, *pp* 96–7)

Since the appearance of Chomsky and Halle's *Sound Pattern of English* in 1968, there has been a great deal of work in generative phonology, but not a great deal of it has been concerned with dialects. Chomsky and Halle made no attempt to handle dialectal varieties in any but a superficial way. They make their position quite clear in their Preface:

> The dialect of English that we study is essentially that described by Kenyon and Knott (1944). . . . In fact, their transcriptions are very close to our own speech, apart from certain dialectal idiosyncrasies of no general interest, which we omit. It seems to us that the rules we propose carry over, without major modification, to many other dialects of English, though it goes without saying that we have not undertaken the vast and intricate study of dialectal variation. For reasons that we will discuss in detail, it seems to us very likely that the underlying lexical (or phonological) representations must be common to all English dialects, with rare exceptions, and that much of the basic framework of rules must be common as well. Of course, this is an empirical question, which must be left to future research. (Chomsky and Halle 1968, *pp* ix–x)

The 'vast and intricate study of dialectal variation' in English has yet to be undertaken, though there have been individual studies that point the way it may go (*eg* Keyser 1963; Troike 1971; Whitley 1974). Full-scale studies of other languages have, however, appeared, notably two that came out in the same year (Brown 1972; Newton 1972). Brown's study of Lumasaaba, a Bantu language spoken by 250,000 people in eastern Uganda, not only develops in detail the phonological rules needed to derive the various dialects of this language, but contains a particularly clear and convincing exposition of the theory of generative phonology and its application to dialect variation. One problem Brown faced is the identification of the proper underlying forms from which to derive the various dialectal variants. Clearly, when one is dealing with a single homogeneous dialect, the underlying forms must be only such as will allow the simplest derivation of morphophonemic variants, as in the forms of *desk* in American Black English, discussed above. But in dealing with two or more dialects, underlying forms must be set up that permit the most economical derivations of variant forms of the same words, as we saw in the case of words with surface [š] and [ž] in Netherlandic, Limburgish, and German. In general, Brown accepts the assumption quoted above from Chomsky and Halle – that in general the dialectal variants within a given language derive from the same underlying forms, and differ in the number and ordering of the rules. After attempting to 'construct a form for Common Lumasaaba which would be neutral as between southern and northern realisations', she found that 'fewer rules were needed if a northern form was taken as the base form, and that these rules were much more general' (*p* 169). On this ground, she used the northern forms as basis. She carefully disclaims that this represents the actual historical development, but speculates that: 'If, at any time in the historic past, Lumasaaba was one homogeneous language ... it seems probable ... that northern dialectal forms resemble this putative Common Lumasaaba more closely than southern forms.' (*p* 171) This conclusion is similar to that reached about Faroese by O'Neil (1963), who found that by adopting as basic the vowel system of one locality (Tórshavn), he could present the others most simply in terms of rules accounting for their departures from that system.

In contrast, Alan Thomas found that to account most economically for the situation in Welsh, it was not possible to use an existing dialect as base, from which the others could be derived, but that it was necessary to 'postulate ... a set of abstract underlying forms, which are explicitly established on the basis of an investigation of correspondences between all the dialects being investigated'. He points out that:

> The prevailing control on the establishment of the underlying forms is that of economy: a set of underlying forms which permits the genera-tion of all dialect forms with a shorter set of rules is to be preferred over one which requires a longer set of rules. (Thomas 1967, p 193; see also Thomas 1968)

This principle was also followed by both O'Neil and Brown; it simply turned out that in Faroese and Lumasaaba, probably for reasons connected with their history, one dialect could be used as a basis for the most economical set of underlying forms.

In his study of Greek dialects, Newton also accepts the Chomsky–Halle assumptions of common underlying forms and differing rules. But because the Hellenic *koiné*, which is the source of almost all the present-day Greek dialects, is well documented, he adds a historical dimension. As he puts it:

> Because dialects arise from an originally more or less uniform lan-guage it is possible to show that they can for the most part be de-scribed in terms of a common set of underlying forms; variation is introduced by the phonological processes which operate on these forms. (Newton 1972, p 5)

An important phrase here is 'for the most part'; Newton leaves an opening for some variation in the underlying forms. As we saw above in our discussion of *desk* and *post*, it may be most econ-omical in some cases to hypothesize restructuring of some under-lying forms which may occur in some dialects (*eg* American Black English) but not in others. It does not seem wise in all cases to re-quire a single set of underlying forms for all dialects of a given language, though certainly if variation in underlying forms be-comes pervasive, we must assume that we are dealing with differ-ent languages rather than dialects of the same language (as is the case, for example, with French and Occitan in the south of France). In fact, this is one of the most satisfactory criteria for settling the old problem of distinguishing between dialects and separate languages.

In spite of the opening clause in the quotation from Newton given above, and the fact that the underlying forms he uses are close to, though not always identical with, the *koiné*, he is care-ful, as are all the writers we are dealing with, to dissociate the synchronic analysis from the diachronic record or reconstruction:

> ... while the 'rules' we shall require reflect in general historical pro-cesses, and their ordering recapitulates the actual temporal sequence

of events, there may very well be discrepancies between historical fact
and synchronic description. (*p* 7)

We saw a minor example of this above, where Widén suggested
the interpretation of syllabic plurals of nouns like *post* as a synchronic response by epenthesis to the problem of difficult consonant clusters rather than the retention of the syllabic ending
from pre-fifteenth-century English.

Although the dialect situation in modern Greek is more complicated than that in Lumasaaba – Newton describes it as 'a linguistic continuum criss-crossed in all directions by a vast number
of isoglosses marking the geographical limits of the different phonological features' (*p* 13) – yet he was able to characterize these
differences clearly and convincingly by a set of a score or so of
rules, their presence or absence, and their ordering. His study is
an admirable demonstration (as is Brown's on a smaller scale) of
the elegant analysis which the generative approach can bring to
complicated dialect data.

Chapter 8

Dialectology and linguistic theory:
II Sociolinguistic

The sociolinguistic approach to dialectology differs from those discussed in the preceding chapter not so much in theory as in objectives and emphasis. It is compatible with either structural or generative theory, both of which have been applied to sociolinguistic data. But where the traditional dialectologists were primarily concerned with the 'local dialect' and the measure of its differences from other local dialects and the standard language, and where the structuralists were concerned with the organizational concept of the diasystem, the sociolinguistic dialectologists are primarily interested in language variation as a correlate or indicator of social variation and as a source of language change. As we have said earlier (Ch. 1), the focus shifts from the language itself to the people who use the language, their social orientations and contrasts. The balance is delicate here; insofar as the linguistic concerns become secondary to the social concerns, the study becomes a form of sociology – linguistic sociology rather than sociological linguistics. It is difficult to serve both disciplines equally effectively, though some modern workers (eg Pellowe 1976) are attempting to do so. Since the emphasis in this book is on dialectology as a branch of linguistics, much sociolinguistic research is outside our field. But there remains a considerable body of sociolinguistic dialectology which is making important contributions to linguistic theory, as we shall see in the latter part of this chapter.

Assumptions, methods, and results

The sociological approach involves major shifts in basic assumptions and procedures from those of traditional dialectology.

These affect respectively the population sampling, the language sampling, the technique of collection, and the presentation of the data.

1. As has already been discussed in Chapter 4, the sociolinguist derives his population sampling procedures from sociology, which has a long history of this kind of sampling. The aim is to secure a representative cross-section of the population, proportionally distributed so far as possible according to such parameters as social class, age, sex, occupation, education, socioeconomic level, and any others (eg ethnicity, religious affiliation) which may be significant in the population under study. Informants are thus identified in advance according to their position in the social framework and selected by random procedures. The population studied is usually considerably smaller than that of a traditional survey, allowing a larger proportion to be used as informants. The sampling methods employed by Labov in New York City, Trudgill in Norwich, and Pellowe et al. in Newcastle have been described above in Chapter 4.

2. On the basis of either the investigator's foreknowledge or a preliminary survey, the language sample is commonly selected to include broad representation of a relatively small number of features which (it is expected) correlate significantly with social differences. A few features – such as postvocalic /r/ or [t d] for /θ ð/ in New York City – are investigated in detail for their supposed diagnostic value, rather than a broad questionnaire of more than 1,000 items, chosen for their relevance for establishing a full picture of a local speech variety.

3. Collection techniques are less often confined to a pre-established questionnaire and rely much more on capturing free discourse as 'natural' as possible. The portable high-fidelity tape recorder has made this feasible, since it obviates the cumbersome, conspicuous, and time-consuming practice of making written records during the interview. Since the studies are usually concerned not only with social variation between individuals of different social rank but also with stylistic variation within the speech of a single informant or socially equivalent group, varying situations are arranged which will put the informant into various contexts – casual, excited, careful, formal, reading. The aim here is not only to get at the basic dialect of the informant, but to exercise and record his COMMUNICATIVE COMPETENCE (Hymes 1974, p 75) – his knowledge of the appropriate kind of language for the various social situations in which he finds himself and his ability to switch easily from one style to another. It may even be desirable to get the informant to talk about his language and that of

others in his community in order to reveal significant attitudes and prejudices – a practice avoided in traditional dialectology.

4. The data of the sociolinguistically oriented survey is seldom presented in its raw form, by tables or maps. More commonly the results are presented statistically, summarized in charts and graphs. The individual informant often seems to disappear, his responses cumulated with those of others in his particular corner of the social grid. Thus, somewhat paradoxically, in the type of survey that focuses on the speaker's role and the social significance of his linguistic performance, the individual informant may be much less conspicuous than he is in the traditional dialect survey. This is, of course, not always the case. In some of the more sensitive studies, the informant may emerge as the more or less skilled manipulator of a range of language variants appropriate to the changing social environments in which he moves, in contrast to the typical informant in a traditional survey, who is treated as a sort of reservoir of local dialect which, properly handled, can be turned on like a tap.

Those sociolinguistic studies which can properly be called dialectological – that is, whose primary aim is the systematic description of linguistic variation and its significance for language structure and language change – may be said to have added two more dimensions to the three treated by Moulton. Those, it will be remembered, were the geographical, the structural, and the historical. The two new ones are the social and the stylistic. Actually no study has attempted to deal with all five as yet; the volume and complexity of the requisite data make this a forbidding task. Instead, one dimension, the geographical, is commonly neutralized by confining the field of study to one relatively homogeneous area, such as a single city or urban district. We may thus say that the best studies of this sort deal with structured social and stylistic variation within a geographically homogeneous speech area, considered in the light of historical development and ongoing linguistic change. The two we will consider here are those by William Labov (1966) and Peter Trudgill (1974b).

Labov's New York City study

Labov's study of social stratification in the speech of the Lower East Side of New York City is certainly the most detailed example of urban sociolinguistic dialectology so far carried out. It was in many ways a pioneer work, and it is frequently cited as a model for other urban studies. It is far too detailed to be fully described in the space available here; what we can do is state its premises, its procedures, and its results in summary form, with the caution that we will not do justice either to the exhaustive analysis or the cautiously qualified claims that Labov presents in a book of more than 600 pages.

In the first place, Labov assumes (on the basis of prior studies by himself and by others) that New York City is a single speech community, with a common basic linguistic system, rather than 'a disparate collection of individuals with various backgrounds, borrowing randomly from one another's dialect' (Labov 1966, *p* 47). This conclusion justifies the use of one area, the Lower East Side, as a laboratory for a study whose results can be extrapolated to the city as a whole.

Secondly, it is assumed that what to previous investigators appeared to be a chaotic state of free variation, especially in the phonology, will turn out on careful close analysis to be a structured variability which correlates statistically with identifiable and quantifiable differences in the two dimensions of social structure and stylistic function (or REGISTER).

Thirdly, it is expected that this variation will be subjectively recognized (however inaccurately in linguistic terms) by the speakers themselves in their evaluation of their own speech and that of other New Yorkers.

Fourthly, it is assumed, or at least hoped for, that some aspects at least of this phonological variation will be indicative of phonological change in progress.

After a preliminary study which clearly revealed social variation in the percentage of postvocalic /r/ pronounced by department-store employees in New York (the 'fourth floor' experiment described in Chapter 3 above), Labov decided upon five phonological items which in New York clearly exhibit variation not only between individual speakers but also within the speech of individual informants. As he points out:

> The most useful items are those that are high in *frequency*, have a certain *immunity from conscious suppression*, are integral *units of larger structures*, and may be easily *quantified on a linear scale*. (Labov 1966, *p* 49; emphasis his)

These criteria led him to the following five phonological items:
1. postvocalic word-final or preconsonantal /r/;
2. the height of the 'short *a*' vowel in word stems before voiced stops, voiceless fricatives, and the nasals [m] and [n]; *ie* words such as *bad, half, cash, ham*;
3. the height of the mid-back rounded vowel of words like *caught, dog, lost, all*;
4. the pronunciation of phonemic /θ/ as fricative, affricate, or stop (*ie* [θ], [tθ], or [t]);

5. the same for phonemic /ð/.

Each of these was given an appropriate scale: the first a binary one (presence or absence of phonetic [r]), the second and third a range of six heights, the fourth and fifth a three-point scale corresponding to the three types of articulation. These scales permitted the derivation of a single number for each informant on each variable within a given type of discourse which would represent the average of his performance for that item in that style. Cumulative averages could also be obtained by averaging the performance of all informants assigned to a given social class.

Four styles were decided upon, representing four clearly differentiable registers which could be elicited and recognized by identification of situation and context. These were: (A) casual speech; (B) careful speech; (C) reading connected text; (D) word-lists, including rote lists from memory (*eg* days of the week), printed lists grouped according to the five variables, and printed lists of minimal pairs.

A questionnaire was constructed to elicit the five variables in as natural samples as possible of the four styles. As in other types of survey that we have discussed, the questionnaire is at the heart of the collection process, so that the difference between this survey and traditional ones can be measured by the striking contrasts between Labov's questionnaire and those we have described in Chapter 3. Instead of a single approach – fixed questions or 'directed conversation' – many are used, ranging from traditional lexical questions, through five kinds of casual speech either directly stimulated or captured from conversation, including both folklore material (childhood rimes and games) and free narrative of experience ('danger of death'), to reading of formal lists, ending with questions on subjective reactions to various types of New York speech, the evaluation by the informant of his own speech, and his attitudes toward other regional and class varieties of American English. The questionnaire is a model of an instrument carefully designed to elicit exactly the kind of quantifiable data required to fulfil the original plan of the survey. As such, it makes some of the traditional survey questionnaires appear like rather haphazard fishing attempts, rather than scientifically planned research instruments.

The population sampling procedures have already been described in Chapter 4 and need not be repeated here, except to remind the reader that the final list of informants who completed the full questionnaire included 122 persons, ranging in age from 20 to over 70. Of these, 81 who had come to New York before the age of 8 made up the central group used in the social-class study. Using procedures developed by J. A. Michael for a

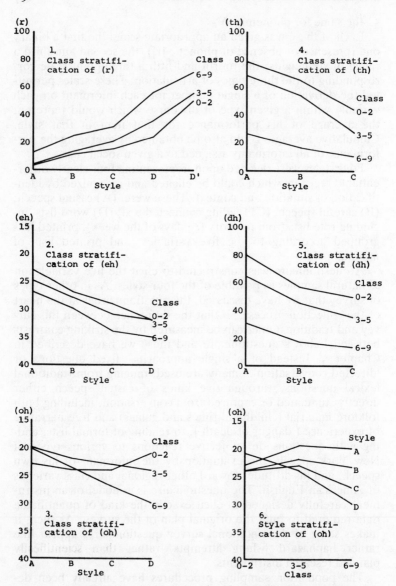

FIG. 8.1 Graphs of style variation in New York City (Labov 1966, *p* 222).

sociological survey called the Mobilization for Youth, each of these was assigned a social rank, one of nine levels on a scale ranging from lower class to upper middle class, based on income, education, and occupation (Americans, at least, will not be surprised to hear that no members of the upper class live on the Lower East Side).

A large part of the analysis, covering over 150 pages, is devoted to a careful study of the realization of the five variables in various registers by members of the different classes. The results are much too detailed even to summarize here, but Fig. 8.1 gives an idea of the kind of information revealed. Each chart here represents the average results for one of the variables as produced by the informants grouped into three social classes: lower class (0–2); working class (3–5); middle class (6–9). Briefly, charts 1–5 display the following:

1. All social levels pronounce fewer than 20 per cent of their postvocalic /r/'s in casual speech, the percentage increasing as the styles change from casual (A) to careful (B) to reading (C) and finally to word-list (D). Style D', tabulated on this chart only, is performance on minimal pairs in the word-lists. It is interesting to note that the working-class speakers, who pronounce fewer than 25 per cent of their /r/'s in any of the other styles, jump to about 50 per cent on the minimal pairs. Since the proportion of /r/'s pronounced increases the higher the class, these data corroborate the conclusion of the 'fourth floor' study that the pronunciation of postvocalic /r/ is a prestige feature in modern New York City speech.

2. All social levels pronounce words like *bag* with a vowel close to a lowered [ε] (25 on the vertical scale) in casual speech, with the vowel lowering as the style becomes more formal, reaching an average of [æ^] for lower- and working-class speakers and [æː] for middle-class speakers on word-lists.

3. For working-class speakers, the /ɔː/ vowel is stylistically stable with an average in the area of a raised [ɔ] with a central off-glide (20–25). The other classes start with a higher vowel approaching [ʊ³] in casual speech, the middle-class lowering to a 'normal' [ɔː^] (30) in formal speech.

4. and 5. Working-class speakers use something like 40 per cent stops and affricates for /θ/ and /ð/ in casual style, lowering to about 20 per cent in reading style. Middle-class speakers are markedly different, using [θ] and [ð] predominantly in all styles and more than 80 per cent of the time in more formal styles. This corroborates the universal feeling that this is a lower-class substandard feature.

Labov subjects his data to various other interesting analyses, which we have not space to go into here. From a linguistic point of view, the most interesting chapter is that in which he analyzes differences from the point of view of 'apparent time' (*ie* age differences of speakers) in order to detect the presence of sound changes in progress, an idea to which in a later article he gave the title 'the use of the present to explain the past' (Labov 1972a; see also Labov, Yeager and Steiner 1972). There is a great deal more, of both sociological and linguistic interest, in this very elaborate study.

Trudgill's Norwich study

Trudgill's study of Norwich speech models its procedures closely upon Labov's. As we saw in Chapter 4, his population was quite close in size to Labov's, but his informant group of 58 represented a smaller percentage of the population. His questionnaire follows Labov's closely in the nature and arrangement of the material sought, differing only in those aspects in which the patterns of life experience of the inhabitants of an English county town or small city may be expected to differ from those of a relatively depressed area within a large American metropolis. Unlike Labov, who was able to base his social criteria on the conclusions of the Mobilization for Youth study, Trudgill had to work out his own sociological analysis. He used six criteria: occupation, income, education, housing, locality, and father's occupation. To each of these he assigned a scale ranging from 0 to 5. It was thus possible for the informants to have cumulative scores ranging from 0 to 30; the actual range was from 3 to 27. The preponderant scores, as might be expected, were toward the lower end of this scale, the majority lying between 6 and 12. He ultimately subdivided his informant group into five social classes on the basis of their variable usage on a single linguistic criterion which is a well-known feature not only of Norwich speech but of Norfolk and East Anglian speech generally – the absence of the third-person concord marker -*s* in the present tense of verbs. His five classes were these:

Class	Social index	Number of informants
I. Middle middle class (MMC)	19+	6
II. Lower middle class (LMC)	15–18	8
III. Upper working class (UWC)	11–14	16
IV. Middle working class (MWC)	7–10	22
V. Lower working class (LWC)	3–6	8

Like Labov, Trudgill proceeds to record the performance of his informants on a set of phonological variables in four different styles of speech: word-list style (WLS), reading passage style (RPS), formal speech (FS), and casual speech (CS). His study differs, however, in that where Labov used only five variables (absence of postvocalic /r/, tensing of 'short *a*', raising of /ɔ/, and substitution of stops or affricates for /θ/ and /ð/), he uses sixteen, three consonantal and thirteen vocalic. The basis of the selection of these variables was '(a) the amount of apparent social significance in the pronunciation of the segment or segments involved; and (b) the amount of phonetic differentiation involved' (Trudgill 1974a, *p* 80). The data upon which the various scales were established included not only Trudgill's own knowledge as a native of Norwich but also earlier work on East Anglian English carried out by Helge Kökeritz in 1932, Guy Lowman in 1936, and W. N. Francis in 1956–57. His overall results are similar in general to those of Labov; that is, he found that performance varied according to the two variables social class and type of speech, approaching the Received Pronunciation (RP) norm as social class became higher and register became more formal. The chart in Fig. 8.2 shows one of these, the variation between [ŋ] and [n] in the verbal *-ing* ending. It can be seen that the middle-middle-class speakers use the [-ɪn] form of the ending only in casual speech and then only about one-fourth of the time, while the lower working class use it always in both formal and casual speech, employing [-ɪŋ] only in the two reading styles. The other three classes fall between these two. The overall pattern is quite similar to those obtained by Labov (Fig. 8.1 above).

Not all of Trudgill's variables, however, follow this pattern of social and stylistic variation. In some of them the social variation is wide but there is little or no stylistic variation; for others the reverse is true: the data show little difference between the classes, but considerable variation across the range from casual to formal language. Trudgill comes to the following conclusion:

Although related to social class differentiation, [stylistic variation] is not an automatic consequence of class differentiation. Stylistic variation takes place in the case of variables subject to class differentiation only when social consciousness is directed towards these variables by reason of the fact that they are:

(i) undergoing linguistic change; or
(ii) subject to overt corrective pressures; or
(iii) involved in surface phonological contrasts; or
(iv) markedly different from prestige accent equivalents (in the case of those speakers who have some contact with the prestige accent). (*p* 103)

	Class	Style			
		WLS	RPS	FS	CS
I	MMC	000	000	003	028
II	LMC	000	010	015	042
III	UWC	005	015	074	087
IV	MWC	023	044	088	095
V	LWC	029	066	098	100

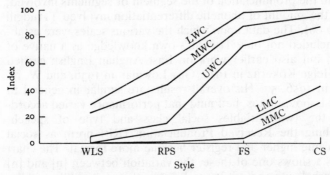

FIG. 8.2. Variable (ng) by class and style in Norwich (Trudgill 1974a, *p* 92).

These are valuable conclusions from a linguistic as well as a sociological point of view. They indicate above all that the forces producing linguistic variation and those inhibiting it within a complex speech community are themselves very complex and difficult to measure, and that a linguistic change which in retrospect may seem as simple as the Neogrammarian Hypothesis supposes may be the final resolution of cooperating and conflicting social and psychological motives. Studies of this sort are already forcing linguists to revise their views of linguistic change.

The remainder of Trudgill's study is given over to a detailed and ambitious investigation of what he calls 'the Norwich diasystem'. He uses the term in much the same sense as Pulgram did (1964b), to stand for all those aspects of Norwich English which establish it as a distinctive variety of English, in spite of the large amount of social and stylistic variation which he has been at pains to discover and analyze. As he puts it:

> It must of course be recognised that Norwich English is not an isolated, distinct or discrete linguistic variety. Geographically, it merges into the other varieties of Norfolk, East Anglian and southern British English. Socially, it merges with the non-localised varieties of RP and

standard English. It is not, however, unreasonable to regard Norwich as if it were a distinct variety. . . . Speakers of Norwich English, that is to say, belong to a particular speech community which has very many common linguistic features. Many of these features are not shared by any other speech community. (*p* 133)

He goes on to state that these common linguistic features can best be conceived of not as a loose, haphazard collection, but as deriving from 'a single underlying framework that is the same for the whole community' – the Norwich diasystem.

There are two main justifications for attempting to establish this kind of diasystem. The first is that a model of this nature provides a common basis for the description and comparison of closely related varieties. The second is that there is some sense in which members of, in this case, the Norwich speech community, can be said to have internalised this diasystem, in that they are able to draw upon it in their variable speech production, and to use it in the comprehension and social interpretation of utterances produced by other speakers. We therefore believe that there is a need to establish some kind of model of this internalised diasystem. The diasystem can be said in some sense to 'exist', and must therefore be described in order correctly and fully to describe the native speaker's linguistic competence. The diasystem, that is, should provide a model of the linguistic competence of the individual as a native speaker of Norwich English *and* as a member of the Norwich speech community. (*p* 134)

This conclusion, if it is indeed true, as Trudgill believes, is a vitally important one for dialectology and for linguistics. For what it does is to establish on a firm linguistic ground the conviction which has been shared in one way or another by all those – amateurs, students, and scholars alike – who have faced the paradox with which we began this book: the belief that there are such things as local dialects in spite of the fact that their boundaries and distinguishing criteria seem to elude precise definition and description. It carries us back to Gauchat's belief in the psychological reality of a dialect, as expressed in the passage from his 1903 article quoted in the last chapter: 'all users of a dialect have something in common, so that one perceives that when they encounter one another in a foreign land, a joyful feeling of home is awakened in them' (Gauchat 1903, *p* 396). It corroborates Séguy's view that there is such a thing as 'Gascon', even though he may measure linguistic distances within the Gascon area that are greater than some which cross its borders.

The diasystem which Trudgill develops for Norwich English is a complicated one, which we cannot attempt to go into here. It is based on a rather abstract type of generative phonology originated by E. C. Fudge in a series of articles published in the late 1960s (Fudge 1967, 1969a, 1969b). It assumes a common underlying system for all Norwich varieties, with phonological and phonetic rules that account for the surface variations between social class dialects and stylistic registers. He finds that even the slurring and elision that characterize fast speech can be attributed to phonetic rules rather than mere random carelessness. It is thus a refutation of the too-ready adoption of notions like 'free variation' and 'dialect mixture'. In short, it goes far toward vindicating the view that has been a governing principle throughout this book: that dialectology is properly a branch of linguistics and has the potential of contributing importantly to that science.

Theoretical implications

The development of sophisticated methods of sociolinguistic dialectology has had the effect of moving the study of language variation from its former peripheral position in linguistics to a position much nearer the center. As we have seen, Weinreich in 1954 found dialectology and theoretical (structural) linguistics completely at odds. His efforts, together with those of dialectologists like Pulgram and Moulton, succeeded in bringing about a kind of reconciliation, as described by Dahlstedt in the passage quoted on p 171. But meanwhile the structural emphasis in linguistics had given way to — or developed into — the generative-transformational one, which had as its focus, in the words of its founder and most distinguished exponent, 'an ideal speaker-listener, in a completely homogeneous speech-community, who knows its language perfectly...' (Chomsky 1965, p 3). Once again it looked as though language variation as well as dialectology, the discipline which makes language variation its field of study, were to be relegated to the untidy outskirts of linguistics, dealing with 'mere performance', about which viable linguistic theories were impossible to construct. The sociolinguistically oriented dialectologists have challenged this position by demonstrating that some aspects of variation, at least, are amenable to systematic quantitative study, and that rather than exemplifying random free variation they are correlated in measurable ways with the social status of speakers. This development is usually dated, quite justly, from Labov's 1966 New York study, though there had been earlier work which anticipated the trend, such as Reichstein's thoroughgoing sociolinguistic analysis of phonological variance in Parisian French (Reichstein 1960). In the face of these carefully controlled studies, it is no longer possible to dismiss social and stylistic variation as of only casual or peripheral concern. It is increasingly coming to be recognized that linguistic theory must be extended so as to incorporate variation, both within the speech community and within the competence (not just the performance) of the individual speaker.

On this necessity, all those linguists (including dialectologists) who accept the sociolinguistic point of view are agreed. Perhaps the most forceful statement of this necessity is a seminal article, virtually a manifesto, entitled 'Empirical foundations for a theory of language change', by three distinguished American linguists, all of them theoreticians as well as dialectologists: the late Uriel Weinreich, William Labov, and Marvin Herzog (1968). Their paper begins with a succinct but clear and illuminating review of major linguistic theories from the neogrammarians to Chomsky, demonstrating that their formulations not only avoided the question of variation within the speech community and the competence of the individual speaker, but actually made it impossible or at least irrelevant to make that question a part of linguistic theory. From Hermann Paul's focus on the idiolect, through Saussure's emphasis on the systematic homogeneity of *langue* and the Bloomfieldian abstraction from individual differences, to the Chomskyan assertion of the central importance of the 'ideal speaker-listener in a completely homogeneous speech-community', linguists excluded variation, among and within the usages of speakers, from central theoretical importance, while at the same time recognizing it as a fact which, on the more practical plane, 'the linguist is forced to consider... very carefully' (Bloomfield 1933, *p* 45). As Weinreich, Labov, and Herzog point out, this focus upon the systematic homogeneity of language resulted in a paradox:

> We have seen that for Paul as well as for Saussure, variability and systematicity excluded each other. Their successors, who continued to postulate more and more systematicity in language, became ever more deeply committed to a simplistic conception of the homogeneous idiolect. They provided no effective means for constituting a speech community out of several such idiolects, nor even of representing the behavior of a single speaker with several idiolects at his disposal. Neither did they offer an effective method for constituting a single language out of chronologically disparate homogeneous stages. Yet most linguists acknowledge the evidence which demonstrates that language change is a continuous process and the inevitable by-product of linguistic interaction. (*p* 150)

The answer, they find, is to change the theoretical model of language from systematic homogeneity to 'orderly heterogeneity', an idea whose origin they trace to the Prague School theorists from Mathesius (1931) to Martinet (1955) and Vachek (1964). But, they maintain, the Praguians never adequately developed this idea:

> Despite our profound theoretical sympathy for the position of the Prague School, it must be conceded that they have not presented their views with a formal precision adequate for the complexity of the linguistic data. . . . Certainly it is not enough to point out the existence or importance of variability: it is necessary to deal with the facts of variability with enough precision to allow us to incorporate them into our analyses of linguistic structure. (p 169)

The remainder of the article outlines how the study of variability can contribute to the theory of language change, with illustrations from the work of Labov with New York City English and that of Weinreich and Herzog with Central European Yiddish. It ends with a set of seven 'general statements about the nature of language change', of which the most important for dialectology are the second and fourth:

> 2. The association between structure and homogeneity is an illusion. Linguistic structure includes the orderly differentiation of speakers and styles through rules which govern variation in the speech community; native command of the language includes the control of such heterogeneous structures. . . .
> 4. The generalization of linguistic change throughout linguistic structure is neither uniform nor instantaneous; it involves the covariation of associated changes over substantial periods of time, and is reflected in the diffusion of isoglosses over areas of geographical space. (pp 187–8)

Social variability and code-switching

Granted, then, that variability between speakers and within the competence of individual speakers is to be incorporated into linguistic theory, the question arises as to how this is to be done. It is generally agreed that it is not sufficient to speak of a local dialect or even of an individual idiolect. Both must be subdivided into lects which differ quantitatively from one another in relation to social status and style. For example, as Labov demonstrated, the pronunciation of postvocalic /r/ in New York City is a variable feature, varying directly in relation to the social class of the speaker and the degree of formality of the style. This can be expressed formulaically in this fashion:

$$/r/ \rightarrow g[r] / \underline{\qquad} \begin{cases} K \\ \# \end{cases}$$

where $g[r] = f(\text{Class, Style})$
$$1 \geq g \geq \emptyset$$
K = any consonant
$\#$ = word boundary

This can be read 'underlying /r/ before a consonant or word-boundary is pronounced [r] 100*g* per cent of the time, *g* being a variable function between Ø and 1 of social class and register'. Other parameters such as age, sex, race, occupation could also be included. This is not a direct statement about a single speaker and style but a statistical average across speakers. That is, the variable *g* is arrived at by averaging the performance of a number of speakers who can be demonstrated by non-linguistic criteria to belong to the same social class, and whose utterances can be reliably placed on a stylistic scale measured by such qualities as formality and precision of speech, social relationship between speaker and audience, type of discourse, situational context, etc. It is obvious that if rules of this sort are to be given reliable status, the variables of class and style must be measured by replicable and objective criteria. It cannot be said that this problem has been completely solved, though the work of linguists like Reichstein, Labov, Trudgill, and others has made notable advances toward solution. They have at least established that the variable *g* does not conceal wide differences between individuals of the same class using the same style, though occasional 'maverick speakers' may depart widely from the norm.

Idiolectal variability

When we look at the individual speaker, whose linguistic competence is the ultimate problem for linguistic theory, it becomes apparent that the two variables class and style have quite different status. In fact, class normally ceases to be a variable at all, except perhaps in the receptive component of the individual's competence. There are, of course, some individuals who, for personal or professional reasons, develop the ability to make major shifts in their social orientation and hence behavior, including use of language – actors, spies, undercover policemen, even linguistic fieldworkers. But most people remain within the class to which birth, education, and experience have assigned them. Thus the class variable can be factored out of the formula we have been looking at, which can be re-expressed as

$$/r/ \rightarrow k \times g[r] \ / \ \underline{\quad\quad} \begin{cases} K \\ \# \end{cases}$$

where $g[r] = f(\text{Style})$
$\quad k = $ a constant set by Class
$\quad K = $ any consonant

In other words, for the individual speaker of a given class, the percentage of postvocalic /r/ that he will produce varies directly with the degree of formality of the utterance. A variable feature, style, has been pinpointed within the linguistic competence of the individual speaker. According to Labov's data, the percentage of postvocalic [r] used by a working-class speaker in New York may range from around 5 per cent in casual style to over 50 per cent in the most formal style, reading minimal pairs from a word-list (see Fig. 8.3).

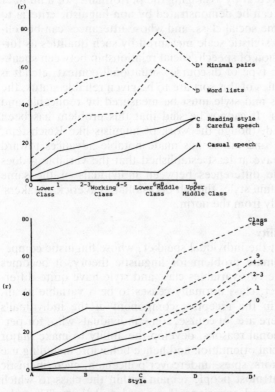

FIG. 8.3. Stylistic and class variation of postvocalic (r) in New York (Labov 1966, *p* 240).
(a) Simplified style stratification of (r): six class groups.
(b) Redefined class stratification of (r): six class groups.

It remains to account for two factors here: (1) the ability of a speaker to vary his performance in an orderly way according to circumstances, and (2) the fact that even when all social and stylistic variables are held constant (so far as this can be managed realistically in the field), a rule such as that for the realization of underlying /r/ as [r] in postvocalic position has to be stated in terms of probability, rather than as a categorical rule which always applies when its input conditions are met.

The first of these problems has generally been explained in various ways as bi- or multi-dialectalism or 'code-switching'. The theory simply states that virtually all speakers are masters of two or more dialects which differ to a greater or less degree in their rules, and that the speaker's competence includes the ability to shift, consciously or unconsciously, from one to another as circumstances direct. Apart from the fact that this greatly extends the concept of competence and complicates the process of language learning, this is an acceptable solution, which has been established by sociolinguistic research and poses a challenge to dialectologists of the future.

The quantitative paradigm: variable rules
The second factor, rule variation within a single lect for which all social and stylistic variables have been controlled, is still a source of considerable controversy. As one sociolinguist has put it:

> Although it may be a heuristically useful procedure to admit inherent variability only after an exhaustive attempt to account for fluctuating variants in categorical terms, we still are left with the fact that our best powers of observation leave us with inexplicable fluctuation. (Wolfram 1973, p 2)

Two hypotheses have been offered to account for this, which have been called the QUANTITATIVE PARADIGM and the DYNAMIC PARADIGM (Bickerton 1973, p 24). The first of these maintains that rule variability is inherent in the language, ie that we must accept the fact that in any situation where a given rule should apply, the outcome may be unpredictable between two alternatives except on a basis of statistical probability. In the example we have been following, this means that when our hypothetical New York City working-class speaker, in the course of reading a list of minimal pairs, comes across a word containing postvocalic /r/ before a final consonant, he makes use of a rule which says, in effect, 'the odds that you pronounce this /r/ as [r] are 55 out of 100', or, formulaically:

$$/r/ \rightarrow \begin{cases} \alpha[r] \\ \beta[\emptyset] \end{cases} / \text{———} C$$

where $\alpha = 0.55$
$\beta = 0.45$

This type of rule, which was first formulated and extensively exemplified by Labov (1969), is called a VARIABLE RULE. It is an essential part of the quantitative paradigm. As Bickerton summarizes it:

> Variable rules ... attempt to deal with variation directly: that is to say, when confronted with a situation in which for many if not all speakers two features equivalent in meaning and function are seen to alternate, they specify as precisely as possible the environments within which the alternation occurs and, then, for each environment estimate relative probabilities for either feature. (Bickerton 1973, p 26)

In addition to social and stylistic correlates of variation, variable rules must therefore specify linguistic correlates such as the phonological environment of a variable feature. Thus Labov writes the Black English rule for the simplification of /-sp -st -sk/ clusters, which we discussed in categorical terms in the last chapter, in this way:

$$[-\text{cont}] \rightarrow \emptyset \ / \ [+\text{strid}] \text{———} \#(\#) \begin{Bmatrix} *[+\text{strid}] \\ \alpha[\sim V] \end{Bmatrix}$$

where # = morpheme boundary
  ## = word boundary
  * = obligatorily (ie of probability 1.0)
  α = a variable between $\emptyset$ and 1
  ~V = a non-vowel, ie consonant, liquid, or glide

The rule says that a non-continuant (ie a stop) goes to zero (is deleted) between a strident and a morpheme- or word boundary:
(a) obligatorily, if followed by a strident, or
(b) in proportion α, if followed by a non-vowel other than a strident. This rule would have the following effects:

dɛsk##C → dɛs##C	α per cent of the time
dɛsk#z → dɛs#z	always
dɛsk##V	is unchanged

If α is found to be 0.5 for Black English speakers of a certain social class level using a certain style, this would mean that in phrases such as
  the desk fell
  the desk was broken
  the desk rolled away
these speakers would use [dɛs] half the time and [dɛsk] the remaining half. In phrases such as *the desk is mine* they would always use [dɛsk], and in *desks* or *desk's* they would always delete the /k/ (with subsequent reduction to [dɛs] by voice assimilation and degemination).

If the linguist attempts to include all the factors that may influence a variable – not only class and style but age, sex, occupation, geographical location, etc., as well – three facts are apparent:

1. The collection of data must be arranged to include enough examples from all social levels, age-groups, and the rest to make reliable generalizations possible.
2. The resulting rules may become very complicated if it is found that the features involved vary measurably in proportion to a large number of social, stylistic, and other factors.
3. If the resulting rules are believed to be part of the competence of native speakers, that competence becomes vastly more complicated than had previously been conceived. The individual speaker does not have to master the social and geographical parameters for each rule, except perhaps as part of his ability to comprehend speakers from other social classes or geographical areas. But it is implied that within his own social and geographical dialect he knows the proper percentage of variation for each variable in each environment and at each style level.

This last point has led some linguists to question the value of variable rules as a credible model of linguistic competence. Bickerton points out two major difficulties: the question of acquisition and the question of the employment of such rules in normal speech production. On the question of acquisition he writes:

> According to generative accounts, rules are internalized by the subconscious processing of primary data. There is evidence . . . that this learning process consists of first drawing a generalisation and later noting the exceptions to it. If we accept the variable-rule principle, we must also accept that the mind possesses not only the apparatus necessary for framing two quite different types of rule, but also some kind of recognition device to tell the speaker whether to interpret a particular set of data as rule-plus-exceptions or as area-of-variability. (Bickerton 1971, p 460)

He goes on to point out that even if a child were able to learn the variability coefficients for rules as competently as he learns categorical (*ie* non-variable) rules, there still remains the question as to how these variable factors are controlled in the process of speaking. Let us say that the coefficient for a certain variable, for a certain class of speaker using a certain style, is 50 per cent. How does a speaker's mind keep him at or approximately close to that percentage? It is unlikely that he will delete every other /r/, for example, and pronounce the rest. But somehow his linguistic competence must keep the tally. And if he shifts to another style, in which the coefficient drops to, say, 35 per cent, the internal counter must keep him to this new figure. As Bickerton concludes, 'though our ignorance of the mind is still immense, one may hazard a guess that the processes just described are beyond its unaided and individual power' (Bickerton 1971, *p* 461).

The dynamic paradigm: lexical diffusion

These are, of course, psycholinguistic objections and call for psycholinguistic research to investigate their validity. On the other side one might 'hazard a guess' that if the human mind can learn, store, and have access to a lexicon of tens, perhaps hundreds of thousands of items, it is not impossible that it has the power to learn and store variable rules of the kind of complexity that Labov suggests. Meanwhile, Bickerton and others offer the dynamic paradigm as an explanation of variability. This claims that a linguistic change, however it may originate, moves gradually across the lexicon, the speech community, or both. In the lexicon, it has been proposed by William S.-Y. Wang and others working with Chinese material that phonological changes do not affect all relevant lexical items simultaneously, but proceed through the lexicon word by word. They entitle this process LEXICAL DIFFUSION. Matthew Chen defines this as follows:

> Sound change does not operate on the lexicon en bloc and instantaneously or according to a uniform schedule; rather it spreads itself gradually across the lexicon and operates on words or groups thereof one after another. Since Wang (1969; cf. Wang-Cheng 1970) this gradual spread of phonological change from morpheme to morpheme has become known under the name of 'lexical diffusion'. (Chen 1972, *pp* 468–9)

This sounds like a return to the notion that 'every word has its own history' and in a sense it is. But it is compatible with the Neogrammarian Hypothesis in the sense that the change will ultimately proceed through the whole lexical set unless some factor intervenes to halt the diffusion before it is complete. In that case there would be a split of the lexical set, such as happened in the English -*oo*- words, all deriving ultimately from Middle English long ō. This lexical set has been divided into four (in most dialects; there are dialectal exceptions):

1. Those undergoing the single change ō > [u], *eg: food, pool, spoon, loose*, etc.
2. Those in which the resultant vowel shortened and/or laxed to [ʊ], *eg: good, book.*

3. Those in which the resultant [ɷ] unrounded to [ʌ]; for most speakers only *blood* and *flood*.
4. Those exhibiting variation between [u] and [ɷ], *eg*: *roof, root, coop, room*, etc.

This last group is evidence that the diffusion of the change from [u] to [ɷ] through the lexicon has been interrupted, leaving a large area of variation even within the usage of individual speakers (*cf* Dickerson 1975).

The other aspect of the dynamic paradigm is that linguistic change moves through the speech community in a series of waves:

> Thus, at any given point in time, the output of a speaker A (whom a given rule had not yet 'reached') would differ from that of a speaker B (whom the rule had 'passed') with respect at least to the operation of that rule, and would leave open the possibility of a third speaker, C, whom the rule was just reaching, and who in consequence would sometimes produce A's output, sometimes B's. (Bickerton 1973, *p* 24)

In such a situation, individual transitional speakers exhibit more or less random variation, though as a group they may show the kind of statistical consistency covered by variable rules. This can certainly help to reconcile the two apparently inconsistent views of the neogrammarians and the dialectologists. It is interesting to note that in his presidential address before the Linguistic Society of America, Labov proposed such a reconciliation and suggested the kind of research that may establish it (Labov 1981).

The controversy between the two points of view – the quantitative and the dynamic – has not yet been resolved. The quantitative side has been supported by studies which deal with the interrelationship between co-occurrent influencing features, and which investigate the connection between competence and performance in terms of the mathematical relationship between probability and frequency (*eg* Fasold 1970, 1978; Cedergren and Sankoff 1974; Rousseau and Sankoff 1978). The concept of variable rules has also been extended into syntax, as in G. Sankoff (1973b), where data from Montreal French and New Guinea Tok Pisin are explained in terms of a probabilistic model of inherent variability. Such a model would include variable rules of the sort described above, which would indicate the probability of the occurrence of a phonological development under specific social and stylistic conditions. Sankoff predicts that the same model can be extended to lexicon and semantics:

> Without going too far into problems of lexical choice and lexical insertion, it is not difficult to see how phenomena such as synonymy, over-

lapping meanings, specificity versus generality, and referents which are marginal or on the border between two semantic domains could all lead to probabilistic considerations of the lexicon. (G. Sankoff 1973b, p 59)

Conclusions

It is clear from the examples that have been described or alluded to in this chapter that the sociolinguistic approach has greatly altered the role and function – some would say the importance – of the dialectologist. It is no longer possible for him simply to display his data, however elegantly. Séguy's abjuration of interpretation as being outside the dialectologist's function certainly seems archaic in the light of the extensive interpretation and manipulation of data by the linguists we have been discussing. Their work has opened up areas which the older dialectology avoided, most notably the language of the cities and of the younger speakers as both creators and reflectors of language change in progress. It is to be hoped that what seems to be an abandonment of the geographical orientation of older dialectologists will be corrected, and that the geographical dimension which formerly dominated the discipline will be reintroduced as an interesting and important aspect of language to be studied along with variation based on class and other sociological dimensions. Then linguistic geography will no longer be the humble handmaid in the linguistic household, as Gilliéron designated it in the rather ironic statement I have used as an epigraph to this book, but a full-fledged member of the linguistic family.

Appendix A

A system of distinctive features for English

	Consonants														
	Obstruents														
	Stops								Fricatives							
	p	b	t	d	k	g	č	ǰ	f	v	θ	ð	s	z	š	ž
Syllabic	–	–	–	–	–	–	–	–	–	–	–	–	–	–	–	–
Sonorant	–	–	–	–	–	–	–	–	–	–	–	–	–	–	–	–
Consonantal	+	+	+	+	+	+	+	+	+	+	+	+	+	+	+	+
Continuant	–	–	–	–	–	–	–	–	+	+	+	+	+	+	+	+
Strident									+	+	–	–	+	+	+	+
Nasal																
Lateral																
Anterior	+	+	+	+	–	–	–	–	+	+	+	+	+	+	–	–
Coronal	–	–	+	+	–	–	+	+	–	–	+	+	+	+	+	+
Voiced	–	+	–	+	–	+	–	+	–	+	–	+	–	+	–	+
Round																
High																
Low																
Back																
Front																
Tense																

			Sonorants		Glides			Vowels													
	Nasals			**Liquids**		**Glides**		**Front**					**Back**							**Central**	
n̩	n	ŋ	r	l	j	w	h	i	ɪ	e	ɛ	æ	ɑ	ɔ	ɒ	ʊ	u	ɯ	ʌ	ə	ɜ
−	−	−	−	−	−	−	−	+	+	+	+	+	+	+	+	+	+	+	+	+	+
+	+	+	+	+	+	+	−	+	+	+	+	+	+	+	+	+	+	+	+	+	+
+	+	+	+	+	−	−	−	−	−	−	−	−	−	−	−	−	−	−	−	−	−
+	+	+	−	−																	
			−	+																	
+	+	−																			
−	+	−																			
					−	+		−	−	−	−	−	−	+	+	+	+	+	−	−	−
								+	+	−	−	−	−	−	−	−	+	+	−	−	−
								−	−	−	−	+	+	+	+	−	−	−	−	−	−
								−	−	−	−	−	+	+	+	+	+	+	+	−	−
					+	+														−	−
								+	−	+	−	−	−	+	−	+	+	−	−	−	+

Appendix B

Dialect atlases

It is customary to refer to dialect atlases by acronymic abbreviations. The following have been used in this book.

AIS *Sprach- und Sachatlas Italiens und der Südschweiz*, Karl Jaberg and Jakob Jud. 8 vols. Zofingen: Ringier, 1928–43.

ALF *Atlas linguistique de la France*, publié par J. Gilliéron et E. Edmont. 13 vols. Paris: Champion, 1902–10. Reprinted by Forni: Bologna, 1968.

ALG *Atlas linguistique et ethnographique de la Gascogne*, Jean Séguy et al. 6 vols in 9 parts. Paris: Centre National de la Recherche Scientifique, 1954–73.

ALLy *Atlas linguistique et ethnographique du Lyonnais* (2nd edn), Pierre Gardette et al. 4 vols. Paris: Centre National de la Recherche Scientifique, 1967–70 (original edn 1950).

ALMC *Atlas linguistique et ethnographique du Massif Central*, Pierre Nauton et al. 4 vols. Paris: Centre National de la Recherche Scientifique, 1957–63.

ALW *Atlas linguistique de la Wallonie*, Louis Remacle and Élisée Legros. vols 1 and 3 so far published. Liège: Vaillant-Carmanne, 1953–55.

DSA *Deutscher Sprachatlas*, auf grund des von Georg Wenker begründeten Sprachatlas des Deutschen Reichs... unter Leitung von Ferdinand Wrede. 23 sheets in 2 vols. Marburg: N. G. Elwert'sche Verlagsbuchhandlung, 1926–56.

DWA *Deutscher Wortatlas*, Walther Mitzka and Ludwig Erich Schmitt (eds). 22 vols. Giessen: W. Schmitz, 1951–80.

LAGS   *Linguistic atlas of the Gulf States*, Lee Pederson (ed.). In progress.

LAMSAS   *Linguistic atlas of the Middle and South Atlantic States*, Raven I. McDavid and R. K. O'Cain. Chicago: University of Chicago Press, 1980–

LANCS   *The linguistic atlas of the North Central States*. Basic materials (microfilm and microfiche). Chicago: University of Chicago Library, 1977.

LANE   *Linguistic atlas of New England*, Hans Kurath et al. 3 vols. Providence: Brown University Press, 1939–43.

LAS   *The linguistic atlas of Scotland*, Scots section, J. Y. Mather and H. H. Speitel. 2 vols. London: Croom Helm, 1975–77.

LAUMW   *The linguistic atlas of the Upper Midwest*, Harold B. Allen. 3 vols. Minneapolis: University of Minnesota Press, 1973–76.

LGW   *The linguistic geography of Wales*: a contribution to Welsh dialectology, Alan R. Thomas. Cardiff: University of Wales Press, 1973.

RNDA   *Reeks Nederlandse Dialektatlassen*, E. Blancquaert and W. Pée (eds). 16 vols (12 so far published). Antwerp: Van de Sikkel, 1930–67.

SDS   *Sprachatlas der deutschen Schweiz*, Rudolf Hotzenköcherle. 4 vols. Berne: Francke Verlag, 1962–75.

SED   *Survey of English dialects*, Harold Orton et al. Introduction and 4 vols in 12 parts. Leeds: E. J. Arnold & Son, Ltd., for the University of Leeds, 1962–71. (For detailed information on separate volumes, see Bibliography.)

WGE   *A word geography of England*, Harold Orton and Nathalia Wright. London, etc.: Seminar Press, 1974.

WGEUS   *A word geography of the eastern United States*, Hans Kurath. Ann Arbor: University of Michigan Press, 1949.

References and bibliography

This list includes all works cited in the text, as well as a selection of other items which may be of interest for further reading.

ABERCROMBIE, DAVID (1965) 'R.P. and local accent', in *Studies in phonetics and linguistics*. Oxford University Press, pp. 10–15.

ABERCROMBIE, DAVID (1967) *Elements of general phonetics*. Edinburgh: University Press.

AGARD, FREDERICK B. (1971) 'Language and dialect', *Linguistics* **65**, 1–24.

ALLEN, HAROLD B. (1973–78) *The linguistic atlas of the Upper Midwest*. 3 vols, Minneapolis: University of Minnesota Press.

ALLEN, H. B. and G. N. UNDERWOOD (eds) (1971) *Readings in American dialectology*. New York: Appleton-Century-Crofts.

ALVAR LOPÉZ, MANUEL (1960) *Los nuevos atlas lingüísticos de la Romania*. Granada.

ATWOOD, E. BAGBY (1953) *A survey of verb forms in the eastern United States*. Ann Arbor: University of Michigan Press.

ATWOOD, E. BAGBY (1955) 'The phonological divisions of Belgo-Romance', *Orbis* **4**, 367–89.

ATWOOD, E. BAGBY (1962) *The regional vocabulary of Texas*. Austin: University of Texas Press.

ATWOOD, E. BAGBY (1963) 'The methods of American dialectology', *Zeitschrift für Mundartforschung* **30**(1) 1–29. (Also in Allen and Underwood (1971) pp. 5–35. German translation, *Amerikanische Dialektologie*, by Frank Schindler, in Schmitt (1968) pp. 565–600, with extra bibliography.)

BACH, ADOLF (1950) *Deutsche Mundartforschung: ihre Wege, Ergebnisse, und Aufgaben: eine Einführung* (2nd edn). Heidelberg: Carl Winter Universitätsverlag.

BADIA MARGARIT, ANTONIO (1952) *Sobre metodología de la encuesta dialectal*. Zaragoza: Consejo Superior de Investigaciones Científicas (*Filología* **15**, No. general 92).

BAILEY, CHARLES–JAMES N. (1973a) *Variation and linguistic theory*. Washington: Center for Applied Linguistics.

BAILEY, CHARLES–JAMES N. (1973b) 'The patterning of language variation', in Bailey and Robinson (1973) pp. 156–86.

BAILEY, RICHARD W. and JAY L. ROBINSON (eds) (1973) *Varieties of present-day English*. New York: Macmillan.

BAILEY, CHARLES–JAMES N. and ROGER W. SHUY (eds) (1973) *New ways of analyzing variation in English*. Washington, D.C.: Georgetown University Press.

BECKER, DONALD A. (1967) 'Generative phonology and dialect study: an investigation of three modern German dialects'. University of Texas Ph.D. dissertation in Linguistics.

BELASCO, SIMON (1972) 'Phonemics as a discovery procedure in synchronic dialectology', in *Papers in linguistics and phonetics to the memory of Pierre DeLattre*, A. Valdman (ed.), pp. 45–64. The Hague: Mouton.

BERGMAN, GUNTER (1964) *Mundarten und Mundartforschung*. Leipzig: VEB Bibliographisches Institut.

BERRUTO, GAETANO (1970) 'Il concetta di fonema e il diasistema', *Bollettino dell'Atlante Linguistico Italiano* N.S. Nos. 17–18, pp. 12–17.

BEYER, E. (1970) 'Structuralisme et dialectologie moderne: points de vue d'un dialectologue', in *Actes du Xe Congrès International des Linguistes*, 2, 5–12. Bucharest: Académie de la République Socialiste de Roumanie.

BICKERTON, DEREK (1971) 'Inherent variability and variable rules', *Foundations of Language* 7, 457–92.

BICKERTON, DEREK (1973) 'Quantitative versus dynamic paradigms: the case of Montreal *que*', in Bailey and Shuy (1973) pp. 23–43.

BLANCQUAERT, E., J. C. CLAESSENS, W. GOFFIN and A. STEVENS (eds) (1962) *Dialektatlas van Belgische-Limburg en Zuid Nederlands-Limburg*. 2 vols, 150 maps (*Reeks Nederlandse Dialectatlassen*, E. Blancquaert and W. Pée (eds), 8). Antwerp: Van de Sikkel.

BLANCQUAERT, E. and W. PÉE (1933) *De nederlandse Dialectnamen van de Spin, den Ragebol, en het Spinneweb*. 's-Gravenhage: M. Nijhoff.

BLOOMFIELD, LEONARD (1933) *Language*. New York: Holt.

BOTTIGLIONI, GINO (1954) 'Linguistic geography: achievements, methods and orientations', *Word* 10, 375–87.

BROWN, GILLIAN (1972) *Phonological rules and dialect variation: a study of the phonology of Lumasaaba* (Cambridge Studies in Linguistics 7). Cambridge: University Press.

BURGHART, LORRAINE H. (ed.) (1971) *Dialectology: problems and perspectives*. Knoxville: University of Tennessee.

CALLARY, ROBERT E. (1975) (for 1971) 'Dialectology and linguistic theory', *American Speech* 46, 200–9.

CASSIDY, FREDERICK G. (1953) *A method for collecting dialect* (Publication of the American Dialect Society, No. 20). Gainesville, Florida: American Dialect Society.

CATFORD, J. C. (1957) 'Vowel-systems of Scots dialects', *Transactions of the Philological Society* 107–17.

CEDERGREN, H. J. and D. SANKOFF (1974) 'Variable rules: performance as a statistical reflection of competence', *Language* 50, 333–55.

CHAMBERS, J. K. and PETER TRUDGILL (1980) *Dialectology* (Cambridge Textbooks in Linguistics). Cambridge: University Press.

CHEN, MATTHEW (1972) 'The time dimension: contribution toward a theory of sound change', *Foundations of Language* 8, 457–98.

CHOMSKY, NOAM (1957) *Syntactic structures* (Janua linguarum, series minor 4). The Hague: Mouton.

CHOMSKY, NOAM (1965) *Aspects of the theory of syntax*. Cambridge, Mass.: M.I.T. Press.

CHOMSKY, NOAM and MORRIS HALLE (1968) *The sound pattern of English*. New York: Harper and Row.

COCHRANE, G. R. (1959) 'The Australian English vowels as a diasystem', *Word* 15, 69–88.

COSERIU, EUGENIO (1975) *Die Sprachgeographie* (Tübinger Beiträge zur Linguistik, 57). Tübingen: Verlag Gunter Narr.

DAHLSTEDT, KARL-HAMPUS (1970) 'The dilemmas of dialectology', in *The Nordic languages and modern linguistics*, Hreinn Benediktsson (ed.). Reykjavík: Visindafélag Íslendinga, pp. 158–84.

DAUZAT, ALBERT (1922) *La géographie linguistique*. Paris: Flammarion.

DAVIS, ALVA L., RAVEN I. MCDAVID, JR. and VIRGINIA G. MCDAVID (1969) *A compilation of the work sheets of the Linguistic Atlas of the United States and Canada and associated projects* (2nd edn). Chicago and London: University of Chicago Press.

DAVIS, LAWRENCE M. (1969) 'Dialect research: mythology vs. reality', *Orbis* 18, 332–7.

DAVIS, LAWRENCE M. (1973) 'The diafeature: an approach to structural dialectology', *Journal of English Linguistics* 7, 1–20.

DeCAMP, DAVID (1971a) 'Toward a generative analysis of a post-creole speech continuum', in *Pidginization and creolization of languages*, Dell Hymes (ed.). Cambridge: University Press, pp. 349–70.

DeCAMP, DAVID (1971b) 'Implicational scales and sociolinguistic linearity', *Linguistics* 73, 30–43.

DeCAMP, DAVID (1973) 'What do implicational scales imply?', in Bailey and Shuy (1973) pp. 141–8.

DICKERSON, WAYNE B. (1975) 'Variable rules in the language community: a study of lax [u] in English', *Studies in the Linguistic Sciences*. Urbana: University of Illinois, pp. 41–68.

DIETH, EUGEN (1932) *A grammar of the Buchan dialect (Aberdeenshire) descriptive and historical*. Cambridge: W. Heffer & Sons Ltd.

DOROSZEWSKI, W. (1958) 'Le structuralisme linguistique et les études de géographie dialectale', in *Actes du Huitième Congrès International des Linguistes*, Eva Sivertsen (ed.). Oslo: University Press, pp. 540–64.

DURRELL, M., et al. (1969) *Sprachatlanten: Berichte über sprachgeographische Forschungen 1 (Zeitschrift für Dialektologie und Linguistik, Beihefte*, N.F.8). Wiesbaden: Franz Steiner Verlag.

ELLIS, ALEXANDER J. (1889) *The existing phonology of English dialects*.

Being Part V of Early English pronunciation ... London: Trübner & Co., for the Philological Society, the Early English Text Society, and the Chaucer Society.

ELLIS, STANLEY (1970) 'The assessment of linguistic boundaries by local dialect speakers', in *Actes du Xe Congrès International des Linguistes*, 2, 109–12. Bucharest: Académie de la République Socialiste de Roumanie.

ELLIS, STANLEY (1976) 'Regional, social and economic influences on speech: Leeds University studies', in *Sprachliches Handeln – Soziales Verhalten*, W. Viereck (ed.). Munich: Wilhelm Fink Verlag, pp. 93–103.

FASOLD, RALPH (1970) 'Two models of socially significant linguistic variation', *Language* **46**, 551–63.

FASOLD, RALPH (1978) 'Language variation and linguistic competence', in *Linguistic variation: models and methods*, David Sankoff, (ed.). New York: Academic Press, pp. 85–95.

FERGUSON, C. A. (1972) '"Short A" in Philadelphia English', in *Studies in Linguistics in honor of George L. Trager*, M. Estellie Smith (ed.) (1972) The Hague: Mouton, pp. 259–74.

FOSSAT, JEAN-LOUIS (1977) 'Vers un traitement automatique des données dialectologiques, en dialectométrie', In Putschke (ed.) (1978) pp. 311–34.

FOURQUET, J. (1956) 'Linguistique structurale et dialectologie', in *Fragen und Forschungen in Bereich und Umkreis der germanischen Philologie* (Deutsche Akademie der Wissenschaften zu Berlin 8). Berlin: Akademie-Verlag, pp. 190–203.

FRANCESCATO, GIUSEPPE (1964) 'Dialect borders and linguistic systems', in *Proceedings of the Ninth International Congress of Linguists*, H. G. Lunt (ed.). The Hague: Mouton, pp. 109–14.

FRANCESCATO, GIUSEPPE (1965a) 'Structural comparison, diasystems, and dialectology', *Zeitschrift für Romanische Philologie* **81**, 484–91.

FRANCESCATO, GIUSEPPE (1965b) 'Struttura linguistica e dialetto', in *Actes du Xe Congrès International de Linguistique et Philologie Romane*, G. Straka (ed.). Paris: Klincksieck, pp. 1011–17.

FRANCIS, W. N. (1959) 'Some dialect isoglosses in England', *American Speech* **34**, 243–50.

FRANCIS, W. N. (1961) 'Some dialectal verb forms in England, *Orbis* **10**, 1–14.

FRANCIS, W. N. (1969) 'Modal *daren't* and *durstn't* in dialectal English', in *Studies in honour of Harold Orton*, Stanley Ellis (ed.) (Leeds Studies in English, N.S., vol. II), pp. 145–63.

FUDGE, E. C. (1967) 'The nature of phonological primes', *Journal of Linguistics* **3**, 1–36

FUDGE, E. C. (1969a) 'Mutation rules and ordering in phonology', *Journal of Linguistics* **5**, 23–38.

FUDGE, E. C. (1969b) 'Syllables', *Journal of Linguistics* **5**, 253–86.

GÁLFFY, MÓZES (1969) 'Questionnaire et structure de l'atlas dialectal: observations basées sur les travaux de l'atlas dialectal sicule', *Orbis* **18**, 405–11.

GARDE, P. (1961) 'Réflexions sur les différences phonétiques des langues slaves', *Word* 17, 34–62.

GARDETTE, PIERRE (1968) *Atlas linguistique et ethnographique du Lyonnais*. Vol. IV: *Exposé méthodólogique et tables*. Paris: Centre National de la Recherche Scientifique.

GARDETTE, PIERRE et al. (eds) (1973) *Les dialectes romans de France à la lumière des atlas régionaux*. Paris: Centre Nationale de la Recherche Scientifique.

GAUCHAT, LOUIS (1903) 'Gibt es Mundartgrenzen?', *Archiv für das Studium der neueren Sprachen* 111, 365–403.

GILLIÉRON, JULES (1912) *L'aire clavellus d'après l'atlas linguistique de la France*. Neuveville.

GILLIÉRON, JULES (1915) *Étude de géographie linguistique, Pathologie et thérapeutique verbales*. Neuveville.

GILLIÉRON, JULES (1918) *Généalogie des mots qui désignent l'abeille* (Bibliothèque de l'École des Hautes Études, Fasc. 225). Paris: Champion.

GILLIÉRON, JULES (1921) *Pathologie et thérapeutique verbales*. Paris: Edouard Champion.

GILLIÉRON, JULES (1923) *Thaumaturgie linguistique*. Paris: Edouard Champion.

GILLIÉRON, JULES and M. ROQUES (1910) 'Études de géographie linguistique XII: Mots en collision, A. Le coq et le chat', *Revue de Philologie Française et de Littérature* 24, 278–88.

GLAUSER, BEAT (1974) *The Scottish-English linguistic border: lexical aspects* (The Cooper Monographs, 20, English Dialect Series, Basle). Berne: Francke Verlag.

GOOSSENS, JAN (1969) *Strukturelle Sprachgeographie: ein Einführung in Methodik und Ergebnisse*. Heidelberg: Carl Winter Universitätsverlag.

GOOSSENS, JAN (1977) *Deutsche Dialektologie* (Sammlung Göschen 2205). Berlin: de Gruyter.

GOOSSENS, JAN and A. STEVENS (1964) 'Funktionale Abhängigkeit von Isophonen: ein Beispiel aus Belgisch-Limburg', *Orbis* 13, 545–55.

GROOTAERS, W. A. (1970) 'Nouvelles méthodes et nouveaux problèmes: le nouvel Atlas Linguistique du Japon', in *Actes du Xe Congrès International des Linguistes*, 2, 113–18. Bucharest: Académie de la République Socialiste de Roumanie.

GUITER, HENRI (1973) 'Atlas et frontières linguistiques', in Straka (ed.) (1973) pp. 61–107.

HÄGERSTRAND, T. (1952) 'The propagation of innovation waves', in *Lund Studies in Geography Series B, Human Geography* 3, Lund: Royal University of Lund.

HALLE, MORRIS (1962) 'Phonology in generative grammar', *Word* 18, 54–72.

HALLE, MORRIS (1964) 'On the bases of phonology', in *The structure of language*, J. A. Fodor and J. J. Katz (eds). Englewood Cliffs NJ: Prentice-Hall, pp. 324–33.

HANLEY, M. L. (1933) 'Note on the collection of phonographic records',

Dialect Notes, vol. VI, Part VII, p. 368.

HARD, GERHARD (1966) *Zur Mundartgeographie: Ergebnisse, Methoden, Perspektiven* (Beihefte zur Zeitschrift 'Wirkendes Wort' 17). Düsseldorf: Pädagogischer Verlag Schwann.

HAUGEN, EINAR (1966) 'Dialect, language, nation', *American Anthropologist* 68, 922–35. Reprinted in *Sociolinguistics*, J. B. Pride and J. Holmes (eds) (Penguin 1972), pp. 97–111.

HEISER, MARY M. (1972) 'Linguistic atlases and phonological interpretation', *Linguistics* 80, 56–64.

HEISER, MARY M. (1977) 'A diasystem of four south central French dialects', *Word* 28, 323–33.

HIRSHBERG, JEFFREY (1981) 'Regional morphology in American English: evidence from DARE', *American Speech* 56, 33–52.

HOUCK, CHARLES I. (1969) 'Methodology of an urban speech survey', in *Studies in honour of Harold Orton*, Stanley Ellis (ed.) (Leeds Studies in English, N.S., vol. II), pp. 115–28.

HUGHES, ARTHUR and PETER TRUDGILL (1979) *English accents and dialects: An introduction to social and regional varieties of British English*. With cassette tape. London: Edward Arnold.

HYMES, DELL (1974) *Foundations in sociolinguistics: an ethnographic approach*. Philadelphia: University of Pennsylvania Press.

IVIĆ, PAVLE (1962) 'On the structure of dialect differentiation', *Word* 18, 33–45.

IVIĆ, PAVLE (1963) 'Importance des caractéristiques structurales pour la description et la classification des dialectes', *Orbis* 12, 117–31.

IVIĆ, PAVLE (1964) 'Structure and typology of dialectal differentiation', in *Proceedings of the Ninth International Congress of Linguists*, H. G. Lunt (ed.). The Hague: Mouton, pp. 115–21.

JABERG, KARL (1936) *Aspects géographiques du langage* (*avec* 19 *cartes*). *Conférences faites au Collège de France* (*décembre 1933*) (Société de Publications Romanes et Françaises, xviii). Paris: Librairie E. Droz.

JABERG, KARL (1955) 'Grossräumige und kleinräumige Sprachatlanten', *Vox Romanica* 14, 1–61.

JABERG, KARL & JAKOB JUD (1928) *Der Sprachatlas als Forschungsinstrument. Kritische Grundlegung und Einführung in den Sprach- und Sachatlas Italiens und der Südschweiz*. Halle (Saale): Max Niemeyer Verlag.

JOCHNOWITZ, G. (1973) *Dialect boundaries and the question of Franco-Provençal: a methodological quest* (Janua linguarum, series practica, No. 147). The Hague: Mouton.

JONES, VALERIE M. (1979) 'Some problems in the computation of sociolinguistic data'. Doctoral thesis, University of Newcastle upon Tyne. (British Library microfilm D26800/79).

KÁLMÁN, BÉLA (1964) 'Remarques sur quelques isoglosses dialectales', in *Proceedings of the Ninth International Congress of Linguists*, H. G. Lunt (ed.), The Hague: Mouton, pp. 130–4.

KAY, PAUL (1978) 'Variable rules, community grammar, and linguistic change', in *Linguistic variation: models and methods*, David Sankoff (ed.), New York: Academic Press, pp. 71–83.

KEYSER, SAMUEL J. (1963) 'Review of Kurath and McDavid (1961)', *Language* **39**, 303–16.

KIPARSKY, PAUL (1973) 'Phonological representations', in *Three dimensions of linguistic theory*, Osamu Fujimura (ed.). Tokyo: Institute for Advanced Studies of Language, pp. 1–136.

KLIMA, EDWARD S. (1964) 'Relatedness between grammatical systems', *Language* **40**, 1–20.

KÖKERITZ, HELGE (1932) *The phonology of the Suffolk dialect, descriptive and historical* (Uppsala Universitets Årsskrift). Uppsala: A.-E. Lundequistska Bokhändeln.

KOLB, EDUARD (1966) *Linguistic atlas of England: Phonological atlas of the northern region*. Berne: Francke Verlag.

KURATH, HANS (1934) 'Progress of the Linguistic Atlas and proposals for the continuation of the work', *Dialect Notes*, vol. VI, Part IX, pp. 417–24.

KURATH, HANS (1949) *A word geography of the eastern United States*. Ann Arbor: University of Michigan Press.

KURATH, HANS (1964) 'Interrelation between regional and social dialects', in *Proceedings of the Ninth International Congress of Linguists*, Horace G. Lunt (ed.). The Hague: Mouton, pp. 135–43.

KURATH, HANS (1968) 'The investigation of urban speech', *Publication of the American Dialect Society* **49**, 1–7.

KURATH, HANS (1972) *Studies in area linguistics*. Bloomington: Indiana University Press.

KURATH, HANS and GUY S. LOWMAN, JR (1970) *The dialectal structure of southern England: phonological evidence* (Publication of the American Dialect Society, No. 54). University, Alabama: Univ. of Alabama Press.

KURATH, HANS and RAVEN I. MCDAVID, JR (1961) *The pronunciation of English in the Atlantic States*. Ann Arbor: University of Michigan Press.

KURATH, HANS et al. (1939, 1954) *Handbook of the linguistic geography of New England*. Providence: Brown University Press; Washington: American Council of Learned Societies.

KURATH, HANS et al. (1979) 'Preview: the Linguistic Atlas of the Middle and South Atlantic States', *Journal of English Linguistics* **13**, 37–47.

KYPRIOTAKI, LYN (1973) 'A study in dialect: individual variation and dialect rules', in Bailey and Shuy (eds) (1973) pp. 198–210.

LABOV, WILLIAM (1963) 'The social motivation of a sound change', *Word* **19**, 273–309.

LABOV, WILLIAM (1966) *The social stratification of English in New York City*. Washington: Center for Applied Linguistics.

LABOV, WILLIAM (1969) 'Contraction, deletion, and inherent variability of the English copula', *Language* **45**, 715–62.

LABOV, WILLIAM (1972a) 'On the use of the present to explain the past', in *Proceedings of the Eleventh International Congress of Linguists*, L. Heilmann (ed.), pp. 825–51.

LABOV, WILLIAM (1972b) *Sociolinguistic patterns*. Philadelphia: University of Pennsylvania Press.

LABOV, WILLIAM (1973) 'Some features of the English of Black Americans'. In Bailey and Robinson (eds) (1973) pp. 236–55.

LABOV, WILLIAM (1981) 'Resolving the neogrammarian controversy', Language 57, 267–308.

LABOV, WILLIAM, M. YAEGER and R. STEINER (1972) A quantitative study of sound change in progress. Report on National Science Foundation contract NSF-GS-3287. 2 vols. Philadelphia: The U.S. Regional Survey.

LANE, LEA BUSSEY (1980) (for 1976) 'Automotive terms in British and American English', American Speech 51, 285–91.

LÖFFLER, HEINRICH (1974) Probleme der Dialektologie: eine Einführung. Darmstadt: Wissenchaftliche Buchgesellschaft.

LOMAN, BENGT (1970) 'Social variation in the syntax of spoken Swedish', in The Nordic languages and modern linguistics, Hreinn Benediktsson (ed.). Reykjavík: Visindafélag Íslendinga, pp. 211–31.

MCDAVID, RAVEN I., JR (1961) 'Structural linguistics and linguistic geography', Orbis 10, 35–46.

MCDAVID, RAVEN I., JR (1967) 'Dialectology: where linguistics meets the people', Emory University Quarterly 23, 203–21.

MCDAVID, RAVEN I., JR (1974) 'Field procedures: instructions for investigators, Linguistic Atlas of the Gulf States', in Pederson et al., A manual for dialect research in the Southern States. University, Alabama: University of Alabama Press, pp. 35–60.

MCDAVID, RAVEN I., JR (1978) 'The gathering and presentation of data', Journal of English Linguistics 12, 29–37.

MCDAVID, RAVEN I., JR and R. K. O'CAIN (1980) Linguistic Atlas of the Middle and South Atlantic States. Fascicle 1. Chicago and London: University of Chicago Press.

MCDAVID, RAVEN I., JR and R. C. PAYNE (eds) (1976) Linguistic atlas of the North Central States. Basic materials (unaltered field records). Microfilm or Xerox prints. Chicago: University of Chicago Press.

MCINTOSH, ANGUS (1961) Introduction to a survey of Scottish dialects. Edinburgh: Nelson (originally published 1952).

MALKIEL, YAKOV (1967) 'Each word has a history of its own', Glossa 1, 137–49.

MALKIEL, YAKOV (1976) 'From Romance philology through dialectology to sociolinguistics', Linguistics 177, 59–84.

MARCHAND, HANS (1969) The categories and types of present-day English word-formation: a synchronic–diachronic approach (2nd edn), revised. Munich: C. H. Beck'sche Verlagsbuchhandlung.

MARKEY, THOMAS I. (1977) Prinzipien der Dialektologie: Einführung in die deutsche Dialektforschung (Giessener Beiträge zur Sprachwissenschaft 8). Grossen-Linden: Hofman Verlag.

MARTINET, ANDRÉ (1955) Economie des changements phonétiques. Berne: Francke Verlag.

MATHER, J. Y. (1965) 'Aspects of the linguistic geography of Scotland: I', Scottish Studies 9(2), 129–44.

MATHER, J. Y. (1966) 'Aspects of the linguistic geography of Scotland. II:

East Coast fishing', *Scottish Studies* **10**, 129–53.

MATHER, J. Y. (1969) 'Aspects of the linguistic geography of Scotland. III: Fishing communities of the East Coast (Part 1)', *Scottish Studies* **13**, 1–16.

MATHER, J. Y. and H. H. SPEITEL (eds) (1975) *The linguistic atlas of Scotland: Scots Section*, vol. 1. London: Croom Helm.

MATHESIUS, V. (1931) 'Zum Problem der Belastungs- und Kombinationsfähigkeit der Phoneme', *Travaux du Cercle Linguistique de Prague*, **4**, 148–52.

MITZKA, WALTHER (1952) *Handbuch zum Deutschen Sprachatlas*. Marburg: Elwertsche Universitätsbuchhandlung.

MOULTON, WILLIAM G. (1960) 'The short vowel systems of Northern Switzerland: a study in structural dialectology', *Word* **16**, 155–82.

MOULTON, WILLIAM G (1961a) 'The dialect geography of *hast, hat* in Swiss German', *Language* **37**, 497–508.

MOULTON, WILLIAM G. (1961b) 'Lautwandel durch innere Kausalität: die ostschweizerische Vokalspaltung', *Zeitschrift für Mundartforschung* **28**, 227–51.

MOULTON, WILLIAM G. (1962) 'Dialect geography and the concept of phonological space', *Word* **18**, 23–32.

MOULTON, WILLIAM G. (1963) 'Phonologie und Dialekteinteilung', in *Sprachleben der Schweiz*, Paul Zinsli et al. (eds). Berne: Francke Verlag, pp. 75–86.

MOULTON, WILLIAM G. (1964) 'Phonetische und phonologische Dialektkarten: Beispiele aus dem Schweizerdeutschen', in *Communications et rapports du Premier Congrès International de Dialectologie Générale (Louvain)*, Pt. 2, 117–28.

MOULTON, WILLIAM G. (1965) 'Die schweizerdeutsche Hiatusdiphthongierung in phonologischer Sicht', in *Philologia Deutsch: Festschrift zum 70. Geburtstag von Walter Henzen*, Werner Kohlschmidt and Paul Zinsli (eds). Berne: Francke Verlag, pp. 115–29.

MOULTON, WILLIAM G. (1968a) 'Structural dialectology', *Language* **44**, 451–66.

MOULTON, WILLIAM G. (1968b) 'The mapping of phonemic systems', in *Verhandlung des zweiten internationalen Dialektologenkongresses (Zeitschrift für Mundartforschung, Beihefte*, Neue Folge, 4.2), pp. 574–91.

MOULTON, WILLIAM G. (1970a) 'Opportunities in dialectology', in *The Nordic languages and modern linguistics*, Hreinn Benediktsson (ed.). Reykjavík: Vísindafélag Íslendinga, pp. 143–57.

MOULTON, WILLIAM G. (1970b) 'Contributions of dialectology to phonological theory', in *Actes du Xe Congrès International des Linguistes*, **2**, 21–26. Bucharest: Académie de la République Socialiste de Roumanie.

MOULTON, WILLIAM G. (1972) 'Geographical linguistics', in *Current Trends in Linguistics*, T. A. Sebeok (ed.), vol. 9, *Linguistics in Western Europe*. The Hague: Mouton, pp. 196–222.

MOULTON, WILLIAM G. (1980) 'Review of H. Orton et al., *The Linguistic*

Atlas of England', *General Linguistics* **20**, 151–63.

NAUTON, PIERRE (1963) *Atlas linguistique et ethnographique du Massif Central*; vol. IV, *Exposé général, Table-questionnaire, Index alphabetique*. Paris: Centre National de la Recherche Scientifique.

NEWTON, BRIAN (1972) *The generative interpretation of dialect: a study of Modern Greek phonology* (Cambridge Studies in Linguistics 8). Cambridge: University Press.

NIDA, EUGENE (1960) *A synopsis of English syntax* (3rd edn). Norman, Okla.: Summer Institute of Linguistics.

NORDBERG, BENGT (1970) 'The urban dialect of Eskilstuna: methods and problems', in *The Nordic languages and modern linguistics*, Hreinn Benediktsson (ed.). Reykjavík: Visindafélag Íslendinga, pp. 426–43.

O'NEIL, WAYNE A. (1963) 'The dialects of Modern Faroese: a preliminary report', *Orbis* **12**, 393–7.

O'NEIL, WAYNE A. (1968) 'Transformational dialectology: phonology and syntax', in *Verhandlungen des zweiten internationalen Dialektologenkongresses* (*Zeitschrift für Mundartforschung, Beihefte*, Neue Folge, 4.2), pp. 629–38.

ORTON, HAROLD and NATHALIA WRIGHT (1974) *A word geography of England*. London, etc.: Seminar Press.

ORTON, HAROLD et al. (1962–71) *Survey of English Dialects*. Introduction and 4 vols. in 12 parts. Leeds: E. J. Arnold & Son Limited, for the University of Leeds.

Introduction, Harold Orton (1962)

Vol. 1, *The six northern counties and the Isle of Man.*, Harold Orton and Wilfrid J. Halliday (eds) (1962–63).

Vol. 2, *The West Midland counties*, Harold Orton and Michael V. Barry (eds) (1969–71).

Vol. 3, *The East Midland counties and East Anglia*, Harold Orton and Philip M. Tilling (eds), (1969–71).

Vol. 4, *The southern counties*, Harold Orton and Martyn F. Wakelin (eds) (1967–68).

ORTON, HAROLD, S. SANDERSON and J. WIDDOWSON (1978) *The linguistic atlas of England*. London: Croom Helm.

OSTHOFF, HERMANN and KARL BRUGMANN (1878) *Morphologische Untersuchungen auf dem Gebiete der indogermanischen Sprachen*. 2 vols. Leipzig: Verlag von S. Hirzel.

PEDERSON, LEE (1973) 'An approach to urban word geography', *American Speech* **46**, 73–86.

PEDERSON, LEE (1974) 'Tape/text and analogues', *American Speech* **49**, 5–23.

PEDERSON, LEE (1976a) 'Aims and methods in a Chicago dialect survey', in *Sprachliches Handeln–soziales Verhalten. Ein Reader zur Pragmalinguistik und Soziolinguistik*, Wolfgang Viereck (ed.). Munich: Wilhelm Fink Verlag, pp. 193–202.

PEDERSON, LEE (1976b) 'The Linguistic Atlas of the Gulf States: interim report three', *American Speech* **51**, 201–7.

PELLOWE, JOHN (1976) 'The Tyneside Linguistic Survey: aspects of a

developing methodology', in *Sprachliches Handeln–soziales Verhalten.*
Ein Reader zur Pragmalinguistik und Soziolinguistik, Wolfgang
Viereck (ed.). Munich: Wilhelm Fink Verlag, pp. 203–17.

PELLOWE, JOHN et al. (1972) 'A dynamic modelling of linguistic variation: the urban (Tyneside) Linguistic Survey', *Lingua* 30, 1–30.

PETROVICI, E. (1956) *Atlasul lingvistic Roman*, Serie Nova, vols 1 and 2.
Bucharest: Editura Academici Republicii Socialiste Romania.

PETYT, K. M. (1980) *The study of dialect: an introduction to dialectology.*
London: André Deutsch.

PICKFORD, GLENNA R. (1956) 'American linguistic geography: a sociological appraisal', *Word* 12, 211–33.

PILCH, HERBERT (1975) 'Structural dialectology', *American Speech* 47,
165–87 (1975 for 1972).

POP, SEVER (1938) *Micul atlas lingvistic Român.* Cluj: Muzeul Limbii
Române.

PULGRAM, ERNST (1953) 'Family tree, wave theory, and dialectology',
Orbis 2, 67–72.

PULGRAM, ERNST (1964a) 'Proto-languages as proto-diasystems: Proto-
Romance', *Word* 20, 373–83.

PULGRAM, ERNST (1964b) 'Structural comparison, diasystems, and dialectology', *Linguistics* 4, 66–82.

PUTSCHKE, WOLFGANG (ed.) (1978) *Automatische Sprachkartographie:
Vorträge des internationalen Kolloquiums zur automatischen Sprach-
kartographie in Marburg vom 11–16. September 1977. Germanistische
Linguistik* 3–4, 1977.

RAVIER, XAVIER (1976) 'Jean Séguy et la traversée du langage gascon.
Réflexions sur une topogenèse géolinguistique', *Revue de linguistique
Romane* 40, 389–402.

REICHSTEIN, RUTH (1960) 'Étude des variations sociales et géographiques
des faits linguistiques (observations faites à Paris en 1956–1957)',
Word 16, 55–95.

REID, T. B. W. (1960) *Historical philology and linguistic science.* Oxford.

ROQUES, MARIO (1957) 'Souvenirs de Gilliéron', *Orbis* 6, 7–10

ROSS, ALLAN S. C. and A. W. MOVERLY (1964) *The Pitcairnese language.*
London: André Deutsch.

ROUSSEAU, PASCALE and DAVID SANKOFF (1978) 'Advances in variable
rule methodology', in *Linguistic variation: models and methods*, D.
Sankoff (ed.). New York: Academic Press, pp. 57–69.

RUSU, V. (1970) 'Tradition et innovation dans le domaine de la dialectologie', in *Actes du Xe Congrès International des Linguistes*, 2, 95–100.
Bucharest: Académie de la République Socialiste de Roumanie.

RYDLAND, KURT (1972) 'Structural phonology and the Survey of English
Dialects: a critical evaluation of the material', *Zeitschrift für Dialektologie und Linguistik* 39, 309–26.

SALTARELLI, M. (1966) 'Romance dialectology and generative grammar',
Orbis 15, 51–9.

SALTARELLI, M. (1968) 'Marsian vocalism: intelligibility and rules of
grammar', *Orbis* 17, 88–96.

SANKOFF, DAVID (ed.) (1978) *Linguistic variation: models and methods*. New York: Academic Press.

SANKOFF, GILLIAN (1973a) 'Dialectology', in *Annual Review of Anthropology*, B. J. Siegel et al. (eds) vol. 2. Palo Alto: Annual Reviews, Inc., pp. 165–77.

SANKOFF, GILLIAN (1973b) 'Above and beyond phonology in variable rules', in Bailey and Shuy (eds) (1973) pp. 44–61.

SAPORTA, SOL (1965) 'Ordered rules, dialect differences, and historical processes', *Language* **41**, 218–24.

SAUSSURE, FERDINAND DE (1915, 1959) *Course in general linguistics*, Charles Bally and Albert Sechehaye (eds), in collaboration with Albert Reidlinger. Translated by Wade Baskin. New York: Philosophical Library.

SCHEUERMEIER, PAUL (1943–56) *Bauernwerk in Italien, der italienischen und rätoromanischen Schweiz. Eine sprachsachkundliche Darstellung landwirtschaftlicher Albeit und Geräte*. 2 vols. Erlenbach-Zürich: Eugen Rentsch Verlag.

SCHLEICHER, AUGUST (1863) (1871) *Die Darwinsche Theorie und die Sprachwissenschaft* (3rd edn). Weimar: Hermann Bohlau.

SCHMITT, LUDWIG ERICH (ed), (1968) *Germanische Dialektologie. Festschrift für Walther Mitzka zum 80. Geburtstag*. 2 vols. (*Zeitschrift für Mundartforschung, Beihefte*, Neue Folge 6). Wiesbaden: Franz Steiner Verlag.

SCHMITT, LUDWIG ERICH and PETER WIESINGER (1964) 'Vorschläge zur Gestaltung des phonetischen Transkriptionssystems', *Zeitschrift für Mundartforschung* **31**, 57–61.

SÉGUY, JEAN (1971) 'La relation entre la distance spatiale et la distance lexicale', *Revue de Linguistique Romane* **35**, 335–57.

SÉGUY, JEAN (1973a) 'La dialectométrie dans l'*Atlas linguistique de la Gascogne*', *Revue de Linguistique Romane* **37**, 1–24.

SÉGUY, JEAN (1973b) 'La fonction minimale du dialecte', in Straka (ed.) (1973) pp. 27–37.

SÉGUY, JEAN (1973c) 'Les atlas linguistiques de la France par régions', *Linguistique Française* **18**, 65–90.

SÉGUY, JEAN (ed.) (1973d) *Atlas linguistique de la Gascogne*, vol. VI. Paris: Centre National de la Recherche Scientifique.

SHAW, DAVID (1974) 'Statistical analysis of dialectal boundaries', *Computers and the Humanities* **8**, 173–7.

SPEITEL, H. H. (1969) 'An areal typology of isoglosses: isoglosses near the Scottish–English border', *Zeitschrift für Dialektologie und Linguistik* **36**, 49–66.

STANKIEWICZ, E. (1956) 'The phonemic patterns of the Polish dialects: a study in structural dialectology', in *For Roman Jakobson*, M. Halle (ed.). The Hague: Mouton, pp. 518–30.

STANKIEWICZ, E. (1957) 'On discreteness and continuity in structural dialectology', *Word* **13**, 44–59.

STERN, GUSTAF (1931, 1964) *Meaning and change of meaning, with special reference to the English language* (Göteborgs Högskolas Årsskrift

38, 1932:1). Göteborg: Elanders Boktryckeri Aktiebolag; Bloomington: Indiana University Press.

STOCKWELL, R. P. (1959) 'Structural dialectology: a proposal', *American
Speech* **34**, 258–68.

STRAKA, GEORGES (ed.) (1973) *Les dialectes romans de France, à la
lumière des atlas régionaux* (Colloques nationaux du Centre de la
Recherche Scientifique, No. 930). Paris: Éditions du Centre de la
Recherche Scientifique.

STRANG, BARBARA M. H. (1968) 'The Tyneside Linguistic Survey', in *Verhandlung des zweiten internationalen Dialektologenkongresses (Zeitschrift für Mundartforschung, Beihefte*, Neue Folge, 4.2), pp. 788–94.

TEUCHERT, H. (1924–25) 'Lautschrift des Teuthonista', *Teuthonista* **1**, 5.

THOMAS, ALAN R. (1967) 'Generative phonology in dialectology', *Transactions of the Philological Society*, pp. 179–203.

THOMAS, ALAN R. (1968) 'Generative phonology and the statements of
morphophonological variants in Welsh dialects'. In *Verhandlung des
zweiten internationalen Dialektologenkongresses (Zeitschrift für Mundartforschung, Beihefte*, Neue Folge, 4.2), pp. 795–803.

THOMAS, ALAN R. (1973) *The linguistic geography of Wales: a contribution to Welsh dialectology*. Cardiff: University of Wales Press.

THOMAS, ALAN R. (1975) 'Dialect mapping', *Orbis* **24**, 115–24.

THOMAS, ALAN R. (1977) 'Derivational complexity in varieties of contemporary spoken Welsh', *Word* **28**, 166–86.

THOMAS, ALAN R. (1980) *Areal analysis of dialect data by computer: a
Welsh example*. Cardiff: University of Wales Press.

TRAGER, G. L. and H. L. SMITH, JR (1951) *An outline of English
structure*. Norman, Oklahoma: Battenburg Press.

TRIER, JOST (1973) *Aufsätze und Vorträge zur Wortfeldtheorie*, Anthony
van der Lee and Oskar Reichmann (eds) (Janua linguarum series
minor 174). The Hague: Mouton (selections from various works 1931–
72).

TROIKE, RUDOLPH C. (1971) 'Overall pattern and generative phonology',
in Allen and Underwood (eds), (1971). New York: Appleton-Century-
Crofts, pp. 324–42.

TRUBETZKOY, N. S. (1931 1969) 'Phonology and linguistic geography',
Appendix I to *Principles of Phonology*, translated by C. A. M.
Baltaxe. Berkeley and Los Angeles: University of California Press,
pp. 298–304.

TRUDGILL, PETER (1972) 'Sex, covert prestige, and linguistic change in
the urban British English of Norwich', *Language in Society* **1**, 179–95.

TRUDGILL, PETER (1974a) *The social differentiation of English in Norwich*. (Cambridge Studies in Linguistics 13). Cambridge: University Press.

TRUDGILL, PETER (1974b) *Sociolinguistics: an introduction*. Penguin
Books.

TRUDGILL, PETER (1974c) 'Linguistic change and diffusion: description
and explanation in sociolinguistic dialect geography', *Language in
Society* **3**, 215–46.

TRUDGILL, PETER (ed.) (1978) *Sociolinguistic patterns in British English*.

London: Edward Arnold.

TUAILLON. G. (1958) 'Exigences théoriques et possibilités réelles de l'enquête dialectologique', *Revue de Linguistique Romane*, 22, 293–316.

TUAILLON, G. (1973) 'Frontière linguistique et cohésion de l'aire dialectale', in Straka (ed.) (1973) Paris: Centre National de la Recherche Scientifique, pp. 174–206.

VACHEK, JOSEF (1964) 'On peripheral phonemes of Modern English'. *Brno Studies in English* 4, 7–110.

VASILIU, E. (1966) 'Towards a generative phonology of Daco-Rumanian dialects', *Journal of Linguistics* 2, 79–98.

VASILIU, E. (1967) 'Transformational vs. bi-unique phonemic typology', in *Phonologie der Gegenwart*, J. Hamm (ed.) (Wiener Slavistisches Jahrbuch, Supplement 6), pp. 254–61.

VEITH, W. H. (1975) 'Moderne Linguistik in deutscher Dialektologie', *Michigan Germanic Studies* 1, 68–79.

VIERECK, WOLFGANG (1968) 'Englische Dialektologie', in Schmitt (ed.) (1968) vol. 2, 542–64.

VIERECK, WOLFGANG (1969) 'A diachronic–structural analysis of a northern English urban dialect', in *Studies in honour of Harold Orton*, Stanley Ellis (ed.) (Leeds Studies in English, N.S., vol. II), pp. 65–79.

VIERECK, WOLFGANG (1973) 'The growth of dialectology', *Journal of English Linguistics* 7, 69–86.

VIERECK, WOLFGANG (1975) *Regionale und soziale Erscheinungsformen des britischen und amerikanischen Englisch* (Anglistische Arbeitshefte 4). Tübingen: Max Niemeyer Verlag.

VIERECK, WOLFGANG (1980) 'The dialectal structure of British English: Lowman's evidence', *English World-Wide* 1, 25–44.

WAKELIN, MARTYN F. (ed.) (1972) *Patterns in the folk speech of the British Isles*. London: Athlone Press.

WAKELIN, MARTYN F. (1972) *English dialects: an introduction*. London: Athlone Press.

WANG, WILLIAM S.-Y. (1969) 'Competing sound changes as a cause of residue', *Language* 45, 9–25.

WANG, WILLIAM S.-Y. AND CHIN–CHUAN CHENG (1970) 'Implementation of phonological change: the Shuang–feng Chinese case', *Papers from the Sixth Regional Meeting of the Chicago Linguistic Society*, 552–59.

WANG, WILLIAM S.-Y. and M. CHEN (1970) 'Diachronic phonology and lexical diffusion'. Paper from the 23rd University of Kentucky Foreign Languages Conference. Unpublished.

WEINREICH, URIEL (1954) 'Is a structural dialectology possible?', *Word* 10, 388–400.

WEINREICH, URIEL, WILLIAM LABOV and MARVIN I. HERZOG (1968) 'Empirical foundations for a theory of language change', in *Directions for historical linguistics*, W. P. Lehmann and Yakov Malkiel (eds). Austin and London: University of Texas Press, pp. 97–195.

WELLS, RULON (1947) 'Immediate constituents', *Language* 23, 81–117.

WHITLEY, M. STANLEY (1974) 'Toward a generative theory of dialectology, with reference to English, Scots, Spanish, and German dialect areas'. Unpublished dissertation in Linguistics, Cornell University (DAI 35/06 p. 37 19-A).

WIDÉN, BERTIL (1949) *Studies on the Dorset dialect* (Lund Studies in English xvi). Lund: C. W. K. Gleerup.

WILLIAMSON, JUANITA V. and VIRGINIA M. BURKE (eds) (1971) *A various language: perspectives on American dialects.* New York: Holt, Rinehart and Winston.

WÖLCK, WOLFGANG (1976) 'Community profiles: an alternative approach to linguistic informant selection', *Linguistics* 177, 43–57.

WOLFRAM, WALTER A. (1969) *A sociolinguistic description of Detroit Negro speech.* Washington: Center for Applied Linguistics.

WOLFRAM, WALTER A. (1973) 'On what basis variable rules?', In Bailey and Shuy (eds) (1973) pp. 1–12.

WOLFRAM, WALT and DONNA CHRISTIAN (1976) *Appalachian speech.* Arlington, Va.: Center for Applied Linguistics.

WOLFRAM, WALT and RALPH W. FASOLD (1974) *The study of social dialects in American English.* Englewood Cliffs, NJ: Prentice-Hall.

WOOD, GORDON R. (1975) 'The computer in analysis and plotting', *American Speech* 47, 195–202 (1975 for 1972).

WRIGHT, JOSEPH (1898–1905) *The English dialect dictionary.* 6 vols. London: H. Frowde.

Index

Page numbers in **bold** indicate the place where the definition or explanation of a technical term is to be found.